TC 3-04.81 (FM 3-04.303)
OCTOBER 2010

I0022103

AIR TRAFFIC CONTROL FACILITY OPERATIONS, TRAINING, MAINTENANCE, AND STANDARDIZATION

Headquarters, Department of the Army

Published by Books Express Publishing
Books Express Publishing, 2011
ISBN 978-1-78039-951-5

Books Express publications are available from all good retail and online booksellers. For
publishing proposals and direct ordering please contact us at: info@books-express.com

*TC 3-04.81 (FM 3-04.303)

Training Circular
No. 3-04.81

Headquarters
Department of the Army
Washington, DC, 29 October 2010

Air Traffic Control Facility Operations, Training, Maintenance, and Standardization

Contents

PART TWO   TACTICAL AIR TRAFFIC SERVICES

Figures

Tables

Preface

Training circular (TC) 3-04.81 provides administrative and operational standards for United States (U.S.) Army air traffic control (ATC) facilities and units. This publication is intended for use by all Active Army, Army National Guard (ARNG), United States Army Reserve (USAR), Department of the Army civilians (DACs), and contract personnel who perform ATC duties for the U.S. Army. TC 3-04.81 consists of two parts—part one (chapters one through four) applies to installation (fixed) ATC facilities only and part two (chapters five through eight) applies to tactical ATC facilities. The appendices are common to both installation and tactical ATC facilities.

This publication supplements applicable Department of the Army (DA), Federal Aviation Administration (FAA), and International Civil Aviation Organization (ICAO) publications; Air and Space Interoperability Council (ASIC) Air Standards; and North Atlantic Treaty Organization (NATO) standard agreements (STANAGs) to be used in providing air traffic services (ATS). When the U.S. Army provides ATC services in overseas areas or tactical deployments necessitate deviations from these standards, it may be necessary to outline these deviations in an agreement between the theater commander and the host nation to conform to foreign government regulations.

The proponent for this publication is U.S. Training and Doctrine Command (TRADOC). Submit comments and recommendations using DA Form 2028 (Recommended Changes to Publications and Blank Forms) to Commander, U.S. Army Aviation Center of Excellence (USAACE), ATTN: ATZQ-TD-D, Fort Rucker, AL 36362; or email the Directorate of Training and Doctrine (DOTD) at av.doctrine@us.army mil. Other doctrinal information can be found on the internet through Army Knowledge Online.

This publication has been reviewed for operations security (OPSEC) considerations.

PART ONE. Installation (Fixed) Air Traffic Control Operations

Chapter 1

Facility Administration

This TC provides direction and guidance for the day-to-day operation of facilities and DA air traffic organizations. A well-managed ATC facility results in trained, qualified, and proficient air traffic controllers ensuring safe and efficient use of airspace while supporting Army aviation operations.

SECTION I – GENERAL

1-1.   The procedures within part one (chapters one through four) of this publication standardize U.S. Army ATC training, operations, management, and maintenance of installation (fixed site) facilities. U.S. Army ATC managers and supervisors will use this publication as a reference to establish training, certification, and facility standards.

1-2.   This chapter details the processes, procedures, and requirements for ATC facility administration. ATC facilities should use local standing operating procedures (SOPs) to supplement these requirements when necessary.

Contents

APPLICABILITY

1-3.   This publication provides U.S. Army guidance for supplying ATC services and operating ATC facilities. This publication incorporates U.S. Army applicable facility management guidance established in Federal Aviation Administrative Joint Order (FAA JO) 7210.3, FAA JO 7220.1B, and contingency planning guidance in response to the National Airspace System (NAS) equipment failures established in FAA JO 1900.47. Additionally, the following FAA publications and ARs apply to all Army controllers and contractors providing ATC support to the Army:

- FAA JO 7110.65T, Air Traffic Control.
- FAA JO 7610.4, Special Operations.
- FAAO 8240.41, Flight Inspection/Air Traffic On-Site Coordination Requirements.
- FAA JO 7220.1B, Air Traffic Control Certification Procedures.
- FAA JO 7340.2, Contractions.
- FAAO 8200.1, United States Standard Flight Inspection Manual (USSFIM).
- FAAO 8260.15, United States Army Terminal Instrument Procedures Service.
- FAAO 8260.19, Flight Procedures and Airspace.
- FAAO 8260.3, United States Standards for Terminal Instrument Procedures (TERPS).
- AR 95-2, Airspace, Airfields/Heliports, Flight Activities, Air Traffic Control, and Navigational Aids.

1-4.   National regulations or agreements adopted for Army use in overseas areas take precedence over this publication; however, every effort should be made to conform to this publication. Refer conflicting procedures to higher headquarters for review and direction. This TC supplements applicable DA, FAA, and ICAO publications to be used in providing ATS. When the U.S. Army provides ATC services in overseas areas, deviations from these standards may be necessary to conform to foreign government regulations. Deviations will be outlined in an agreement between one of the following:

- Theater commander and the host government.
- Host government military commanders and U.S. Army commanders.
- Host government ATC authorities and the U.S. Army commanders.
- Host government ATC authorities and U.S. Army ATC authorities.

1-5. Host regulations and procedures apply to U.S. Army controllers who augment a civil or foreign ATC facility. U.S. Army controllers who augment a facility operated by another branch of the U.S. military will comply with the ATC regulations and procedures of the host service.

1-6. Supervisors of civilian controllers should review local bargaining unit agreements from their civilian personnel office. Labor management relations agreements provide overarching procedures and guidance for managers and supervisors of employees represented by an exclusively recognized union.

SECTION II – FACILITY ADMINISTRATION AND MANAGEMENT

1-7. Army ATC facilities are grouped into five major classifications:

- Airfield/heliport/air traffic control tower (ATCT).
- Ground controlled approach (GCA).
- Airspace information center (AIC).
- Army approach control (non-radar).
- Army radar approach control (ARAC).

COMBINED AIR TRAFFIC CONTROL SERVICES

1-8. Combined ATC services provide two or more of the facility services identified in paragraph 1-7 permanently from one facility. Operations of this type require a combined training program, which qualifies controllers in all functional areas within the combined facilities. When facilities are combined, individual facility characteristics—including separate training and qualification programs, facility management, and administration—are lost. Combined facilities become a larger centralized facility providing ATC services under one management structure and training/rating program.

1-9. Some facilities do not lend themselves to combination and require a distinct management structure for continued safe operations. Even when proximity is advantageous to combine facilities, other factors should be considered before combining ATC services. Facility managers should carefully weigh training, supervision, and diminishment of ATC services when considering the permanent combination of facilities. The Installation Management Command (IMCOM) headquarters will be notified of all restructure actions.

LIMITED POSITION QUALIFICATIONS

1-10. At combined ATC services facilities where specialization is necessary to ensure training opportunities for Army tactical controllers, Army personnel may be designated to perform limited ATC functions—such as "PAR only" and "AIC only".

1-11. Army tactical controllers authorized to operate in a portion of the facility's area of responsibility require a general knowledge of the facility's total area of responsibility. The facility training program (FTP) for these specialized position qualifications will consist of a detailed knowledge and separate training program established for the area in which the controller intends to operate.

1-12. Training conducted for these position qualifications will be annotated in Section II of DA Form 3479 (Training and Proficiency Record-Air Traffic Control), not on FAA Form 7220-1 (Air Traffic Control Specialists Certificate). The training received at installation facilities will satisfy the requirements of phase

II training for tactical facility ratings and will be assessed against the commander's task list (CTL) during tactical exercises and deployments.

MULTIPLE RATINGS

1-13. A controller with multiple ratings is one who holds ratings from two or more different facilities at the same location. Controllers with multiple ratings must meet currency requirements of all facilities as outlined within this publication. A combined facility training manual (FTM) may be prepared at locations where multiple ratings are required as a condition of employment or when a combined FTM format reduces the redundancy of training requirements for controllers pursing multiple ratings.

FACILITY CONSOLIDATION

1-14. Facility consolidation is a temporary operation designated by the ATC chief during non-peak hours of operations. The ATC chief will define consolidated facility operations in a memorandum outlining—
- The facilities to be consolidated.
- The hours the consolidated facilities will operate.
- The maximum traffic density allowed before additional workforce is brought in for duty and notification procedures when traffic conditions exceed maximum levels.
- The required staffing (position manning) and management oversight of the facility during consolidated operations.

Note. Facilities consolidated during non-peak hours will be manned with a minimum of two fully qualified controllers (rated in all facilities consolidated), one of which must be controller-in-charge (CIC) qualified. Position qualified (PQ) controllers authorized under combined positions (paragraph 1-33) will not be used to satisfy this requirement.

STAFFING LEVEL STANDARDS

1-15. An understanding of staffing levels is necessary to effectively manage controller personnel and ensure operational readiness of the facility. Facility managers should review AR 570-4 to better understand the Army's planning, programming, budgeting, and execution polices regarding staffing levels and manpower determinations. For the purpose of this TC, two levels of staffing are presented—required staffing levels and emergency manning levels (EMLs).

REQUIRED STAFFING LEVELS

1-16. Required staffing levels are reflected on a facility's table of distribution and allowances (TDA) and are determined using manpower staffing standards. This staffing level represents the required number of personnel to operate a facility within mission requirements. Staffing levels are validated by the appropriate Army commands (ACOMs), Army Service Component Command (ASCC), or direct reporting unit (DRU) headquarters. Factors relevant to these calculations are—
- Days per week facility is open.
- Hours of operation per day.
- Number of peak and off peak shifts.
- Number of control or operating positions per shift.
- Day-week-month conversion factors.
- Manpower availability factor.

EMERGENCY MANNING LEVEL

1-17. EMLs represent the minimum number of facility-rated and position-qualified controllers necessary to support the mission for limited periods. EMLs should not be confused with required staffing levels as discussed above. EMLs are developed by the ATC/facility chief and validated by the appropriate ACOM,

ASCC, or DRU headquarters. Copies of validated EMLs are furnished to local leadership and maintained by each facility. Once validated, EMLs become the basis for reporting and are used to determine facility actions as identified below. EMLs will be revalidated every two years or when a change to mission requirements is initiated.

1-18. Emergency manning level restricts ongoing controller progression and significantly impairs administration/management functions. Facilities operating at this manning level experience increased payroll expense due to extended work schedules, restrictions of leave and school attendance, and significant changes to workforce scheduling based on unplanned controller illnesses and medical incapacitations. When developing EMLs, the following factors should be applied:—

- Formulated from 70 percent of a facility's required staffing level reflected on approved TDA documents (excluding ATC chief, facility chief, and training supervisor).
- Facility operational hours.
- 50-hour work week per controller.
- Consolidated positions, except when determined by the facility chief based on traffic density and complexity of positions. A statement will be added to the EML validation listing positions that cannot be consolidated, time periods (shifts), and the justification.

1-19. AR 95-2 prohibits facilities from operating at EML for longer than 60 days. Facilities will seek approval of variances to EMLs through local command structure and submit for approval to ACOM, ASCC, or DRU headquarters as appropriate.

1-20. EML computations are based upon absolute minimum position staffing per shift per facility to provide advertised services. A minimum of one supervisor will be assigned per shift unless a variance justifies additional requirements. During known periods of low traffic density, ATC positions can be combined to reduce the number of controllers on shifts; this will afford adequate controller staffing during peak flying periods.

1-21. When a facility reaches EML, the following additional actions should be taken to mitigate the impact on flying operations. These actions require the involvement and support of airfield leadership, local post/camp/station commanders, and when support of adjacent FAA facilities is required, the FAA regional Department of the Army representative (DAR):

- Curtail ATC services, such as multiple precision radar approach capability and monitoring approaches during visual meteorological conditions.
- Request relief from external visits/inspections affecting facilities.
- Curtail ATC facility operating hours and temporarily return the airspace to the FAA.
- Notice to airmen (NOTAM) the facility closed and cease operations according to procedures in the FAA parent facility contingency plan established in accordance with FAA Order 1900.47.

Note. Facility managers will only use facility-rated and position-qualified controllers and exclude medically grounded or otherwise disqualified controllers when determining EML status.

1-22. If personnel actions taken have not alleviated the adverse conditions and the facility remains at EML at the end of the 60-day period, facilities must reduce services or curtail operating hours. If corrective action cannot be taken in time to avoid the curtailment, the post, camp, or station commander will be notified of the anticipated reduction in ATC hours of operation or services and the date normal operations will resume.

1-23. Notification that services or hours of operation have been curtailed is sent through the airfield division chief/commander/manager to the installation commander, ACOM, ASCC, or DRU headquarters and the Air Traffic Services Command (ATSCOM) using standard memorandum format in accordance with (IAW) AR 25-50.

CURRENCY REQUIREMENTS

1-24. Facility chiefs and training supervisors are required to rotate through all positions within the facility for a total of 24 hours each calendar month. Training supervisors will be designated in writing by facility memorandum and reflected in section 1 of DA Form 3479.

1-25. Controllers holding multiple ratings are required to rotate through all positions within those facilities for a minimum of 24 total hours for each facility, each calendar month. Facility chiefs and training supervisors holding multiple ratings are required to rotate through all positions for a total of 16 hours in each facility, each calendar month.

1-26. No more than 50 percent of hours spent providing direct supervision may be used to satisfy currency requirements.

1-27. Distribution of time to meet currency requirements will be determined by the facility chief in a facility memorandum based upon complexity and traffic density. When working combined positions, controllers will equally divide the time between the combined positions.

1-28. All GCA controllers are required to complete ten approaches each month, five of which may be conducted through simulation and one of which must be an emergency or no-gyro approach. At facilities where controllers have multiple ratings and rotate between facilities, controllers will complete five live approaches, one of which must be an emergency or no-gyro approach.

1-29. ARAC facilities will determine PAR currency requirements for assigned controllers detailed in a facility memorandum.

OPENING AND CLOSING FACILITIES

1-30. ATC managers operating facilities less than 24 hours per day, 7 days per week will establish procedures for opening and closing. They will coordinate these procedures with airfield operations and/or the ATC facility having instrument flight rules (IFR) jurisdiction. These procedures will also be included in a letter of agreement (LOA). When opening and closing, part-time facilities will broadcast the service they are resuming or terminating.

1-31. If airfield operations continue to function when the ATC facility is closed, the ATC facility and base/flight operations will exchange pertinent flight data (FD) before the facility opens or closes. The facility will publish hours of operation in the appropriate flight information publications (FLIPs)/NOTAMs.

SHIFT REQUIREMENTS

1-32. Facility shifts and workweeks will be scheduled following guidance outlined in AR 95-2.

CONSOLIDATION OF OPERATING POSITIONS

1-33. The consolidation of operating positions will be determined by the facility chief in a facility memorandum outlining the circumstances in which positions may be combined, to include—
- Specific hours of the duty day that positions may be combined.
- Traffic conditions allowing position consolidation.
- Positions excluded from consolidation.

Note. No less than two controllers will be present for duty in a control TWR, GCA, and AIC—one of which must be CIC qualified. ARAC facilities require one fully qualified (rated) controller per sector (after consolidation) and one rated controller per PAR position— one of which must be CIC qualified. No less than two controllers will be present for duty in an ARAC. The use of PQ controllers to meet manning requirements may be used in TWRs, GCAs and AICs; although, this creates a unique risk when managing rest breaks and other relief periods.

POSITION ASSIGNMENTS

1-34. Only ATC personnel qualified to perform duties outlined in AR 95-2 and this publication will man operating positions. Controllers will be assigned to positions as required by traffic, equipment, and individual qualifications.

1-35. Non-PQ trainees will not be assigned to positions on which they are not qualified unless they are under direct supervision of facility rated controllers. In addition, PQ controllers will not be assigned to more than one position at a time, unless they are qualified on both positions. Non-PQ trainees and PQ controllers may sign on to permanently combined positions at facilities where these positions are reflected on the facility status report and manning documents.

1-36. Facility-rated controllers providing direct one-on-one supervision will sign on behind the non-PQ trainees and are directly responsible for operating the position. Personnel providing direct one-on-one supervision may not be signed on at additional positions. Non-current or non-proficient, facility-rated controllers will not be assigned to a position unless given direct one-on-one supervision by current facility-rated controllers.

1-37. At the discretion of the SL, non-PQ trainees may conduct precision or surveillance approaches during IFR conditions under certain circumstances. They may conduct these approaches if—

- Direct one-on-one supervision is maintained.
- Direct communications override is available at the position of operation.
- Weather conditions are acceptable (not less than a 500-foot ceiling or 1-mile visibility).

Transfer of Position Responsibility

1-38. Position responsibility will be transferred according to FAA JO 7110.65T and appropriate facility directives. All controllers, including supervisors, will know how to perform the duties of any position to which they may be assigned before they assume responsibility. Each controller will—

- Read the recent information file, DA Form 3502 (Daily Report of Air Traffic Control Facility) and any other operational data specified.
- Obtain a briefing on communications, traffic and airfield conditions, equipment outages, and current and forecasted weather.
- Accept responsibility for the position only after ensuring the briefing is complete and all questions about the operation of the position have been resolved.

1-39. The relieving controller and the controller being relieved will share equal responsibility for the completeness and accuracy of the position-relief briefing. The ATC chief/facility chief will provide a tailored checklist of the equipment and conditions that will likely be a factor at each position during relief periods.

OPERATING INITIALS

1-40. The ATC chief/facility chief will assign controllers and maintenance personnel individual two-letter operating initials. The facility chief and maintenance chief will maintain a list of operating initials for all assigned personnel on a facility memorandum. Controllers will use the assigned operating initials on all interphone systems and facility forms and records except where signatures are required.

AIRCRAFT ACCIDENTS AND INCIDENTS

1-41. When a facility, service, or navigational aid (NAVAID) is suspected to have been involved in an aircraft accident or incident, ATC must act immediately. Airfield division chief/commander/manager must perform notifications in accordance with (IAW) AR 95-2. ATC will provide the continuous safe, orderly, and expeditious movement of all air traffic operating under the jurisdiction of the ATC facility. In addition, ATC will obtain accurate and complete information for investigations. When an accident or incident involves, or is suspected to have involved, radar equipment, the facility will discontinue radar service until a flight inspection is performed.

RESPONSIBILITIES OF AIR TRAFFIC CONTROL MANAGERS

1-42. As soon as the ATC chief/facility chief, training supervisor, SL, or CIC receives notification of an accident or incident, he will—

- Notify the chain of command. The notification will include—
  - Date and time of accident/incident.
  - Number and type of aircraft involved.
  - Number of injuries and/or fatalities.
  - Brief synopsis of events to include ATC involvement.
  - Actions taken.
  - A point of contact by name, position, and telephone number to obtain additional information.
- Obtain a written statement about the incident or accident from all controllers and supervisory personnel involved. Written or taped records pertaining to an aircraft accident will be retained for a minimum of six months. Written or taped records pertaining to an aircraft incident will be retained for a minimum of 30 days.
- Request a local weather observation, unless there has been an intervening meteorological aviation report (METAR) or special observation (SPECI).
- Record all appropriate details, including the local weather observation, on DA Form 3502 (see appendix A).

Note. Immediately inform the local weather personnel of each emergency or aircraft mishap. When notified of an emergency, the weather station must intensify the weather watch to ensure the aircraft in distress receives the maximum weather support.

- Mark and safeguard the recording tapes that are (or may be) pertinent to the accident and handle them according to chapter three of this publication. In case of an incident, such as an emergency or a complaint about ATC services that does not result in an accident, removal of recorder tapes before the normal rotation time is unnecessary.
- Relieve the controller for physical and psychological evaluation by the local medical officer or flight surgeon if there is any indication the controller contributed to the accident or incident. The controller will obtain a clearance from the local medical officer or flight surgeon before returning to duty.
- Examine the condition of the equipment, along with technically certified maintenance personnel, to determine whether it could have contributed to the accident or incident.

Note. Additional instruction pertaining to facility actions will be contained in the ATC facility position binder.

INFORMATION RELEASE

1-43. No personnel may give interviews, make statements, or release any written or recorded information to news agencies or unauthorized personnel or organizations. Information on an aircraft accident, incident, or alleged violation of any kind will not be released outside official Army channels without approval from the commander, United States Army Aeronautical Services Agency (USAASA). The identity of personnel involved will be treated as restricted information. The installation commander may approve the release of information to Army organizations and Army press releases after consultation with the Public Affairs Office (PAO) and the Staff Judge Advocate (SJA).

Note. Headquarters, DA Deputy Chief of Staff (DCS) Assistant Chief of Staff, Operations and Plans (G-3) is the release or denial authority for Freedom of Information Act (FOIA) requests. Commander, USAASA serves as the DCS G-3 responsible official for the U.S. Army regarding airspace, aeronautical information, ATC, and flight procedures policy.

SECTION III – PERSONNEL TITLES, QUALIFICATIONS, RESPONSIBILITIES, AND RESTRICTIONS

AIR TRAFFIC CONTROL CHIEF

1-44. The ATC chief must meet all requirements as outlined in AR 95-2. The ATC chief manages multiple ATC facilities at a single airfield, heliport, or installation. The ATC chief's responsibilities include—

- Providing assistance and local expertise on matters of ATC and airspace to the air traffic and airspace officer (AT&AO), DAR FAA, ACOMs, ASCC, direct reporting unit (DRU), local post, camp, or installation commander, and representatives of other units, agencies, or commands.
- Ensuring ATC systems meet all safety and operational requirements.
- Collecting and safe guarding data concerning aircraft mishaps, emergencies, or violations.
- Ensuring ATC personnel maintain currency in assigned facilities.
- Monitoring the establishment and conduct of ATC training and rating programs ensuring compliance with this publication and applicable regulations.
- Serving as air traffic control specialist (ATCS)/control tower operator (CTO) examiner IAW AR 95-2, FAAO JO 7220.1B, and this publication.
- Administering biennial written exams and conducting skill evaluations.
- Ensuring all facilities comply with applicable Army and FAA regulations and publications regarding ATC facility operations.

FACILITY CHIEF

1-45. The facility chief manages a single ATC facility. His duties include—

- Ensuring the facility operates according to military and FAA rules and regulations applying to ATC.
- Developing and maintaining a FTP.
- Developing and maintaining a FTM.
- Serving as ATCS/CTO examiner IAW AR 95-2, FAAO JO 7220.1B, and this publication.
- Ensuring all controllers meet the physical standards of AR 40-501, AR 95-2, Department of the Army Pamphlet (DA Pam) 611-21, the Office of Personnel Management (OPM) handbook X-118, their official job descriptions, and/or local/host nation requirements.
- Ensuring the operational readiness of facility equipment and associated NAVAIDs.
- Maintaining a current file of pertinent regulations, manuals, charts, maps, and training material IAW this publication and AR 95-2.
- Ensuring assigned personnel maintain currency.
- Maintaining custodial control of all facility forms, records, and publications and ensures their accuracy, completeness, and distribution.
- Initiating and maintaining a facility duty schedule.
- Conducting testing and practical evaluation for PQ or rating of trainee controllers.
- Administering biennial written exams and conducting skill evaluations.
- Ensuring the number of non-ATC personnel in an ATC facility to a minimum. The chief will be the final authority on the admittance of non-ATC personnel to the facility and the number permitted at any one time. (In the chief's absence, the SL or CIC will assume this responsibility.)

● Must be facility rated and have completed facility management and administration training prior to assuming the duties of this position.

AIR TRAFFIC CONTROL TRAINING SUPERVISOR

1-46. The ATC training supervisor is a facility-rated ATC specialist designated by the facility/ATC chief. The training supervisor—

● Plans, schedules, direct, and supervise the facility training of assigned ATC personnel.
● Supervises and conducts classroom and self-study training.
● Develops local course material, training aids, and control scenarios to supplement and enhance the FTP.
● Evaluates and analyzes the capabilities and progress of the ATC personnel assigned to that facility.
● Maintains training records.
● Conducts position qualification evaluations.
● Recommends to the facility chief those controllers who require proficiency or remedial training. The training supervisor bases his recommendations on—
  ▪ Personal observations.
  ▪ SL comments.
● Serves as ATCS/CTO examiner IAW AR 95-2, FAAO JO 7220.1B, and this publication.
● Administers biennial written exams and conducts skill evaluations.
● Must be facility rated and have completed facility management and administration training prior to assuming the duties of this position.

AIR TRAFFIC CONTROL AUTOMATION SYSTEMS ADMINISTRATOR

QUALIFICATIONS

1-47. The ATC automation systems administrator duties are performed by either ATC (general schedule [GS]-2152 or 15Q) and/or ATC maintenance technicians (GS-856 or 94D), and/or foreign national equivalent employees employed by the Department of the Army in U.S. Army ATC facilities provided they meet the training requirements in accordance with regulatory guidance. Contractors in the aforementioned specialties may perform ATC automation systems administrator duties but shall not certify systems for use. ATC personnel are required to be facility rated and maintain proficiency within the associated facility. All ATC automation system administrators are required to complete the systems specialist course prior to performing these duties. Recognized training course are the following:

● Systems Administrators Course, (Keesler AFB, MS).
● Systems Administrators Course, (FAA Mike Monroney Aeronautical Center, OKC, OK).
● Systems Administrators Training associated with the installation of new systems.
● As applicable, Network+ certification and other information assurance requirements.

RESPONSIBILITIES

1-48. The ATC automation systems administrator is an assigned additional duty. The automation systems administrator ensures that the facility computer and related equipment function properly. He also–

● Analyzes, logs, tracks and resolves software/hardware matters of significance pertaining to networking connectivity issues, printer, servers, and applications to meet mission needs.
● Coordinates hardware/software installations and upgrades to ensure work is properly performed in accordance with established policy.
● Coordinates and monitors troubleshooting to isolate and diagnose common system problems.

- Coordinates testing, upgrades and configuration of system files and services. Ensures changes are in accordance with appropriate operating procedures.
- Installs, configures and maintains workstations and servers, including web based servers.
- Performs software installations and upgrades to operating systems and layered software packages and maintains them in accordance with established policies and procedures.
- Conducts routine hardware and software audits of workstations/servers for compliance with established standards, policies, procedures and configuration guidelines.
- Directs automation activities for systems analysis, program updates, security management, technical support, and resource management.
- Maintains control over the configuration of ATC automation systems, ensuring compliance with FAA, US Army, and National Airspace System specifications.
- Assists functional users define requirements to sustain or improve facility operations.
- Coordinates with ATC maintenance personnel with active certification authority to conduct systems or subsystems certification following events that effect equipment certification.

SHIFT LEADER

1-49. During the SL's tour of duty, he is responsible to the facility chief for the efficiency of facility operations. He also performs normal ATC duties in addition to those of the SL. The SL—

- Assigns and directs all phases of the subordinates' work.
- Ensures personnel receive on-the-job training (OJT) and conducts assessments of training through the administration of controller evaluations (DA Form 3479-1 [Trainee/Controller Evaluation]).
- Conducts position qualification evaluations when directed by the facility chief/training supervisor but are restricted from conducting biennial skill evaluations.
- Assists and advises controllers during emergencies.
- Maintains facility records.
- Ensures personnel are current and proficient.
- Notifies search and rescue facilities of aircraft in distress and provides assistance and advice.
- Delegates responsibility to subordinates and assists the training supervisor.
- Evaluates the operational effectiveness of facility systems, subsystems, and equipment.
- Records and reports outages and takes action to correct discrepancies.
- May serve as ATCS/CTO examiner IAW AR 95-2, FAAO JO 7220.1B, and this TC.
- Must be facility rated and have completed facility management and administration training prior to assuming the duties of this position.

CONTROLLER-IN-CHARGE

1-50. A CIC will be designated to assume the duties of the SL under the following conditions:

- When supervisory personnel leave the facility or are off duty, the facility chief will designate a CIC for the period the supervisor is absent. Assigning a CIC assures coordination and cooperation will continue when the SL is not available.
- The CIC will assume the duties and responsibilities of the SL. He also performs his normal ATC duties in addition to those of the SL.
- CICs may conduct controller evaluations but are restricted from conducting position qualification assessments and biennial skill evaluations.

1-51. Prior to being designated as a CIC, controllers will meet the following prerequisites:

- Be operationally current in the facilities CIC duties are to be preformed.
- Be selected by the ATC/facility chief.
- Successfully complete administration and management training.

1-52. The ATC/facility chief may designate more than one CIC per shift to ensure coverage is achieved during leaves, illnesses, or temporary groundings. The CIC duties should be rotated to expose the controller to supervisory duties and responsibilities.

1-53. ATC/facility chiefs and training supervisors will determine facility requirements for CICs considering facility operational needs such as scheduling concerns, staffing concerns, special events, and other issues. ATC managers will evaluate controllers for CIC duties based on their knowledge, skills, and abilities. Included in these three areas are problem solving and analytical ability, planning and organizing, decisiveness, judgment, communication skills, and interpersonal skill.

AIR TRAFFIC CONTROL MAINTENANCE CHIEF

1-54. The ATC maintenance chief is responsible for all ATC equipment maintenance. Duties include—

- Coordinating maintenance-related issues, such as LOA, on-call rosters, and NAVAID scheduled maintenance with the ATC chief/facility chief.
- Ensuring maintenance facilities are maintained according to applicable military and FAA publications and standards.
- Ensuring the qualifications of maintenance personnel.
- Establishing a maintenance training and certification program for the local facility.
- Coordinating facility configuration changes with the ATC chief or higher headquarters.
- Maintaining "as built" diagrams and drawings for ATC facilities and equipment IAW AR 95-2.
- Maintaining a file of pertinent regulations, manuals, and training material IAW appendix A.
- Serving as a maintenance training program certifier.

CONTROL TOWER OPERATOR AND AIR TRAFFIC CONTROL SPECIALIST EXAMINERS

1-55. CTO and ATCS examiners will be designated and assume duties as follows:

- CTO and ATCS examiners will be designated according to AR 95-2, FAA JO 7220.1B and this publication. AR 95-2 explains how to request examiner designations.
- A primary and alternate ATCS and CTO examiner may be appointed per facility.
- Examiners will conduct CTO/ATCS facility rating or certifications IAW Title 14 Code of Federal Regulation (CFR) Part 65, FAA JO 7220.1B, and AR 95-2. The required documentation for rating and certifications will be prepared and processed as per guidance provided in FAA JO 7220.1B and AR 95-2.
- PQ controllers in the absence of the facility managers provided they hold a rating for the facility and are current.
- Conduct biennial skill evaluations.

Note. CTO and ATCS examiners not meeting medical requirements may only administer the written portion of ratings and biennial skill evaluations.

OPERATING POSITIONS

1-56. Operating and controlling an ATC facility may require the following positions and responsibilities in addition to the supervisory positions:

- **Local control (LC).** Issues information and clearance for properly separating and sequencing aircraft under his control.
- **Ground control (GC).** Issues information and instructions for the orderly movement of traffic (aircraft, vehicles, and pedestrians) on the movement area.
- **Flight data (FD).** Receives, posts, and relays FD clearances and messages and assists in facility operations, as directed.

- **Coordinator (CI).** Coordinates the flow of air traffic between other positions or facilities, as required.
- **Clearance delivery (CD).** Delivers clearances to departing aircraft. The function of the CD is separate from that of the GC or FD.
- **Flight following (FF).** Issues information and advisories to arriving, departing, and en route aircraft and monitors the flight progress of aircraft. The FF also receives, posts, and relays progress reports and posts information to FD strips, boards, charts, and tactical situation maps.
- **Radar position (R).** Ensures separation, initiates control instructions, monitors and operates radios, accepts and initiates automated handoffs, assists the radar associate position with non-automated handoff actions when needed, assists the radar associate position in coordination when needed, and scans radar display. Correlates flight progress strip information, ensures computer entries are completed on instructions or clearances issued or received, ensures strip marking are completed on instructions or clearances issued or received, adjusts equipment at radar position to be usable by all members of the team.
- **Radar assistant (RA).** Assists the radar controller by accepting or initiating automated handoffs as directed by the radar position for the continued smooth operation of the facility/sector and ensures the radar position is made immediately aware of any actions taken.
- **Feeder control (FDC).** Provides for the radar sequencing and separation of aircraft vectored to intercept the final approach courses for handoff to precision approach radar (PAR) or for the conduct of a surveillance approach.
- **Final control (FC).** The FC issues instructions to the pilot based on the position of the aircraft relative to the final approach course, glide path, and distance from touchdown. The FC also monitors certain non-radar instrument approaches.

Note. The facility chief in a facility memorandum may further define radar positions such as radar North (RN), radar South (RS).

SECTION IV – FACILITY EQUIPMENT

1-57. This section discusses ATC facility equipment, equipment checks, and facility maintenance. It includes information on recorded media and procedures for the reproduction and accountability of recorded data. Information concerning equipment requirements, layouts, and navigational aid equipment standards is contained in appendix E.

EQUIPMENT OUTAGES

1-58. ATC facilities responsible for notifying the designated facility or office of any equipment outage, service curtailment, or airfield activity that may require a NOTAM will establish written procedures for the notification process.

FACILITY MAINTENANCE

SCHEDULING

1-59. The maintenance chief at each facility will ensure personnel schedule services, inspections, and repairs of ATC equipment according to AR 750-1, DA Pam 750-8 and the applicable operator/maintenance manual. Personnel will coordinate scheduling with the ATC/facility chief.

COORDINATION

1-60. The maintenance chief and facility chief will ensure certified maintenance personnel are available to perform any phase of the cursor alignment or adjustment requiring the use of test, measurement, and diagnostic equipment (TMDE). Maintenance of a NAVAID servicing two or more airfields or is a part of the NAS must be coordinated with the air route traffic control center (ARTCC) and other facilities affected.

SCHEDULING PERSONNEL FOR DUTY

1-61. Certified ATC maintenance personnel will be scheduled for duty during normal duty hours, Monday through Friday. However, such factors as equipment outages, mission requirements, maintenance schedules, and the number of assigned personnel may require the scheduling of certified maintenance personnel at times other than normal duty hours.

PROCEDURES FOR RECALLING AIR TRAFFIC CONTROL MAINTENANCE PERSONNEL

1-62. The facility chief/airfield management, in coordination with the maintenance chief, will develop written procedures for recalling ATC maintenance personnel if ATC or NAVAID equipment fails. These written procedures will be readily available to controllers on duty.

Note. ATC equipment with backup systems or NAVAIDs that do not provide the only means of an IFR approach to the active runway normally would not require a recall of maintenance personnel. However, other factors to consider before recalling maintenance personnel include amount of time before maintenance personnel arrive for scheduled duty, current and forecast weather conditions, and aircraft traffic.

EQUIPMENT CHECKLIST

1-63. The equipment checklist will be a locally produced form; the checklist may be a separate form, or it may be placed on the back of DA Form 3502. This form is not intended to circumvent the Army maintenance system but only to serve as a list of equipment that must be checked. Controllers must complete standard Army maintenance forms on equipment requiring them. The equipment checklist will be initiated at opening of the facility and reviewed at the beginning of each shift. Completed checklists will be filed with and retained the same as DA Form 3502.

1-64. The facility chief will establish an equipment checklist to be completed at the opening of the facility. This checklist often includes communication systems, light guns, digital bright radar indicator tower equipment (DBRITE), and automatic terminal information service (ATIS) checks. If radio checks cannot be completed during the facility's duty day this will be annotated on the DA Form 3502 in the closing statement. Recording equipment may be included in the equipment checklist.

1-65. If all equipment is operational, the entry on the form may be limited to "checklist complete." If outages occur, the entry must identify those outages, the name of the agency notified, and their operating initials, for example, "checklist complete; DBRITE OTS MAINT/CB NTFYD."

1-66. If an operational check of the primary crash alarm system cannot be conducted when a facility begins operation, this system will not be included on the equipment checklist. This system will be checked at least once a day and the results entered on DA Form 3502.

1-67. On DA Form 3502, a capital "E" (equipment) will be placed in the coordinated universal time (UTC) column to the left of entries showing equipment out-of-service time and return-to-service time. The "E" for a specific equipment outage need not be repeated each day thereafter unless the equipment returns to service. Examples of these are E0800, checklist complete, 126.2T OTS MAINT/CB NTFYD" and "E 0810, 126.2T RTS, radio and recorder checks complete."

AUTOMATIC TERMINAL INFORMATION SERVICE

1-68. ATIS provides advance operational and meteorological information for terminal areas and non-control airports using a controller-prepared recording. This information is repetitively broadcast on a voice outlet for aircraft arriving/departing an airport or operating within the terminal area. FAA JOs 7110.65T and 7210.3 contain further guidance on ATIS.

COORDINATED UNIVERSAL/LOCAL TIME

1-69. All ATC facilities will use UTC and date in all operational activities. Local time will be used for facility duty schedules and other administrative forms and correspondence.

1-70. A reliable clock depicting hours, minutes, and seconds will be visible from each operating position in all ATC facilities. Except for those facilities with digital, or direct coded time source clocks, time checks will be conducted at the beginning of each shift. The results of time checks will be logged on DA Form 3502. Time checks will be performed according to FAA JO 7210.3. Check clocks immediately after the facility goes to emergency/backup power and again 30 minutes later if found to be inaccurate. Check clocks hourly until restored to normal power.

LIGHT GUNS

1-71. ATC light gun color codes and meanings will be attached to the back or side of the light guns. ATC light guns will be adjusted to provide a red light when activated (if applicable).

CRASH ALARM SYSTEM

1-72. Crash telephone and radio receiver/transmitter keys should be centrally located so they are readily available to all control positions. DA Pam 385-10 and AR 420-1 prescribe the policies, procedures, and guidelines on the primary and secondary crash alarm system and local crash grid maps.

1-73. The ATC chief/facility chief will develop procedures for each position in the event of an aircraft accident/incident. These procedures will be published in the FTM and be contained within the separate operating position files.

TELEPHONE LINES

1-74. When possible, all non-commercial telephone lines to installation ATC facilities will terminate in the communications console key system. Commercial telephones should be provided on separate instruments. When this is not possible and commercial telephones are recorded, a beeper tone is required.

1-75. Direct telephone lines are required between ATC facilities. Their use will be restricted to the relay of essential movement and control instructions and advisories. Calls on direct telephone lines are handled secondarily to the primary function of ATC services. The lines should not be used to relay information such as departure or arrival times and load messages that can be handled by other means. If an ATC facility requires immediate priority over another, it will on initial contact state, "stand by for emergency instructions." These occurrences will be entered on DA Form 3502.

RADIO EQUIPMENT

1-76. ATC facilities are authorized to join radio nets with the crash and rescue team, airfield services, weather station, fire station, ambulance service, and security agency. To the extent possible, these radios will terminate within the communications console.

1-77. During the hours of operation, ATC facilities will continuously monitor all assigned radio frequencies. Facilities sharing radios will establish procedures to ensure one of the facilities continuously monitors these frequencies.

1-78. All ATC facilities should have transmit/receive capability on emergency frequencies 121.5 and 243.0-megahertz (MHz). When ATC facilities are close, they will share transmitters and receivers if services will not be degraded. If transmitters and receivers are shared, geographical area coverage will not be reduced. In addition, voice communications switches will be equipped with lockout devices to avoid inadvertent interference between facilities.

1-79. The two emergency frequencies will not be terminated on the same transmit-receive key selector of any other frequency. When a remote communications console is provided to a non-ATC facility at an airfield that has an ATC facility, only the emergency receiver will be provided.

1-80. As a minimum, two-way transmitter and receiver checks will be conducted daily on all radio frequencies. These checks will also be conducted following recording equipment and other equipment repairs and normal preventive maintenance.

NAVIGATIONAL AIDS

1-81. All NAVAIDs must pass an FAA flight inspection before IFR operations are conducted. The procedures contained in FAA 8260.3 will be used to construct a precision or non-precision approach that will service the terminal area. The following actions will be accomplished to prepare for a flight inspection:

- Ensure all personnel are familiar with FAAO 8200.1.
- Provide accurate facility data for new or relocated facilities.
- Develop an LOA concerning the airspace used for the approach procedure.
- Assign the best-qualified controller available.
- Establish communications on a single dedicated frequency.
- Ensure all facility equipment is calibrated IAW applicable manuals.
- Ensure certified maintenance personnel will be available to make corrections and adjustments.
- Provide transportation to move flight inspection equipment and personnel.

MONITORS

1-82. The approach control facility normally is designated the primary NAVAID monitoring facility. At locations without an approach control, the TWR is designated the primary NAVAID monitoring facility.

1-83. Some ATC facilities do not operate continuously. If the NAVAID is to remain on the air continuously, another facility or agency will be assigned monitoring responsibility. This facility or agency will also provide continuous manning and respond quickly to the call for maintenance personnel. In addition, it will establish written procedures concerning equipment outages and submission of NOTAMs.

1-84. If another facility or agency is not available to perform this function, the IFR supplement must indicate that the particular NAVAIDS are unmonitored when the facility is closed.

1-85. Monitors that do not provide an automatic visual or aural alarm will be checked at least once an hour. When an ATC facility is responsible for monitoring NAVAIDs, the facility chief will include monitoring instructions in the FTM. If a NAVAID monitor alarm is received, the identification feature will be checked aurally and the responsible maintenance authority notified immediately. If the alarm cannot be silenced and the identification feature cannot be heard, the NAVAID is considered inoperative.

1-86. If personnel suspect a control line or monitor failure rather than a malfunction of the NAVAID causes an alarm, they must take the appropriate action per FAA JO 7110.65T. If a malfunction is confirmed, use of the NAVAID will be discontinued. A NOTAM will be published showing NAVAIDs with inoperative monitors as unmonitored. A Department of Defense (DOD) FLIP, en route supplement, and IFR supplement will also show those NAVAIDs without installed monitors as unmonitored.

INTERRUPTIONS AND MALFUNCTIONS

1-87. The ATC chief/facility chief establishes procedures for reporting interruptions to NAVAIDs and malfunctions in communications and radar equipment. He ensures the timely response of maintenance personnel to a report of an interruption or a malfunction.

1-88. The on-duty SL or CIC will report any known or reported malfunction in equipment or interruption to a NAVAID to the appropriate office; for example, maintenance personnel, ARTCC, approach control facility, and any other facility that may be affected. The malfunction or interruption is reported to the airfield division chief/commander/manager.

RECORDED MEDIA

RECORDER CHECKS AND TAPE CHANGES

1-89. A facility memorandum will be developed outlining the procedures for changing, marking, loading, and securing recorded media, and for controller/maintenance responsibilities. If the recording device is not convenient to operating areas, the facility chief and the responsible maintenance chief will develop a written agreement assigning this responsibility. It is imperative that all controllers and maintenance personnel are properly trained to check the recorder, change the recorded media, and perform preventive maintenance checks and services (PMCS). This training will be noted in the training records.

1-90. Controllers are required to monitor the quality of recordings. At the beginning of each shift, the SL or CIC will ensure all recording channels are operating properly.

1-91. The facility chief and the maintenance chief will establish written procedures to ensure the recording quality is checked after all radio, recorder, or telephone equipment maintenance. These checks will be noted on DA Form 3502. At dual facilities, the ATC chief may designate one facility to make all tape changes and recorder checks. This facility will have the responsibility to document the results of tape changes and recorder checks on DA Form 3502.

Recording Equipment Labels

1-92. An identification number will be assigned and attached to each recorded media. At the beginning of each day, the number of the recorded media and the device number used to record will be entered on DA Form 3502. If it is necessary to change the recorded media during the shift, the reason for the change, the number of the recorded media removed, and the number of the recorded media and the device used to record will be entered on DA Form 3502 and the initials of the individual making the change.

DIGITAL AUDIO LEGAL RECORDER

1-93. As part of the NAS ATC modernization program, the digital voice recorder system (DVRS) is being phased out and replaced by the DALR system. The completion of installation, testing, and switchover will create an inability to playback any voice data retained from old media tapes/cassettes. Old media storage requirements remain in effect to satisfy retention directives. Any facility requiring the playback of DVRS media will contact ATSCOM fixed-base systems division.

USE OF RECORDERS

1-94. Controllers and maintenance personnel will use the following information for configuring, certifying, maintaining, and operating DALR systems until the appropriate maintenance technical handbook(s) and technical instruction book(s) are distributed:

- Air traffic facilities will record operational communications to the maximum extent practicable.
- If combined positions are periodically split into individual positions, record them on separate channels when so used.
- Operational voice recorders will be provided a time source.
- Recorders may be used to monitor any position for evaluation, training, or quality control purposes.
- The ATC/facility chief will develop a facility memorandum, or LOA identifying those personnel who have access to the DALR system, their access privileges, and identify a systems administrator for the DALR. The intent of this memorandum is to ensure system security and the integrity of the media being recorded.

ASSIGNMENT OF RECORDER CHANNELS

1-95. Assign position recording channels in the following order of priority:

Primary

- Radar position.
- Radar position.
- LC.
- Radar position.
- FD (TWR).
- FF.
- Clearance delivery.
- GC.
- FD (radar).
- FD (AIC).
- Coordinator.
- Supervisory.
- Primary crash line from ATC facility to local crash net.
- ATIS.
- Point to point telephone lines between ATC facilities.

1-96. After the requirements listed above are met, the remaining spare channels may be used for channel clearing and recording the primary radio frequencies. These frequencies are recorded in the following order.

Secondary

- Very high frequency (VHF) and ultra high frequency (UHF) emergency.
- Approach control (radar or non-radar).
- Departure control.
- LC.
- GC.
- Pilot to dispatch positions.

MAINTENANCE/CONFIGURATION/CHECKS

1-97. FAA policy will be used to establish essential maintenance activities for DALR system. FAA policy identifies the performance checks (tests, measurements, and observations) of normal operating controls and functions, which are necessary to determine whether operation of the DALR is within established tolerances/limits. This document is available on the ATSCOM homepage.

1-98. All performance and maintenance checks will be accomplished by ATS maintenance personnel with the exception of the daily checks for indications of alarm conditions on the maintenance workstation. These checks may be performed by either ATS or maintenance personnel. If ATS personnel are to conduct the daily alarm condition checks, the ATC facility chief and maintenance chief will establish a written agreement outlining the responsibilities and procedures for conducting these checks. The results of all system checks will be annotated on the FAA Form 6030-1 (Facility Maintenance Log 1).

1-99. The ATC chief and maintenance chief will establish written procedures to ensure the quality of recordings are checked and documented after all radio, recorder, or telephone equipment maintenance. The results of these checks will be annotated on the DA Form 3502.

SOFTWARE VIRUS PROTECTION

1-100. The DALR system is a computer-based, software-driven recording system running on its own private local area network (LAN) without virus protection software: as such, it can be vulnerable to software viruses. The primary method of protection from the introduction of viruses is system isolation from any outside LAN. The system will not be connected to any external LAN administrative or otherwise.

1-101. Except for the types listed below, no other programs and/or software packages will be loaded and/or executed on any of the computer systems (logger and computer workstations) part of the DALR system. This applies to logger(s), and all computer workstations part of the DALR and the systems isolated LAN:

- Logger Software.
  - Nice administrator application.
  - Nice monitor application.
  - Nice log setup tool.
  - Nice inform.
- Workstation Software.
  - Castle rock Secure Network Management Program-computers (SNMPc).
  - Microsoft internet explorer.
- User Installed Workstation Software.
  - Microsoft office suite (Army approved version).
  - WAV player utility.

RECORDED MEDIA ACCOUNTABILITY

1-102. The facility chief has custodial responsibility for tape recordings made on equipment furnished or maintained by the Army. When another service or agency has custodial responsibility for the recorder tapes, an LOA will be initiated to specify access and retention policies and procedures.

RECORDED MEDIA RETENTION-DIGITAL AUDIO LEGAL RECORDER

1-103. The DALR system will be set to retain normal day-to-day activities for 45 days. Media containing information on emergencies or alleged violations will be reconstructed and filed utilizing the "create new incident" feature of the system. If no request for transcript has been received within the allotted retention timeline, the media may be deleted. If there is a request for information, the recording will be distributed on a compact disk/digital video device (DVD) with an embedded Time stamp and retained for 30 days from time of extraction. In the event items are added to the original distribution, they will be placed on the original compact disk/DVD.

1-104. Recordings containing accident information will be retained for a minimum of six months. These recordings will be reconstructed and filed utilizing the "create new incident" feature of the system. Additionally, these recordings will be extracted as soon as possible and labeled. Recordings related to hijackings will be retained for three years. If no request for transcript has been received within six months, the data in the incident folder may be deleted and the related compact disk/DVD destroyed. When creating accident files for retention, ensure all audio starts five minutes prior to first contact and continues five minutes after the accident or last contact. For detailed information regarding aircraft accident and incident notification, investigation and reporting refer to FAAO 8020.16 and AR 95-30. Figure 1-1 outlines the format used for certified copies of tapes containing accident information.

I certify that this is the original recording made in _____(facility)_____ containing all conversation
on ____(position)____ at ____(channel)____ pertaining to (accident or emergency (aircraft ID) on ___(date)___

Signature:

Name:

Grade:

Title:

Date:

Figure 1-1. Certification of tapes containing accident information

RECORDED MEDIA TRANSCRIPTIONS

1-105.   The memorandum format contained in AR 25-50 is the Army standard. The required contents of
the memorandum are—

- Subject.
- Recording facility.
- List of transmitting facilities.
- Facility, landline, or position being recorded.
- Date of transcription and the time covered by transcript.
- Certification.

1-106.   FAAO 8020.11 appendix 2 contains detailed information and instructions for the transcription of
recorded media.

WIND INDICATOR EQUIPMENT

1-107.   Windsocks and wind cones used at Army facilities will comply with standards in unified facilities
code (UFC) 3-535-01 Wind sensors will comply with standards in UFC 3-260-01.

1-108.   Controllers can determine estimated winds after comparing readouts from transmitters and visual
observations of windsocks and wind cones using the Beaufort scale shown in FAAO 7900.5. Windsock
values must be known by the controllers prior to any attempt to estimate winds using visual observations of
windsocks.

ALTIMETERS

SETTING COMPARISONS

1-109.   ATC facilities will compare official altimeter reports with facility instruments at the beginning of
each shift. Any difference will be posted next to the face of the instrument and recorded on DA Form 3502.
The correction factor will be applied to the reading obtained from the facility instrument before the
altimeter setting is transmitted to a pilot or another facility. Use of the facility instrument will be
discontinued at—

- Non-precision approach locations when the correction factor exceeds ±0.05-inches of mercury.
- Precision approach locations when the correction factor exceeds ±0.02-inches of mercury.

1-110.   When weather conditions indicate the probability of a steep pressure gradient between the two
locations or the elevation difference exceeds 1,000 feet, altimeter settings are not compared. At locations
that do not meet the 10- and 25-nautical mile limitations, a mercurial barometer or altimeter-setting
indicator is required to make comparisons.

Obtaining Official Altimeter Settings

1-111. Altimeter-setting indicators inspected and calibrated according to Air Force weather service guidance may be used to obtain the official altimeter setting at locations that have no local weather service support. At facilities with no weather reporting station and only one altimeter device, the altimeter setting may be compared with values obtained from adjacent weather stations if at locations where—

- Precision Instrument Landing System (ILS) or PAR approaches are conducted, the distance to the weather station is not more than 10 nautical miles, and the wind speed is 25 knots or less.
- Non-precision approaches are conducted, the distance to the weather station is not more than 25 nautical miles, and the wind speed is 30 knots or less.

Estimated Settings

1-112. Air traffic controllers will issue an altimeter setting as estimated according to FAA JO 7110.65T.

SECTION V – MEDICAL

MEDICAL RESTRICTIONS TO AIR TRAFFIC CONTROL DUTIES

1-113. The duties of a controller require a certain level of health status or fitness due to the nature of the high degree of responsibility toward the public. The aeromedical technical bulletin (ATB) titled *"Department of the Army Civilian (DAC) and Civilian Contract Air Traffic Control (ATC) Medical Examination Qualification Standards",* dated July 2003, will serve as a guide for the conduct of the air traffic controller medical examination (ATCME) for DAC and contract civilian ATC. The ATCME may be completed by a flight surgeon or aeromedical physician's assistant (APA) from any branch of the service and will be completed annually for all DAC/contract ATC. Medical qualification requirements for DA civilian air traffic controllers are outlined in OPM operating manual: Qualification standards for general schedule positions, GS-2152: ATC series are IAW section 339.202, Title 5, CFR.

1-114. Current OPM standards address both application and retention for ATC. ATC medical examinations fall in two broad categories:

- **Initial ATCME** - preformed for initial employment purposes. They are valid for up to 18 months from the date of examination.
- **Retention ATCME** - performed on ATC once in service. This is performed for re-certification for DAC and civilian ATC on an annual basis. It is generally valid for 12 months and is synchronized with the ATC's birth month.

Note. Specific requirements and medical standards to be met are contained within the ATB.

1-115. FAA physicals for either category of ATC will not be accepted by the United States Army Aeromedical Activity (USAAMA) as certification of medical fitness. Any DAC or civilian contract ATC who pursues a FAA certificate does so at their own expense unless specifically covered by their contract. A DA Form 4186 (Medical Recommendation for Flying Duty) signed by a flight surgeon of any military service must be completed as part of the ATCME and serves as a recommendation to the local airfield division chief/commander/manager of the individual's medical fitness for execution of ATC duties. Flight surgeons will not issue a DA Form 4186 based on presentation of an FAA examination or certificate. Failure to comply with the annual requirement for an ATCME or current, valid DA Form 4186 may result in medical disqualification. The signed DA Form 4186 will be maintained in the controller's training records (see appendix F, figure F-9).

1-116. If a supervisor determines a controller's physical or mental health is questionable, he will relieve the controller of ATC duties. The supervisor will refer the controller to a flight surgeon/medical examiner for an evaluation and a ruling. If a controller is receiving a substance or medical procedure that is likely to provoke an adverse systemic reaction, he will be restricted from ATC duties. The controller will not perform ATC duties until declared fit IAW AR 40-501. AR 40-8 addresses the factors to consider and the appropriate medical restrictions to ATC duty.

1-117. A Class II FAA medical certification is not required by DA or FAA for contract ATCs to control air traffic in DOD facilities (14 CFR 65.31, 33). The initial and subsequent determinations of medical fitness for ATC duties are made as outlined in the above-mentioned regulation. The contract will state that DA contract ATCs will meet the same medical qualification requirements as those for DA civilians set forth in paragraphs above.

This page intentionally left blank.

Chapter 2

Air Traffic Control Operations

The ATC chief/facility chief will coordinate closely with airfield management to establish written procedures for ensuring the most efficient use of runways. Compliance with established procedures ensures positive control and coordination of personnel, ground vehicles, and aircraft on or near taxiways, runways, and landing areas. Personnel in or near these areas will maintain two-way radio communications with the control TWR to the maximum extent possible and will be familiar with TWR light gun signals.

SECTION I – CONTROL TOWER OPERATIONS

COMMUNICATION PROCEDURES

2-1.   The SL on duty is responsible for all communications emanating from the facility. The facility chief will ensure periodic checks are made to detect and prevent superfluous or unauthorized transmissions, as follows:

Contents

- The SL takes action to detect and prevent radio or telephone transmission of false or deceptive communications and obscene, indecent, or profane language. The SL is also responsible for detecting unauthorized or unassigned identifications and preventing willful or malicious interference with other communications.

- Besides normal ATC transmissions, the facility may need to transmit third-party messages about the safety of aircraft operations or the preservation of life or property. Such transmissions are authorized on ATC radio communications channels. Controller personnel or persons concerned with the emergency may handle these transmissions. Other personnel may be given access to ATC facilities radios if control instructions are not issued and their transmissions can be interrupted to continue ATC services.

- ATC facilities may relay non-ATC instructions only when no other source of communication is available and the transmissions will not interfere with ATC instructions. When it appears that such broadcasts may affect the control of air traffic, ATC personnel will immediately notify the ATC chief/facility chief.

CERTIFIED TOWER RADAR DISPLAY

2-2.   Some towers are combined with full radar approach control facilities, and the controllers rotate between the tower and approach control. Under these conditions, local controllers may use certified tower display workstations or DBRITE displays for the terminal radar function if they can satisfy the FAA air traffic requirements regarding aircraft operating on runways or in the surface area. The conditions and limitations for usage will be specified in an LOA.

2-3.   At locations where controllers do not rotate between the radar facility and the tower, Local controllers may use certified tower display workstations and DBRITE displays to—

- Identify aircraft and their exact location or spatial relationship to other aircraft. (This authority does not alter the visual separation procedures outlined in FAA JO 7110.65T.)
- Provide radar traffic advisories to aircraft.

- Provide directions or suggested headings to visual flight rule (VFR) aircraft as a radar identification method or as an advisory NAVAID.
- Provide information and instructions to aircraft operating in the surface area.

2-4. When the above conditions and the following conditions are present, local controllers may also use certified tower display workstations and DBRITE displays to ensure separation between successive departures, arrivals, and over flights within the surface area. The additional conditions are if—

- Radar separation procedures do not require the tower to provide radar vectors.
- Local controllers have radar training and certification or qualification commensurate with their radar duties.
- A copy of the LOA was submitted to the DAR IAW AR 95-2.

Note. The LOA must authorize the specific function and prescribe the procedures to be used. It must also prescribe the process for a transition to non-radar procedures or the suspension of separation authority in case of a radar outage.

- The procedures for giving and receiving radar handoffs or point-outs do not impair the local controller's ability to satisfy FAA and Army ATC requirements for aircraft operation on runways or within the surface area.

2-5. The TWR facility may be delegated the responsibility for providing the services outlined in the previous paragraphs. In flight-following facilities, tower display workstations and DBRITE will provide traffic advisories and VFR radar services.

2-6. The tower display workstations and DBRITE are IFR-certifiable; at select GCA locations, it will serve as the surveillance radar.

WEATHER

2-7. All controllers should complete initial qualification (Q) weather training before starting PQ phase but must have completed this weather training prior to being position qualified. Weather training is valid for a 12-month period and must be renewed by or prior to the anniversary month of their previous training. The ATC chief/facility chief will ensure comprehensive training is given to controllers by weather personnel on tower (prevailing) visibility. Tower visibility training will include—

- Definitions.
- Visibility determination criteria and procedures.
- Reporting procedures.
- METARS training to include—
  - Reading aviation weather reports.
  - Abbreviations.

2-8. The results of initial (Q) and annual training (P) will be entered on DA Form 3479 in section II. Required entries in section II include the date training was completed, total training time, and test results if applicable. If remedial training is required, it will be completed as previously outlined, except an "R" will indicate the type of training given. Figure 2-1, page 2-3, is an example of a remedial training entry.

2-9. Local weather service authorities will provide a practical training program to certify air traffic controllers as limited weather observers IAW AR 115-10. At airfields where weather support is not available, the facility chief will contact the DAR to secure certified training materials from the FAA and conduct internal facility training.

SECTION II - TRAINING, TESTING, AND EVALUATIONS				
SUBJECT / POSITION / EQUIPMENT	TYPE OF TRAINING	DATE	RESULTS	REMARKS
Weather Certification	Q	3 May 2008	U	USAF
Weather Certification	R	5 May 2008	S	USAF

Figure 2-1. Remedial training entry

RELAY OF WEATHER OBSERVATIONS TO THE TOWER

2-10. The local weather service will make weather observations available through automated means.

Weather Data

2-11. The airfield weather status (IFR or VFRs) will be posted to DA Form 3502 when daily operations begin. As it changes during the day, the status is again posted to the form.

2-12. Controllers do not need to retain weather data received over recorded voice lines or automated systems. However, they will retain with the DA Form 3502, weather data received over unrecorded voice lines and data copied on notepaper. Both the observer and the controller initials will be posted on each observation received.

AUTOMATED METEOROLOGICAL OBSERVING SYSTEMS

2-13. The United States Air Force (USAF) may provide official weather observations at U.S. Army locations worldwide using USAF-owned and certified Automated Meteorological Observing Systems (AMOS) operating in full automated mode. USAF Operations Directorate (A3O) recently issued guidance directing the USAF to operate AMOS fully automated except during periods when human augmentation or backup of AMOS is required.

2-14. The USAF will install or has installed AMOS at designated ATC controlled Army airfields (AAFs) worldwide. When commissioned, the USAF certifies AMOS (Automated Surface Observation System [ASOS], FMQ-19, and TMQ-53) to meet all federal certification requirements to include FAA requirements for establishment and maintenance of Class D airspace.

COOPERATIVE WEATHER WATCH

2-15. The cooperative weather watch is an observation program in which air traffic controllers and other base agencies assist in monitoring weather conditions. A primary concern is the reporting of tower visibility when different from reported surface prevailing visibility, sector visibility, and local pilot reports (PIREPs). Air Force manual (AFMAN) 15-111 mandates a cooperative weather watch for USAF weather agencies. When a cooperative weather watch is mandated, an LOA is required to document procedures and responsibilities of the agencies participating in the program. This LOA will include as a minimum:

- Training requirements and certification of tower personnel to provide tower visibility observations (TVOs).
- Review of tower visibility checkpoint charts (VCCs).
- Requirement for ATC controllers to make tower prevailing or sector visibility observations when visibility at usual points of observations or at tower level is less than 4 miles.
- Notification requirements when tower prevailing visibility differs from reported values.
- Notification requirements to the servicing radar facility.
- Procedures for reporting and relaying PIREPs.
- Procedures for reporting of weather phenomenon.

Visibility Checkpoint Charts

2-16. VCC are a means of accurately making TVOs by identifying prominent lights or objects located near the tower. All control tower facility chiefs will prepare VCCs. These charts will be used to report TWR visibility and observe changes in the reported visibility. Charts will clearly identify both day and night visibility checkpoints. The most suitable day markers are dark or nearly dark colored objects such as:

- Buildings.
- Chimneys.
- Hills.
- Tree line.

2-17. The most desirable night visibility markers are lights of moderate intensity such as:

- Television station tower obstruction lights.
- Radio station tower obstruction lights.

2-18. Checkpoint charts may be map-type charts depicting the prominent lights or objects to be used with their distances and directions from the control tower using range rings as appropriate or be high quality (color/digital) photos taken on a predominantly cloud and obstruction-free day.

Advisories

2-19. TVOs are advisories unless weather station personnel verify them or the individuals taking the observations have been certified to make official weather reports. This information may include thunderstorm location, movement, and rapidly deteriorating visibility. TWR controllers must also advise terminal radar facilities of any observed phenomena not in the current weather report.

Support to the Cooperative Weather Watch Program

2-20. TWR controllers must relay TVOs to weather station personnel to support the cooperative weather watch program. This requirement is particularly important during severe weather, and when conditions observed by non-weather personnel and those reported in the current weather observation are different. The local situation and weather observation site location influence how the weather station reports or relays information. The station will issue a new observation or include reports of differing conditions, such as runway visual range (RVR) and prevailing visibility, in an official weather observation (METAR, SPECI, or local). The local weather unit and the organizations to which certified non-weather personnel are assigned will establish the criteria and procedures for weather reporting. Facility chiefs will contact the nearest weather station to visit and review regulations concerning weather observation, reporting, and personnel training.

2-21. Tower facilities will perform TVOs at the request of the local weather station or airfield division chief/commander/manager. Facilities that perform TVOs will develop a LOA between the ATC facility and weather station. The LOA will state the weather elements to be reported, responsibilities, and coordination procedures. Air Force weather stations, for example, normally publish these requirements in regulations or supplements.

2-22. Tower personnel will—

- Notify the surface-based observer when the tower prevailing visibility decreases to less than or, increases to equal or exceed, four miles.
- Report all changes of one or more reportable values to the surface-based observer when the prevailing visibility at the tower or the surface is less than four miles.

2-23. Tower personnel will record on graphic transcription equipment, or a separate tabulation sheet, the following information for each control TVO:

- Time of observation.
- Prevailing visibility at the tower level.
- Remarks (such as visibility in different sectors).
- Observer's initials.

NIGHT VISION SYSTEM OPERATIONS

2-24. Tower facilities using night vision systems (NVS) will establish a training program for their use. This program will include—

- Identification of aircraft using NVS.
- Night vision device (NVD) routes.
- Traffic density and restrictions.
- Hours of operation.
- Emergency procedures.
- Weather requirements.
- Nonparticipating traffic.
- Aircraft lighting (lights out or dim mode).
- Publication of a NOTAM, if required.

SECTION II – RADAR OPERATIONS

RADAR SERVICE

2-25. Radar service will be provided only when the controller has a suitable target and is satisfied that the presentation and equipment performance are adequate for the service provided.

DAILY PERFORMANCE CHECKS

2-26. Radar controllers determine if the quality of radar display is satisfactory for ATC purposes. Radar performance quality is determined by comparing identified targets against data obtained during the commissioning flight inspection. Controller and certified maintenance personnel may also determine the quality of the radar display jointly through minimum performance criteria. Radar controllers will be familiar with the commissioning flight inspection and minimum performance data. The facility chief will make this information available to the controllers.

2-27. The SL will ensure each radar controller completes the necessary radar alignments and adjustments at the beginning of each facility workday or as soon as practicable thereafter, according to the appropriate manuals. The daily radar performance check will be part of routine equipment checks. Controllers will accomplish this check once each shift, unless lack of traffic makes it impossible. For radar performance checks, area surveillance radar (ASR) systems will conform to the following tolerances:

- **Coverage.** A usable target return will be maintained along the entire airway/route or arrival/ departure control route for which radar service is provided. Tracking accuracy along these routes will be within the fix/map accuracy. Radar services for arrival or departure routes exist between the normal handoff point and a point one-half mile from the end of the runway.
- **Fix/map accuracy.** Radar accuracy must be such that reporting aircraft are within a circular area about the fix. The radius of this area is three percent of the fix-to-station distance or 500 feet (1,000 feet for the Air Traffic Control Radar Beacon System [ATCRBS]) whichever is greater. Tolerances are not assigned for fixed target identification or moving target indicator.

DISPLAY INDICATORS

2-28. Radar approach, departure control, and VFR radar advisory functions are normally conducted from a radar approach control. A tower display workstation or a DBRITE display may be used. Radar approach and departure control functions may be performed from the tower cab if—

- Not more than two radar-operating positions are required, and DBRITE display indicators are used on a permanent basis.
- More than two operating positions are required, and DBRITE display indicators are installed on an interim basis pending the establishment of a radar approach control.

● Temporarily, when radar display indicators other than DBRITE display indicators are installed.

2-29. If a scan conversion DBRITE is used, the standard installation will consist of one operational and one standby scan conversation unit. The range and center selected for the master DBRITE display will be the same on all slaved display indicators.

2-30. If the radar operating positions concerned require individual beacon decoding, each DBRITE display position will need a separate scan conversion unit. A DBRITE display installed in the tower cab for LC will be positioned where it can be viewed easily from the local controller's normal sitting or standing position. At least one direct-view indicator must be retained if the surveillance-approach capability would be lost when only the scan conversion DBRITE display is used.

AUTOMATION PROGRAM CHANGES

2-31. Facility chiefs of automated facilities will review each site program bulletin (terminal) issued by FAA ATS or the U.S. Air Force and local program patches to determine their impact on operations and procedures. When necessary, a facility directive will be issued to describe functional changes and resulting procedural changes. When a facility has a DBRITE hosted by an FAA or Air Force radar automation system, the facility chief will coordinate with the host facility chief to determine the impact of a site program bulletin.

AUTOMATIC ACQUISITION AND TERMINATION AREAS

2-32. The facility chief will—

● Establish automatic acquisition areas for arrivals and over-flights at ranges that permit automatic acquisition of targets before the ARTCC/Automated Radar Terminal System (ARTS)-to-ARTS automatic handoff area when the center is in the radar data processing (RDP) mode.
● Coordinate with adjacent automated facilities to ensure computer handoffs will be initiated only after the aircraft are within their facility automatic acquisition area.

Note. Coordination may not be feasible because of airspace assignment. Therefore, a LOA will prescribe the use of an appropriate procedure according to FAA JO 7110.65T to confirm the identity of all aircraft handed off before ARTS acquisition.

● Establish automatic acquisition areas for departing aircraft one mile or less from the end of the runway.
● Establish automatic termination areas for arriving aircraft one mile or less from the runway threshold.
● At satellite airfields, for arriving aircraft at minimum radar coverage range or altitude, whichever is greater.

2-33. Prescribe, in a LOA, the operating position responsibility for determining if an automatic acquisition of a departure track has occurred. Distances greater than those specified above may be authorized when operational conditions dictate. FAA concurrence may be obtained through the DAR.

AIR TRAFFIC CONTROL RADAR BEACON SYSTEM

2-34. The FTM will specify the discrete codes assigned to each operating position from the code subsets allocated to the facility. The ATC chief/facility chief will develop local procedures, operating instructions, and training materials to standardize intra-facility operations of the ATCRBS. Before the ATCRBS is used, its operational status will be verified. When the system is released to maintenance technicians, ATCRBS data will not be used and the affected facilities will be informed of scheduled and unscheduled shutdowns.

RADAR MAPPING

2-35. Facility chiefs will coordinate with adjacent radar facilities and the responsible authority for flight inspections to ensure the accuracy and adequacy of common reference points on radar maps when they are used to provide ATC services. To increase operational efficiency, data on video maps should be limited to—

- Handoff points.
- Reporting points.
- Major obstructions.
- Range accuracy marks.
- Airfields and heliports.
- Airway/route centerlines.
- Map alignment indicators.
- Hospital emergency landing areas.
- Radio navigational and approach aids.
- Special-use tracks such as scramble, recovery, and standard instrument departure (SID).
- Runway centerline extensions to a minimum of six miles.
- Prominent geographic features such as islands and mountains.
- MVA in hundreds of feet (for example, 25 equals 2,500 feet).
- Boundaries such as controlled special-use areas, terminal buffer areas, or outer fix holding-pattern areas.
- Airports immediately outside the area of jurisdiction but within the airspace used to receive radar handoffs and depicted by the facility having jurisdiction over the airspace.

2-36. The guidance in the previous paragraph will assist controllers in making emergency airport recommendations when in-flight emergencies occur near facility boundaries. There is no intent to establish criteria for airfield depiction. Because facilities having jurisdiction depict airfields on their video maps, those same airfields will be depicted on the adjacent facility video map. FAA JO 7110.65T provides additional information on airfield depiction.

AIRPORT SURVEILLANCE RADAR

2-37. To provide surveillance approaches, ASR indicators will display an electronic cursor as a reference to the runway centerline extended. This centerline reference will be extended to a minimum of six miles or the final approach fix (FAF) whichever is greater. The use of grid indicator lines on the face of the surveillance scope to form the ASR final approach course is not authorized. The facility chief will prepare a chart with recommended altitudes for surveillance approaches. This chart will be maintained in the facility and made readily available to controllers.

MINIMUM SAFE ALTITUDE WARNING AND CONFLICT ALERT

2-38. MSAW is a software function of the ARTS designed to generate an alert when an associated aircraft with Mode-C is at, or predicted to be at, an unsafe altitude. MSAW monitors aircraft for terrain and obstacle separation and will generate an alert, both aural and visual, on the display of the air traffic controller. MSAW consists of two detection components; the general terrain map (GTM) and the approach path monitor (APM). The facility chief may temporarily inhibit the MSAW, the APM portion of the MSAW, and conflict alert (CA) functions if their continual use would impact adversely on operational priorities. The chief is authorized to inhibit CA at specific operating positions, if advantageous to operations.

2-39. MSAW digital terrain maps (DTMs) will be kept current. The DAR will ensure FAA regional airspace branches furnish all automated radar facilities copies of newly received FAA Forms 7460-2 (Notice of Actual Construction or Alteration). The DAR will also ensure all automated radar facilities receive emergency notices of the erection of structures 200 feet or more above ground level and lie within

60 nautical miles of the radar site. To keep DTMs current, automated radar facilities also require copies of the National Flight Data Digest (NFDD) that contain information pertinent to that facility.

2-40. The ATC chief/facility chief will ensure FAA Forms 7460-2 are reviewed and the appropriate corrections made to the DTMs. He will also ensure the magnetic variation (MAGVAR) of the facility DTMs coincides with the MAGVAR of the facility radar video and geographical maps.

2-41. A DTM is constructed to align with the radar antenna, which has been offset for magnetic north. Therefore, any change in antenna offset will result in a corresponding change in the relative positions of the terrain points and obstacles used to determine DTM bin-altitude assignments. This will require, not only generating and verifying a new DTM, but also readapting the MSAW and CA databases to coincide with the changed declination. These databases would include, for example, airport areas, inhibit volume areas, and capture boxes.

MAGNETIC VARIATIONS OF VIDEO, GEOGRAPHICAL, AND MINIMUM SAFE ALTITUDE WARNING DIGITAL TERRAIN MAPS

2-42. Permanent echoes are the primary references for verifying radar antenna alignment. The facility chief will ensure the MAGVARs of radar video, geographical, and DTMs coincide. The accuracy of new or modified digital maps will be verified by using targets of opportunity that fly over displayed fixes, NAVAIDs, and so forth. Discrepancies will be documented showing the observed direction and displacement. If any discrepancy cannot be corrected or if the results obtained from targets of opportunity are not satisfactory, the facility may request a flight inspection through the DAR.

SECTION III – AIRSPACE INFORMATION CENTER OPERATIONS

PURPOSE

2-43. Flight following is a mission set with the operation of an AIC. Flight following is the observation of the progress of aircraft identified by radar or reports at predetermined times or geographic points. The aviator provides the primary navigation information and the controller receives and correlates the aircraft identity with the appropriate geographic position. Flight following is also a service that may be used to provide pilot briefings and en route communications and to assist aircraft in emergencies. In addition, it may be used to issue and relay ATC clearances and aviation weather information, monitor NAVAIDs, and provide a point-of-flight watch.

RESPONSIBILITIES

2-44. Installation commanders should review their local airspace management measures and determine if an Army AIC facility is required for flight safety in their cantonment areas, training areas, and ranges. Installations should take the following actions to evaluate existing methods of airspace management or to develop and implement additional airspace/aircraft procedures:

- Determine overall requirements for airspace management training based on the number of aircraft.
- Establish and coordinate an air route system with the installation plans and training office, assistant Chief of Staff, G-3, G-3 air, AT&A officer, and other key players in the airspace management arena.
- Establish routes to move aircraft to/from/through cantonment areas, training areas, or ranges.
- Ensure routes of flight do not cross/join or have two-way traffic at the same altitude, or establish procedures to preclude conflict.
- Ensure a common frequency for aircraft using the same routes of flight or training areas.
- Establish adequate reporting points that are easily identifiable and not located in or near brightly lighted or populated areas.

- Establish area, and subdivide free-play areas for mission training based on the overall training/airspace requirements, number of aircraft, and type of training.
- Number, letter, or name subdivided areas and depict them on the installation maps.
- Schedule free-play training areas in advance for specific unit training.
- Establish control procedures that preclude conflict on ingress/egress routes where chokepoints may exist.
- Establish separate routes of flight for NVD/nap-of-the-earth (NOE) training and operations.
- Ensure NVD/NOE routes have easily identifiable start and release points.
- Establish procedures to preclude the mixing of lighted and unlighted aircraft.
- Establish the maximum allowable density for aircraft in each free-play training area, and specify the data in the installation SOP.

2-45. AICs will provide communication and control of corridor feeder-route systems, chokepoints, crossing corridors, and transition areas in cantonment areas, training areas, and ranges. In addition, they will—

- Provide a common frequency.
- Issue advisories that allow pilots to separate their aircraft from other aircraft and activities or adverse weather that may endanger the aircraft.
- Monitor the flight progress of all participating aircraft within the facility area of responsibility.
- Advise other area users of aircraft activity that may affect, or conflict with, the mission or activity.
- Provide assistance during emergencies.
- Assist with search and rescue efforts, as needed.

PROCEDURES

2-46. The procedures developed for conducting day-to-day operations of an AIC depend on a number of circumstances. Local requirements govern exact operational procedures. However, the number and types of operating agencies and the activities in the facility area influence these procedures. Installations needing assistance in determining requirements for facility personnel and equipment will submit a facility request through their ACOM/ASCC/DRU/ARNG to ATSCOM (see AR 95-2 for blank form and procedures). The procedures and requirements outlined below establish a minimum standard and will apply to all Army AICs.

2-47. Each facility will have an up-to-date map of its area of responsibility. Each map will depict the following areas and routes:

- Explosive ordinance disposal (EOD)/hazardous cargo route.
- Impact areas.
- Firing points.
- NAVAIDs.
- Air defense identification zones (ADIZs) and no-fly areas.
- Prominent obstructions.
- NOE, NVD, unmanned aircraft systems (UAS) routes.
- Mandatory reporting points.
- Radio and radar blind spots.
- IFR recovery airfields and landing areas.
- Restricted/prohibited areas.
- Aircraft entry and exit points.
- Changeover points.
- Corridors, transition areas, training areas, and ranges.
- The same grid system as other area ATC and search and rescue facilities.

2-48. The flight progress of participating aircraft will be monitored, and the maximum time between position reports will be 30 minutes. Less time may be required depending on the type, length, and area of routes such as an NOE route.

2-49. The facility's area of responsibility will be divided into as many subareas as necessary to simplify recognition and reporting. Each area will be lettered, numbered, or named. The boundaries of these subareas, such as rivers, roads, and power lines, should be easily recognized from the air.

2-50. Procedures will be developed to ensure the timely receipt and dissemination of area weather information. Each facility should be electronically connected to the same weather dissemination equipment as in other area ATC facilities.

2-51. Procedures will be developed between the AIC facility and other area ATC facilities to ensure timely control information is passed. LOAs will establish procedures concerning hand-offs, control transfers, flight plans, and arrival and departure times.

2-52. The facility should have the capability of communicating with other ATC facilities and agencies that use or operate within the facility area of responsibility. Standard ATC radio and interphone phraseology will be used in all facility communications.

2-53. The facility area and airspace is determined by local, host-nation, post, camp, or station requirements. The area and airspace may or may not contain a restricted or prohibited area, overlap, underlay or join another ATC facility area or airspace. Whether a facility joins another ATC facility area or airspace is determined by local requirements, equipment, and agreements. FAA JO 7400.2 and FAAO 7610.4 contain additional information on the procedures for handling airspace matters and special military operations.

UNMANNED AIRCRAFT SYSTEMS

GENERAL PROCEDURES

2-54. The following procedures will be applied at all non-joint use DOD controlled airfields with approved certificate of authorization (COA). These general procedures are:

- If equipped, unmanned aircraft (UA) will operate with full lighting and transponders.
- Deconfliction of UAS and transient aircraft will be specified in the COA. Possible methods include:
  - Altitude restrictions for UAS.
  - Visual holding points with specific lateral and vertical limits.
  - Use of ground observers.
- Mission commander will advise ATC of initiation and completion of flight operations.
- Radio checks between UAS pilot/operator and ATC will be conducted prior to operations.
- All communications between ATC and UAS pilot/operator will be accomplished on:
  - Designated primary and/or alternate frequencies.
  - Secondary/backup communications.
  - Telephone connectivity will be pre-coordinated.
- UAS operations will be conducted under VFR IAW service regulations and CFRs. Increased ceiling and visibility requirements may be applied.

AIR TRAFFIC CONTROL PROCEDURES

2-55. The following procedures will be adhered to by ATC during UAS operations.

- **Description of aircraft types.** Describe UAS to other aircraft by stating UA.
- **ATIS procedures.** Make a new recording when UAS operations are in effect or have terminated for the day.
- **Sequencing and separation.** UAS pilots cannot be instructed to follow another aircraft.

- **Simultaneous same direction operations.** All UAS will be treated as "other" aircraft.
- **Same runway separation.** All UAS will be treated as category III aircraft.
- **Use of visual separation.** Use of visual separation is not authorized.
- **Special visual flight rules (SVFR).** SVFR operations for UAS are not authorized.
- **Preventive control.** May be applied IAW FAA JO 7110.65T.

Transient Aircraft Procedures

2-56. ATC will keep the UAS pilot/operator apprised of any known transient aircraft that may impact operations. The UAS pilot/operator will take all necessary actions to maintain lateral and vertical separation. ATC should provide UAS pilot/operator recommended altitudes or direct them to predetermined points (UAS zones) to ensure deconfliction.

Wake Turbulence Advisories

2-57. ATC will apply the following procedures:

- Issue cautionary wake turbulence advisories, and the position, altitude and direction of flight to the UAS pilot/operator landing behind all manned aircraft.
- Wake turbulence rules cannot be waived by UA pilot/operator.

No Radio Aircraft Procedures

2-58. ATC will apply the following no radio procedures:

- ATC will notify UAS pilot/operator of any known no radio (NORDO) aircraft.
- ATC will broadcast on emergency frequencies when a NORDO aircraft is present to establish two-way radio communications with the NORDO aircraft.
- UAS pilot/operator, assisted by ATC will determine the best method to separate UAS and NORDO aircraft. Example methods include:
  - UAS may proceed to UA zone and hold.
  - Cease operations and if it will not aggravate the situation.
  - Altitude deconfliction.

Emergency Procedures

2-59. ATC will apply the procedures listed in chapter 10 section 1 of FAA JO 7110.65T. The safety of manned aircraft will take precedence over UA in an emergency.

2-60. If primary radio communications between UA pilot/operator and ATC are lost, UA pilot/operator or ATC will be notified immediately via predetermined alternate communications method. Failure to establish and maintain radio communication between UA pilot/operator and ATC will require termination of UA operations.

2-61. If lost link occurs, the UAS pilot/operator will immediately notify ATC with the following information:

- Time of link loss.
- Last known position.
- Altitude.
- Direction of flight.
- Conformation of execution of lost link procedures.
- Conformation of visual contact with UAS.

Note. UAS lost link is an emergency, but may not require crash rescue services.

2-62. In the event of a lost link, lost communications between UAS and ATC or lost communications between UAS pilot/operator and observer, ATC will:

- Cease aircraft launches until status of affected UAS is determined.
- Recover other UAS as appropriate.
- Issue advisories and ATC instructions as appropriate to ensure the safe operation of all aircraft.

EMERGENCY SECURITY CONTROL OF AIR TRAFFIC

2-63. Emergency security control of air traffic (ESCAT) is described by FAAO 7610.4 as emergency conditions threatening national security, but do not warrant the declaration of a defense emergency, air defense (AD) emergency, or the control of NAVAIDs. Detailed responsibilities and conditions for implementation of ESCAT are contained in FAAO 7610.4.

2-64. The appropriate military authority will take the following actions:

- Notify or coordinate, as appropriate, the extent or termination of ESCAT implementation with Department of Transportation (DOT) and Department of Homeland Security (DHS).
- Disseminate the extent of ESCAT implementation through the Noble Eagle Conferences and the Federal Aviation Administration Domestic Event Network (FAA DEN).
- Specify what restrictions are to be implemented. Some examples of restrictions to be considered include:
  - Define the affected area.
  - Define the type of aircraft operations authorized.
  - Define the routing restrictions on flights entering or operating within appropriate portions of the affected area.
  - Define restrictions for the volume of air traffic within the affected area using the emergency air traffic priority list (EATPL) (paragraph 245.22 of this part) and security control authorizations, as required.
  - Set altitude limitations on flight operations in selected areas.
- Restrict operations to aircraft operators regulated under specified security programs such as:
  - Aircraft operator standard security program and the domestic security integration program (DSIP).
  - Revise or remove restrictions on the movement of air traffic as the tactical situation permits.
  - Air Traffic Control Search Coordination Center (ATCSCC) will direct appropriate ARTCCs and combined/center radar approach controls (CERAPs) to implement ESCAT restrictions as specified by the appropriate military authority.

2-65. ARTCCs/CERAPs will take the following actions when directed to implement ESCAT:

- Provide the appropriate military authority feedback through the ATCSCC on the impact of restrictions and when the restrictions have been imposed.
- Impose restrictions on air traffic as directed.
- Disseminate ESCAT implementation instructions to U.S. civil and military ATC facilities and advise adjacent ATC facilities.

2-66. U.S. civil and military ATC facilities will—

- Maintain current information on the status of restrictions imposed on air traffic.
- Process flight plans IAW current instructions received from the ARTCC. All flights must comply with the airspace control measures in effect, the EATPL, or must have been granted a security control authorization.
- Disseminate instructions and restrictions to air traffic as directed by the ARTCCs.

EMERGENCY SECURITY CONTROL OF AIR TRAFFIC PRIORITY LIST

2-67. When ESCAT is implemented, a system of traffic priorities may be required to make optimum use of airspace, consistent with AD requirements. The EATPL is a list of priorities that may be used for the movement of air traffic in a defined area. Priorities will take precedence in the order listed:

- Priority One:
    - President of the U.S.
    - Prime Minister of Canada.
    - Respective cabinet or staff members essential to national security.
    - Aircraft engaged in active continental defense missions.
    - Military retaliatory aircraft.
    - Airborne command elements.
    - Anchor Annex flights.
- Priority Two:
    - Forces being deployed or in direct support of U.S. military offensive and defensive operations including the use of activated Civil Reserve Air Fleet (CRAF) aircraft as necessary, and/or other U.S. and foreign flag civil air carrier aircraft under mission control of the U.S. military.
    - Aircraft operating in direct and immediate support of strategic missions.
    - Search and rescue aircraft operating in direct support of military activities.
    - Aircraft operating in direct and immediate support of special operations missions.
    - Federal flight operations in direct support of homeland security, law enforcement agencies (LEAs) and aircraft performing security for high threat targets such as nuclear power plants, dams, chemical plants, and other areas identified as high threat targets.
- Priority Three:
    - Forces being deployed or performing pre-deployment training/workups in support of the emergency condition.
    - Aircraft deployed in support of continental United States (CONUS) installation/base defense (aircraft operating in direct/immediate security support or deploying ground forces for perimeter defense).
    - Search and rescue aircraft not included in priority two.
    - Flight inspection aircraft flights in connection with emergency restoration of airway and airport facilities in support of immediate emergency conditions.
    - Continental United States airborne reconnaissance for damage assessment (CARDA) missions in support of immediate emergency conditions.
- Priority Four:
    - Dispersal of tactical military aircraft.
    - Dispersal of U.S. civil air carrier aircraft allocated to the CRAF Program.
    - Repositioning of FAA/DOD/Department of National Defense (DND) flight inspection aircraft.
    - Flight inspection activity in connection with airway and airport facilities.
    - Specific military tactical pilot currency or proficiency in support of homeland defense.
    - Military tactical aircraft post-maintenance test flights.
    - Federal aircraft post maintenance check flights in support of homeland security.
- Priority Five:
    - Air transport of military commanders, their representatives, DOD/DND-sponsored key civilian personnel, non-DOD/DND or other federal key civilian personnel who are of importance to national security.
    - Dispersal of non-tactical military aircraft for their protection.

- ■ Aircraft contracted to and/or operated by federal agencies.
- Priority Six:
  - ■ State and local LEA directly engaged in law enforcement missions.
  - ■ Flight operations IAW approved federal and state emergency plans.
  - ■ Lifeguard and medical evacuation (MEDEVAC) aircraft in direct support of emergency medical services.
  - ■ Flight operations essential to the development, production, and delivery of equipment, personnel, materials, and supplies essential to national security.
  - ■ Other essential CARDA missions not covered in priority three.
- Priority Seven:
  - ■ Other military flight operations.
- Priority Eight:
  - ■ Other flight operations not specifically listed in priorities one through seven.

Chapter 3

Air Traffic Controller Training

The FTP provides standardization and guidance in conducting facility training. The FTP guides newly assigned personnel through an established program of instruction to become facility-rated. Each facility chief will develop a FTP based on established training time limits IAW AR 95-2.

SECTION I – FACILITY TRAINING PROGRAM

PROGRAM OF INSTRUCTION

3-1. The installation FTP consists of three types of training (qualification, proficiency, and remedial), a FTM, four training phases (indoctrination, primary knowledge, position qualification, and facility rating phase), tests, and the appropriate evaluations. In addition to this training, the program will include the knowledge and skill requirements outlined in the 14 CFR, Part 65 for CTO ratings or FAA JO 7220.1B for all other ratings.

Contents

TYPES OF TRAINING

Qualification

3-2. Newly assigned personnel receive qualification training before they can obtain a facility rating. This training is also given to facility-rated controllers when new procedures are instituted or new ATC equipment is installed. This training will be annotated in section II and III (as appropriate) of DA Form 3479.

Proficiency

3-3. Facility-rated or PQ controllers are given proficiency training to remain current and proficient on ATC policies, procedures, and equipment. This type of training includes but is not limited to weather certification, changes to ARs, FMs, TCs, handbooks, and operational procedures. Proficiency training will be annotated in sections II and III (as applicable) of DA Form 3479.

Remedial

3-4. Remedial training will be given only to personnel who have shown they are no longer qualified at a control position, which they were previously qualified for, or failure of a written or oral examination. This training is given to correct a demonstrated weakness and may consist of—

- Classroom instruction.
- Additional time on the position under direct supervision.
- Both.

3-5. The facility chief determines the time limits for the controllers receiving remedial training. This training will be annotated in section II of DA Form 3479. The reason for remedial training, its contents, and time limits will be annotated in section III.

TRAINING PHASES

Indoctrination

3-6. All newly assigned controllers begin the FTP with this phase. The indoctrination phase consists of—
- A briefing on what is expected of the trainee.
- An introduction to AR 95-2.
- Discussion of training time limits.
- Issuance of the FTM.
- A comprehensive review of chapter one of the FTM and a general review of the remaining chapters.
- A review of their FTP schedule.
- A tour of the ATC facility and other airfield facilities.
- A verification of ATCS/CTO card and certificate of CTO grades.
- A written examination on chapter one of the FTM.
- Verification of valid flight physical.

Note. The trainee must successfully complete the written examination before entering the primary knowledge phase of training.

Primary Knowledge

3-7. This phase teaches the general subjects the trainee needs prior to training at an operating position. This phase ends with written closed book examinations on those chapters deemed necessary by the facility chief for the trainee to operate effectively during the position qualification phase of training. As an example, the facility chief for an ATCT FTP may decide chapters two through eight are necessary prior to beginning position training within the position qualification phase. Those chapters deemed appropriate for the primary knowledge phase of training must be indentified within the FTP and outlined in section II of DA Form 3479 under primary knowledge.

Position Qualification

3-8. In this phase, the trainee receives hands-on training at each position with written, oral, and practical evaluations on the FTP requirements. The trainee is then evaluated on each operating position, and the results are recorded on DA Form 3479-1 and section II of DA Form 3479.

3-9. Position qualification training should begin at the least complex control position and advance to the most complex. To become PQ at a control position the trainee must complete all FTP requirements applying to that position. A satisfactory evaluation must be received on DA Form 3479-1 with a comment provided in the "evaluators" section reflecting that the requirements of that position have been met and the trainee is PQ. Record this evaluation in section II of DA Form 3479.

Facility Rating

3-10. A trainee PQ on all operating positions will be given a pre-FAA/ATCS facility rating examination. This written examination will consist of 50 to 100 questions covering the skills and knowledge requirements of Title 14 CFR Part 65 or FAA JO 7220.1B for the rating desired. The questions will focus primarily on those topics the trainee must know to operate as a controller at the facility assigned. A failed examination returns the trainee to classroom study, re-examination, and is annotated in sections II, III of DA Form 3479.

3-11. Once the pre-FAA exam is complete, the trainee will be given a final FAA/ATCS facility rating examination and evaluated by the ATCS/CTO examiner. The written, oral, and practical evaluation for facility rating will be annotated in section II of DA Form 3479. The results of the practical evaluation will be recorded on DA Form 3479-1. This evaluation will be maintained in DA Form 3479 for one calendar year. The written examination will consist of 50 to 100 questions on topics as outlined in Title 14 CFR Part 65 or FAA JO 7220.1B and other areas deemed appropriate by the examiner for the facility rating being sought. A failure of this examination, returns the trainee to classroom study and rescheduling of the examination. This failure is annotated in sections II, III of DA Form 3479.

ADMINISTRATION AND MANAGEMENT TRAINING

3-12. Administration and management training is an ongoing program wherein supervisors continuously train subordinates to assume supervisory positions. Administration and management training will culminate in a written examination of at least 25 questions. As a minimum, this training will include:

- Chapter 13 of the FTM.
- AR 95-2 (chapter 14 and 15 Para 14-6, 14-8, 14-9, 15-2, 15-3, 15-4).
- 14 CFR parts 65.31 to 65.50.
- FAA JO 7220.1B (chapter 5 Para. 9, chapter 6, Para 3 and 5).
- Chapters one, two, and three of this TC.

3-13. The administrative management exam will be administered prior to assuming the duties of CIC, SL, ATC training supervisor, or facility chief. All training and test results will be entered into sections II, III, (as appropriate) of DA Form 3479.

FACILITY TRAINING MANUAL

3-14. The FTM is a locally prepared publication. The facility chief is responsible for its preparation, content, and quality. The quality of the FTM has a direct bearing on the effectiveness of a FTP. FTMs will be reviewed, rewritten, and/or updated at least annually. A memorandum will be attached to the front of each FTM with the date, statement of review or update, and the facility chief's signature. This memorandum will be created even if no changes are made.

3-15. The FTM is used for facility rating preparation, remedial and proficiency training. The manual also serves as a reference. Charts, maps, photographs, and drawings in the FTM make the information more understandable.

3-16. At least three copies of the FTM will be maintained at a facility. Additionally, one copy will be sent to the quality assurance office (if applicable) where it will be maintained on file. The facility may maintain any number of additional copies for controller use.

3-17. The chapters or portions of chapters in the FTM that do not apply to a particular facility may be marked "not applicable" or to be used as determined by the facility chief. The chief may choose to include those chapters that apply to a collocated or adjacent facility to familiarize controllers with that facility. Trainees will not be tested on chapters that do not apply to the rating being sought.

SECTION II – BIENNIAL SKILLS EVALUATIONS

3-18. All rated controllers will be administered biennial skills evaluations consisting of at least a 50 question written test comprised of topics from all ratings held and a practical evaluation on all positions of the facilities in which they are certified. In ARAC facilities, the practical evaluation may be conducted on the most complex radar sector(s) and PAR/AIC positions when established within the facility. Skills evaluations may be administered individually within the controller's anniversary month of their facility rating or during a prescribed month for all rated controllers. The facility chief will establish the evaluation time period through a facility memorandum.

> *Note.* Controllers exceeding the biennial period for skills evaluations will not operate in a facility until successfully completing a both the written and practical portion of the biennial skills evaluation.

3-19. The written test portion of the skills evaluation may be given open book and should consist of the following topics:
- TWR facilities:
  - Weather affecting flight.
  - TWR visibility procedures.
  - Aircraft equipment failure.
  - Hijacking.
  - Flight emergencies.
  - Transitioning, handling, and separation of special flight.
  - Safety alerts.
  - Traffic advisories.
  - Wake turbulence.
  - Taxi into position and hold procedures.
  - Locally developed operating procedures.
  - Bird activity information.
  - Intersection departure procedures (DPs).
  - IFR clearance procedures.
  - SVFR procedures.
  - Same runway separation procedures.
  - Simultaneous arrival/DPs.
  - Intersecting runway procedures.
- Radar facilities:
  - Weather affecting flight.
  - Hijacking.
  - Flight emergencies.
  - Traffic advisories.
  - Wake turbulence.
  - Locally developed operating procedures.
  - Bird activity information.
  - Inadvertent instrument meteorological conditions (IIMC) formation breakup procedures.
  - Airspace intruder training.
  - Tracked and untracked targets (depending on equipment resource capability).
  - Mode C and non-Mode C equipped targets.
  - Airspace violators who have established two-way radio communications and violators who have not established two-way radio communications.
  - Lost aircraft orientation.
  - Radar identification procedures.
  - Radar handoff procedures.
  - Non-radar procedures.
- AIC facilities:
  - Bird activity information.
  - IIMC formation breakup procedures.
  - SVFR procedures.
  - Weather affecting flight.
  - Aircraft equipment failure.
  - Hijacking.
  - Flight emergencies.

- Safety alerts.
- Traffic advisories.
- Locally developed operating procedures.

3-20. Skills evaluations will be documented in section II of DA Form 3479 and DA Form 3479-1. The written exam and DA Form 3479-1 will be maintained on the right side of training records folder and removed when the next evaluation is completed. Biennial skill evaluations may only be given by ATC chiefs, facility chiefs, training supervisors and ATCS/CTO examiners.

Note. ATC managers not holding a rating in the facility and medical clearance may only administer the written portion of the biennial skill evaluation.

SECTION III – INSTALLATION AIR TRAFFIC CONTROL TRAINING FOR WARFIGHTERS

3-21. Army installation ATC facilities (includes Army contract facilities) will be utilized to train Army air traffic controllers assigned to tactical units. These facilities provide essential technical training for certification and proficiency. Installation air traffic density, hours of operation, and internal training requirements will be used to determine the number of military controllers that can be trained in the facility during a given period. An LOA detailing the training program between the respective unit commanders is required.

INSTALLATION FACILITY RESPONSIBILITIES

3-22. Installation facilities provide unique training opportunities for Army controllers. It is essential that DA civilian and U.S. Army contract controllers understand that most Army controllers special duty (SD) to their facilities will not have the experience, expertise, and qualifications of the controllers hired to operate these Army facilities. It is therefore, essential that a formalized technical training program is established, followed, and tracked for certification. This training program must define academic milestones to be met with assigned dates for practical and written evaluations. Fixed-site ATC managers are the Soldier's partners to ensure the Army maintains a trained and competent ATC capability.

3-23. Facility schedules for these Army controllers should be based upon—
- Air traffic density.
- Facility hours of operation.
- Internal training requirements.
- Number of military controllers that can be effectively trained at the facility.

3-24. Prior to Army controllers beginning training, fixed site ATC managers should provide units with copies of the FTM and FTP.

UNIT RESPONSIBILITIES

3-25. Unit commanders must ensure LOAs developed between installation facilities and the unit takes into consideration the following:
- Unit operations.
- Training events.
- Number of personnel committed to fixed site training per cycle.
- Time required for completion of FTP.

3-26. Units must adhere to the agreed upon requirements of the LOA developed for fixed site training. Unit commanders will ensure individual soldiers adhere to the training schedule and training disruptions are kept to emergency type situations. Commanders must prioritize their selection for fixed site training. The following is suggested criteria used in the selection process:
- Soldiers requiring an initial rating prior to deployment.

- Air traffic controllers who have not received a rating in the past five years.
- Prior rated Soldiers requiring an initial rating due to assignment to a different section.

3-27. Units are responsible for ensuring the Soldiers selected for training have the following:
- For initial rating, CTO rating certificate of grade for CTO exam (copies may be obtained through the DAR and FAA website).
- DA Form 3479 (complete and up-to-date).
- Required limited weather observer training complete and documented.
- Current flight physical and signed DA Form 4186 (up slip).

3-28. AR 95-2, table 15-1, outlines training time requirements for rating within each category of Army ATC facilities. These time requirements are the maximum allowed to complete training without a training time extension (TTE). An initial CTO rating is the only type of rating which the FAA specifies a minimum time requirement of six months. Time spent in a tactical TWR training program may be applied to this time requirement.

3-29. Commanders are encouraged to visit fixed site facilities and request progress reports on their controller's training progress and attitude toward training.

INDIVIDUAL SOLDIER RESPONSIBILITIES

3-30. A Soldier's selection for fixed-site training should be viewed as a commitment by the unit to recognize the hard work, diligence, and competence of the Soldier. The controller must make every opportunity of this training to strengthen and hewn their skills as an air traffic controller and broaden their knowledge of airspace and ATC procedures. Soldiers selected for fixed site will be counseled in writing. This counseling will specifically state the soldier's responsibilities and commitment to their unit and the fixed site facility. The soldier's responsibilities are:
- Adhere to the assigned work schedule.
- Complete study assignments and be ready for oral, practical, and written evaluations.
- Stay on or ahead of the FTP schedule.
- Maintain medical standards as outlined in AR 40-501.
- Maintain a positive training attitude.
- Discuss (frequently) training with unit leadership to—
  - Indentify any perceived problems with training.
  - Identify any scheduling conflicts with training.
  - Indentify any weak areas of the trainee and determine corrective actions.

Chapter 4

Air Traffic Control Maintenance

FAAO 6000.6 details ground inspection, certification, and the operation of military facilities used within NAS. The Army has one ground inspection standard that applies to all fixed ATC facilities. This guidance will not relieve maintenance or supervisory personnel from executing procedures or emergency actions warranted by specific situations.

SECTION I – GROUND INSPECTION

4-1. Certification is the form of quality control used by facility maintenance to ensure ATC facilities operate within prescribed standards. Verification is the process by which non-federal personnel (as defined in FAAO 6700.20) perform a similar quality control function. Government facility maintenance personnel are responsible for overseeing the verification process.

Contents
Section I – Ground Inspection.................4-1
Section II – Air Traffic Control Maintenance Certification Program 4-6

4-2. Personnel with specific written certification authority and responsibility on the subject facility will perform certification. Section II describes certification authority credentials. Personnel without certification authority may perform maintenance and logging duties. These activities will either be confined to non-certification parameters or followed with the appropriate certification by a fully qualified system specialist.

4-3. All ATC systems, subsystems, and equipment requiring certification IAW FAA orders or Army guidance will be certified for use in the NAS and outside continental United States (OCONUS) to meet host nation and ICAO requirements.

CERTIFICATION PROCEDURES

4-4. System and service certification will be entered in the appropriate maintenance log prior to commissioning. Log entries for services without a maintenance log will be placed in the associated facility maintenance log IAW DA Pam 750-8. System certification is event based and ties the certification judgment to the decision to place a system or subsystem into service.

4-5. Authorized personnel only will perform event-based certification. The following events define when certification is required, regardless of whether it affects a certification parameter:

- Prior to commissioning.
- Upon request following aircraft accident/incidents.
- Following adjustment to any certification parameter regardless of whether an interruption was required.
- Prior to restoration following flight inspection requiring on-site personnel.
- Prior to restoration following any modification.
- Prior to restoration following maintenance task requiring an interruption or would have required an interruption to a facility without redundancy.
- Prior to restoration following corrective maintenance activity required to restore a facility to operation.

4-6. System and subsystem certification is not required when a facility is restored to operation by restoration of power, initialization, or reset, and no other action was taken.

4-7. Some NAS systems contain user interface controls that can cause a certification parameter to be adjusted beyond its tolerance or limit. Such adjustments will not void the certification.

4-8. The certification statement made in the log must contain only one of the following:

- The prescribed certification statement from the maintenance handbook. Some handbooks require site-specific variables to be included in the certification statement ("Local transmitter [identity of frequency] [main and/or standby] certified" entered as "Local transmitter 123.4 MHz main certified").
- The prescribed certification statement and identification or removal of exceptions (remote transmitter receiver [RTR] certified except main 123.5 MHz transmitter and standby 121.3 MHz receiver).
- A modified certification statement lists a specific subset of multiple-like equipment. (Certifying multiple receivers with one certification statement).

Note. Time-based certification intervals performed by sites in addition to event based certification on systems, subsystems, and services will be listed in the maintenance SOP.

INSPECTION RESPONSIBILITY

4-9. Personnel responsible for ground inspection of Army ATC and NAVAID facilities are required to use the information in this chapter to establish criteria for determining the technical efficiency of these facilities. This guidance does not authorize agencies to assume ground inspection authority over facilities that are not under their jurisdiction. The NAVAID maintenance chief and the ATC chief/facility chief or their representatives are responsible for coordinating ground inspection activities. Maintenance personnel having inspection responsibility for a NAVAID must request a confirming flight inspection when safe operation of the facility is in question.

Note. Special flight inspections will be accomplished per FAAO 8200.1, chapter four.

VERY HIGH FREQUENCY OMNIDIRECTIONAL RANGE/DISTANCE MEASURING EQUIPMENT/TACTICAL AIR NAVIGATION INSPECTIONS

4-10. Circumstances requiring a confirming flight inspection include—

- Accidents/mishaps.
- Major changes in local obstructions or buildings that may affect the signal strength, coverage, or courses.
- Replacement or installation of the tactical (TAC)/distance measuring equipment (DME) antenna or radio frequency (RF) subassemblies (excluding transmission lines) of the antenna.
- Major modernization or corrective maintenance to the counterpoise, such as extension of the counterpoise.
- Change in facility operating frequency.
- Change in output level (power) for the purpose of increasing or decreasing service volume.
- Adjustment or replacement of the very (high frequency) omnidirectional range (VOR) antennas or components (including pedestals, loops, baluns, and supporting braces).
- Installation and operation of the tactical air navigation (TACAN) antenna (with no change to the VOR antenna system).
- Replacement or modification of the test generator, if the tolerances for ground check cannot be met.
- Installation of a modification to improve the RF spectrum for 50 kilohertz (kHz) channel spacing, or to eliminate adjacent channel interference.

4-11. Circumstances not requiring a confirming flight inspection include—

- Replacement of any or all solid-state components.
- Replacement or repair of equipment components or units.
- Complete tuning of the transmitter.
- Measurement and adjustment of all modulation levels.
- Phasing adjustments.
- Installation or relocation of the DME mast, the TACAN monitoring pole, or a remote communication outlet (RCO) antenna pole (if accomplished IAW current instructions).
- Replacement of the polarizer when reset to the previous setting, or readjustment of the polarizer when a portable ground polariscope is used to optimize the facility for minimum vertical polarization.
- Installation or replacement of obstruction lights or the painting of the antenna shelter.
- Replacement of the radio transmitter antenna-2 (RTA-2) upper and lower bearings, spin motor, and the radome.
- Other maintenance procedures, such as refurbishment of VOR counterpoise, wood decking, and/or terneplate, provided conditions are restored to those that existed at the time of the last flight inspection (as reflected in facility records) and ground check is within $\pm$ 0.2 degrees of the reference ground check.
- Other maintenance procedures, such as any or all of the following, provided conditions are restored to those that existed at the time of the last flight inspection (as reflected in facility records).
- Repair, alignment, or replacement of the goniometer.
- Repair, replacement, modification, or repositioning of any fixed field detector used in facility monitoring.
- Replacement or modification of any signal element in the monitors.
- Adjustment or replacement of the RF transmission lines (including feed-lines, stubs, positioner, and bridges, either coaxial or hybrid).
- Replacement, repair, or modification of test equipment. (For the VOR, if unable to make before and after measurements, a confirming flight inspection will not be required if the tolerances for ground check are met.)

4-12. The following applies to maintenance of NAVAIDs facilities and equipment – VOR, VOR/DME, very high frequency omnidirectional radio range tactical air navigation aid (VORTAC), and TACAN:

- **AN/Federal Communication Commission Registration Number (FRN)-41(V).** Army technical manuals (TMs) will be used for ground inspection and preventive maintenance. The equipment will be certified IAW FAA JO 6820.7. Use VOR level 1 performance check data sheet, VOR level 2 ground check data sheet and VOR level 3 test generator calibration data sheet located in TM 11-5825-266-14-1 for equipment maintenance and certification.
- **AN/FRN-47(V).** Army TMs will be used for ground inspection and preventive maintenance. The equipment will be certified IAW FAA JO 6820.7. FAA technical performance records will be used for equipment maintenance.
- **AN/FRN-45.** USAF technical orders will be used for ground inspection and preventive maintenance. The equipment will be certified IAW FAA JO 6820.7. FAA technical performance records will be used for equipment maintenance.
- **AN/URN-25.** United States Navy (USN) TMs will be used for ground inspection and preventive maintenance. The equipment will be certified IAW FAA JO 6820.7. FAA technical performance records will be used for equipment maintenance.
- **415SE.** Ground inspection, preventive maintenance, and certification will be performed IAW FAA JO 6820.7 and applicable TMs. FAA technical performance records will be used for equipment maintenance.

- **WILCOX 5690.** Ground inspection, preventive maintenance, and certification will be performed IAW FAA JO 6820.7 and applicable TMs. FAA technical performance records will be used for equipment maintenance.

NON-DIRECTIONAL RADIO BEACON INSPECTIONS

4-13. Circumstances requiring a confirming flight inspection include—
- Accidents/mishaps.
- Major changes in local obstructions, building, and so forth that may affect signal strength and coverage.
- Changes or modifications to the antenna or ground plane that may affect facility coverage.
- Change in the antenna current to increase or decrease the service volume.
- Frequency change.
- Circumstances not requiring a confirming flight inspection. The circumstances remain unchanged as stated in the appropriate manuals.

4-14. The following applies to maintenance of non-directional beacons (NDBs):
- **T-1428/FRN, TN-588/FRN and R-2176/FRN.** Army TMs will be used for ground inspection and preventive maintenance. The equipment will be certified IAW FAA JO 6740.2. FAA technical performance records will be used for equipment maintenance.
- **ND-500 and ND-4000A.** Ground inspection, preventive maintenance, and certification will be performed IAW FAA JO 6820.7 and applicable TMs. FAA technical performance records will be used for equipment maintenance.

INSTRUMENT LANDING SYSTEM INSPECTIONS OF THE LOCALIZER, GLIDE SLOPE AND 75 MEGAHERTZ MARKER BEACONS

4-15. Circumstances requiring a confirming flight inspection include—
- Accidents/mishaps.
- Changes to obstructions, buildings, power lines, and so forth that may affect the radiated signal.
- Construction, runway repairs, and so forth that were performed in the general localizer or glide slope area, if there is any doubt about how they affect facility performance.
- Change in the facility assigned operating frequency.
- Replacement of critical ILS components (such as RF lines and antenna components, RF bridges, electronic modulators, mechanical modulator troughs or parts, power dividers) and transmitters as complete units if they contain any of these critical components.
- Repair or replacement of any of the localizer antennas in the radiating array.
- Repair, replacement, or repositioning of any of the glide slope antennas in the radiating array.
- Removal, repair, or reinstallation of any of the glide slope antennas in the radiating array.

4-16. Circumstances not requiring a confirming flight inspection include all other maintenance activities that meet the maintenance requirements of FAA JO 6750.49.

4-17. Refer to FAA JO 6750.49 and applicable equipment TMs for ground inspection procedures and certification. FAA technical performance records will be used as directed by FAA JO 6750.49 for ILS and 75 MHz marker beacon maintenance.

PRIMARY AND SECONDARY RADAR FACILITY INSPECTIONS

4-18. Circumstances requiring a confirming flight inspection include the following:
- Accidents/mishaps.
- When a reported deficiency is not susceptible to exact measurement or to verification by ground measurement.
- After an aircraft accident in which the radar facility may have been involved.

- After an antenna change (ASR/PAR) or antenna tilt change (fixed tilt surveillance radars only) or when engineering judgment indicates a probable change in the antenna radiation pattern.
- After a modification or other circumstance that, in the judgment of the facility chief/maintenance chief, requires facility performance to be recertified.
- Anytime secondary radar directional output power is reduced below the minimum output power level or the Omni to directional power ratio is increased above the level previously documented during the flight inspection.

4-19. When circumstances remain unchanged, no confirming flight inspection is required as stated in the appropriate manuals.

Periodic Operational Checks of the Radar System

4-20. In addition to the flight commissioning flight inspection, periodic operational checks of the radar system will be performed by the FAA, Army flight inspection aircraft, air traffic controllers, and maintenance personnel. These checks will supplement the performance assurance obtained from observing the system during daily operations. These checks include—
- Observing identified targets under control within the sector and comparing them against data obtained during the commissioning flight inspection or against minimum performance requirements developed at the facility. These targets may be flight inspection aircraft or targets of opportunity.
- Checking the technical performance of the facility against the established performance database of the facility.

Note. Installation facilities refer to FAA JO 6310.9 (ASR-8), FAA JO 6310.19 (ASR-9), FAA JO 6310.30 (ASR-11), TM 11-5840-377-13-2 (Army-Navy/Federal part number [AN/FPN]-66), TM 11-5840-382-23 (AN/FPN-67), FAA JO 6360.14 (ATCBI-5), and applicable equipment TMs for ground inspection procedures and certification. FAA technical performance records will be used by FAA JO 6310.9, FAA JO 6310.19, FAA JO 6310.30, and FAA JO 6310.14.

AIR TRAFFIC CONTROL AUTOMATION EQUIPMENT INSPECTIONS

4-21. Ground inspections and certification will be performed on radar automations systems IAW applicable TMs and the following FAA orders:
- FAA JO 6191.3, Standard Terminal Automation Replacement System (STARS). FAA technical performance records will be used for equipment maintenance.
- FAA JO 6130.3, Maintenance of Flight Data Input/Output (FDIO) Equipment.

COMMUNICATION FACILITIES INSPECTIONS

4-22. Terminal area and AIC communications are provided by the various types of air/ground facilities. Facilities consist of air/ground transmitter and receiving equipment, recording equipment, and necessary control equipment. Communications facilities will be flight inspected IAW FAAO 8200.1.

4-23. FAA technical performance records and applicable TMs for communications ground inspection procedures and certification will be used for equipment maintenance at remote communications facilities.

4-24. Equipment will be certified IAW FAA JO 6480.6 and 6580.5. FAA technical performance records will be used for equipment maintenance.

4-25. Antenna ground inspection procedures will be accomplished IAW FAA JO 6580.5. Annotate ground inspection results on the appropriate FAA technical performance record used for radio maintenance.

4-26. Refer to FAA JO 6670.13, maintenance of digital voice recorder (DVR) equipment, and applicable TMs for recorder ground inspection procedures and certification. FAA technical performance records will be used for equipment maintenance.

ADDITIONAL REQUIREMENTS

4-27. Facilities should be visited frequently enough to ensure accurate and reliable operation according to the criteria established in this guidance. Each time a facility is visited, the maintenance technician responsible for the facility will verify facility performance on the basis of one or more of the following criteria:

- Visual and aural. On every visit verify, by visual and aural observation, whether equipment is operating normally. This includes, but is not limited to, meter readings, pilot light indications, extraneous noises, and excessive heat.
- Monitoring. On scheduled visits and as required, certify whether the facility operation is satisfactory by noting local monitoring information. Monitoring may include a control line check to determine control and remote monitor functions are satisfactory.
- Meter readings. On scheduled visits, if applicable, record meter readings and compare them with those previously recorded on station records.
- Performance standards and tolerances. On scheduled visits and as required, determine whether the facility meets the performance standards and tolerances established in this guidance, the TMs, or the handbooks.
- System ground check. On scheduled visits and as required, perform a ground check and compare the results with the reference ground check error curve (VOR) and/or with data obtained at the time of the last flight inspection. Evaluate these data, and determine facility performance has not departed appreciably (beyond tolerance) from the previous system ground check recordings.
- Flight inspection. On scheduled visits or as requested, determine whether facility performance is satisfactory based on the flight inspection evaluation. Ground check data will be recorded immediately following any flight inspection.

Note. An accident investigator may request a flight inspection on any NAVAID suspected to have been a contributing factor in an accident or mishap.

SECTION II – AIR TRAFFIC CONTROL MAINTENANCE CERTIFICATION PROGRAM

4-28. This section specifies the procedures for implementing and maintaining a uniform certification program for U.S. Army ATC maintenance technicians. This guidance applies to DA civilians, local national (host nation) civilians, and military personnel (ATC systems and subsystems repair specialists in military occupational specialty [MOS] 94D) who perform maintenance on Army-owned ATC equipment. Contractor personnel are prohibited from certifying U.S. Army NAVAIDs. Contractor personnel may repair and verify the NAVAIDs are operating properly, but NAVAIDs certification is an inherent governmental function.

PROGRAM OBJECTIVES

4-29. The U.S. Army ATC maintenance certification program establishes the uniform standards for measuring the technical proficiency of ATC maintenance technicians. It also ensures the technical competence of all maintenance personnel having direct responsibility for the safe operation of systems/subsystems/equipment critical to air navigation and ATC. The program establishes the procedures for documenting the technicians' proficiency, granting authority, and assigning certification responsibility.

CERTIFICATION RESPONSIBILITY AND AUTHORITY

4-30. The responsibility for the certification program is shared by ACOM/ASCC/DRU/ARNG), ATSCOM, certifiers, and ATC facility maintenance chiefs.

AIR TRAFFIC SERVICES COMMAND

4-31. ATSCOM will—

- Provide overall direction to, and guidance on, the program.
- Identify and specify the theory and performance requirements.
- Standardize and continually evaluate and update all phases of the program.
- Develop, validate, review, and revise theory and performance examinations.
- Determine the systems to be added or deleted from the program and inform the appropriate individuals/elements.
- Print and distribute the examinations and certificates.
- Resolve comments, questions, and disputes about the examinations.
- Maintain database files containing complete verification records.
- Designate examining officials (in writing).
- Determine the acceptability of formal schools.

Note. Only examinations developed or approved by ATSCOM will be used as a basis for issuing certification authority. This certification may be used only for the specified ATC system/subsystem.

CERTIFIERS

4-32. A memorandum nominating maintenance certifiers will be approved by ACOM/ASCC/DRU and forwarded to ATSCOM. Military, DA civilians, and local national civilians qualified to serve as maintenance certifiers will be approved in writing by the commander, ATSCOM.

Maintenance certifiers will—

- Maintain files containing complete technician certification and related training records on each technician.
- Request the theory and performance examinations through the examiner from ATSCOM.
- Conduct and record the annual review on DA Form 3479-9 (ATC Maintenance Personnel Certification and Related Training Record), section II.

SITE MAINTENANCE CHIEF, MAINTENANCE SUPERVISORS

4-33. The site maintenance chiefs/supervisors will—

- Provide the technician with the training materials needed to accomplish comprehensive training on the systems/subsystems/equipment.
- Coordinate with the examiner about administration of the examination.
- Develop and document OJT on the site-specific systems/subsystems to support the certification program.
- Advise the airfield division chief/commander/manager on the status of ATC maintenance certification.
- Coordinate with the ATC facility maintenance chief for NOTAM if training is required on any in-use operational system/subsystem/equipment.

MAINTENANCE TECHNICIAN CERTIFICATION

4-34. Technician certification is completed through an accepted course of study provided by the FAA or through unit certification programs.

FEDERAL AVIATION ADMINISTRATION MAINTENANCE SCHOOLING

4-35. Completion of an accepted course of study offered by FAA, DOD (excluding initial MOS producing schools), or contractors that meet or exceed the objectives required to certify the equipment to FAA (NAS) standards contained in FAAO 8200.1. The FAA course catalog is available at http://www.academy.faa.gov/catalog/. ACOM/ASCC/DRU/ARNGs will send their annual training requirements to ATSCOM for processing by the FAA liaison.

CERTIFICATION BASED ON PROGRAM COMPLETION

4-36. The certification program must be administered efficiently to provide qualified technicians that meet the stringent requirements for properly maintaining ATC equipment. The technician must satisfy the theory concepts and performance requirements specified in this chapter to meet qualification requirements of the assigned position. After completing qualification requirements, the technician may be assigned the responsibility of certifying specific systems/subsystems/equipment. The ATC maintenance technician certification process consists of the following eight steps (figure 4-1):

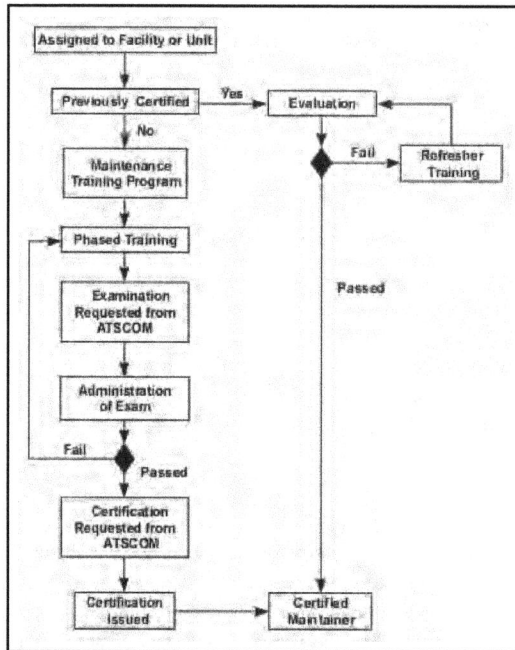

Figure 4-1. ATC maintenance technician certification process

- **Step 1.** The technician is assigned to the facility or unit.
- **Step 2.** The technician has prior certification.

Note. If certified on a particular system/subsystem, the maintenance chief reviews the technician's training records, evaluates him, then takes the appropriate steps. If not previously certified, continue with step 3.

- **Step 3.** The technician enters the maintenance training program. This step includes—
  - Establishing training records.
  - Orientation on equipment.
  - Orientation on facilities and their locations.

- Initial counseling on maintenance and shop operations.
- Statement of performance expectations.
- Orientation on safety.
- Overview of classes.
- SOP requirements.

- **Step 4.** The technician enters a phased training program on individual systems or equipment (for example ASR-9 and Air Traffic Control Beacon Interrogator [ATCBI]-5). This step of the certification process consists of the following three phases:

  - **Phase I.** The technician is trained on the theory of operation, system/subsystem/equipment operational characteristics, power requirements, frequency spectrum, and normal operating standards. Also covered in this phase are the required reference material, forms and records, maintenance allocation charts, PMCS and TMDE procedures and requirements, and local SOP requirements.

  - **Phase II.** The technician is trained on alignment systems and subsystems, sequential and system interface alignment procedures, and TMDE requirements and settings. This training also includes reference material and local SOP requirements, forms, and records completion.

  - **Phase III.** The technician is trained on system and subsystem fault localization, schematic use, maintenance allocation charts, and major and minor component installation/removal procedures. This training also includes tool requirements and usage, safety and quality control requirements, supply procedures, and reference material and local SOP requirements.

- **Step 5.** When the technician has satisfactorily completed the three phases above, the examiner will forward a written request to ATSCOM for the theory examination.

- **Step 6.** The examiner administers the examination to the technician in two parts as explained below. All theory examinations are open book.

  - **Part 1.** The technician completes the comprehensive written examination, which consists of questions on Phases I, II, and III.

  - **Part 2.** The technician is given the hands-on performance examination on Phases II and III.

- **Step 7.** The examiner grades the examination and sends it with the answer sheet to Commander, ATSCOM, AFAT-ATS-CT, 2805 Division Road, Fort Rucker, Alabama 36362-5265. If the technician passes the examination, ATSCOM issues the certification. If the technician fails the examination, the examiner identifies the specific areas in which the technician had problems. The technician is re-entered in the phased training program.

- **Step 8.** The technician is now certified on the applicable system or subsystem. The flow process is continued when the technician encounters a new system or new equipment.

THEORY OF OPERATION AND PERFORMANCE EXAMINATIONS

4-37. All theory and performance examinations used in the certification program are developed or validated by ATSCOM. These examinations will be used to determine whether the examinee knows the theory and practical techniques required to perform maintenance, and diagnose and correct deficiencies on ATC systems/subsystems/equipment. Comprehensive examinations are developed using TMs, FMs, TCs, handbooks, manufacturer manuals, FAA joint acceptance standards, and senior maintenance personnel. Equipment examinations are comprehensive in scope, covering not only the equipment within the system but also the auxiliary equipment considered part of the system.

EXAMINER PREREQUISITES

4-38. The examiner will be designated, in writing, by ATSCOM. The duties of the theory examiner consist of monitoring only. He need not hold certification authority. The performance examiner must possess certification for the entire system on which he examines another technician.

THEORY (CONCEPTS) WRITTEN EXAMINATIONS

4-39. The written examination will test the technician's understanding and knowledge of a wide range of information. The questions will cover system-oriented theory, operational characteristics, subsystems, power requirements, frequency spectrum, and normal operating standards. Some questions require both calculations and analytical reasoning.

Requests for Theory Examinations

4-40. The maintenance supervisor will send written requests for theory examinations through the examiner to ATSCOM. An examination will not be requested unless there is a reasonable expectation the technician will pass it. Under no circumstances will it be used as a screening device.

Administration of Theory Examinations

4-41. When administering the theory examinations, the examiners will—
- Understand and apply mandatory secure-handling requirements to protect program integrity.
- Not discuss or disclose the contents of examinations.
- Prepare an appropriate area for administering examinations and give the examinee required instructions and materials.
- Caution the examinee on the official nature of the examinations and the penalties involved for disclosure of the contents.
- Allow examinees the use of reference material (personal or supplied) during the examinations.
- Control and time examinations as prescribed and process completed examinations as instructed.
- Store examination papers in a secure file.

Grading of Theory Examinations

4-42. The examiner will grade theory examinations; the examinations and the results will be mailed to Commander, ATSCOM, AFAT-ATS-CT, 2805 Division Road, Fort Rucker, Alabama 36362-5265.

If the technician fails to achieve 70 percent on the examination, the examiner will define specific weak areas and the technician will be required to review all areas on the examination.

Security in Handling Theory Examinations

4-43. Everyone in the examination chain concerned with the certification process must maintain security in the handling of written examinations. Compromise of examinations in any form is a serious violation of the rules of conduct and discipline. Any violation will require the appropriate official to take disciplinary action. Any person having personal knowledge of a compromise on any segment of the written examination will advise ATSCOM immediately of the details. The security requirements of theory examinations include but are not limited to—
- Placement of documents in locked storage (secured with a combination lock or the equivalent).
- Accountability for all examinations after their completion.
- Refusal to discuss or transfer examination content.

PERFORMANCE EXAMINATIONS

4-44. Performance examinations are used to demonstrate a technician's proficiency. These examinations vary in length according to the complexity and scope of the system/subsystem/equipment. The use of reference material is encouraged during the examination. The examinee makes the actual adjustments, alignments, or software program changes; evaluates system performance; and corrects equipment maladjustments. The examiner observes the results and verifies the accuracy of the adjustments, alignments, or changes.

4-45. The examiner may deviate from the printed examination to ensure the examinee has the required proficiency. The examinee should be told of any deviations before taking the examination.

4-46. If there is a published OJT course, the performance examination may be incorporated as an integral part of OJT. When there is no published OJT course, the examination may be used as a study outline. When the examination is so used, the individual who provides OJT should not be the examiner.

4-47. The examiner may make only minor changes to the performance examination to make it compatible with the system used. Operations and questions other than those given on the performance examination may be used to ensure the examinee's total system knowledge. When maintenance procedures or system configurations change, facilities will recommend changes be made to the examinations. Recommendations for changes to examinations will be sent to Commander, ATSCOM, AFAT-ATS-CT, 2805 Division Road, Fort Rucker, Alabama 36362-5265.

Administration of Performance Examinations

4-48. The distribution of the performance examination prior to the examination is encouraged. The trainee will be made thoroughly familiar with the examination requirements and related test equipment during OJT.

4-49. Except in instances in which two people are required to make a particular adjustment or alignment, the trainee will complete the examination unassisted.

Grading of Performance Examinations

4-50. Once the trainee has completed an operation, the examiner grades the performance. Failure of only one of certain operations constitutes failure of the entire examination.

Note. Secure handling of the performance examination is not required.

Examination Review and Evaluation

4-51. Certification examinations are constantly reviewed and updated by ATSCOM. Examinations are combined when redundancy is discovered or revised when found to be obsolete. Examiners may detect questions that are not correct or administer an examination that is not relevant to the system/subsystem/equipment for which the technician is being tested. In either case, examiners should include an appropriate comment with the examination and send the results to Commander, ATSCOM, AFAT-ATS-CT, 2805 Division Road, Fort Rucker, Alabama 36362-5265.

Examination Failure Policy

4-52. If a technician requiring certification authority fails an examination, the supervisor will return the technician to the phased training program (figure 4-1, page 4-8). The remedial training will be documented in the technician's official certification and related training record. The program will contain the—

- Training for the deficient areas identified.
- Recommended study material.
- Method for measuring progress.
- Time schedule for improvement program completion.
- Name of instructor(s) and method of documenting training.

4-53. If the technician fails the theory examination, he is ineligible to take the performance examination. If a technician passes the theory examination but fails the performance examination, he is not required to take another theory examination. The examiner must notify ATSCOM, in writing, of the tentative scheduled date for the new performance examination; ATSCOM will then verify the date.

4-54. The examiner will use a different examination each time a technician retakes the examination. A technician may not take a theory or performance examination more than three times in a 12-month period.

4-55. The ATSCOM must retain examinations, answer sheets, comments, and any other information pertaining to a failed examination for not less than two years.

EQUIPMENT CERTIFICATION

4-56. Table 4-1 lists ATC equipment requiring certification. A technician qualified and authorized to do so must perform equipment certification. ATC equipment is unusable until certified or authorized by the commander.

Table 4-1. Equipment certification listing

Name	Nomenclature
ATC landing control system	Army–Navy/tactical signal equipment (AN/TSQ)-71B
Radar set	AN/TPN-18A
Radar set	AN/TPN-31
Interrogator set	AN/TPX-44
Interrogator set	AN/TPX-56(57)
Radar system	AN/FSQ-84
Radar set	AN/FPN-40
Interrogator set	AN/TPX-41
Interrogator set	AN/TPX-42
Radar system	AN/FPN-67
Radar system	AN/FPN-66
Radar system	ASR-8/9/11
Digital bright radar indicator tower equipment	DBRITE
VHF omnidirectional range (VOR)	AN/FRN-41(V)
Instrument landing system	Localizer, glideslope, markers, Mark 20
Non-directional beacon system	NDB
Automation systems	Tower display workstations, ARTS II, IIA, PIDP
Tactical air navigation system	TACAN
ATIS systems	ATIS
Distance measuring equipment	DME
ATS air-to-ground communications	Voice switches, RCE, radios
Recorder	DALR 1

PART TWO. TACTICAL AIR TRAFFIC SERVICES

Chapter 5

Tactical Facility Administration

Part two of this manual (chapters five through eight) standardizes U.S. Army tactical facility administration, operations, training, and maintenance. Procedures dealing with operational requirements, position responsibilities, and duties are the minimum standard, unless stated otherwise.

SECTION I – GENERAL

ARMY AIR TRAFFIC CONTROL GOVERNING DIRECTIVES

5-1. The following FAA directives, and ARs, apply to all Army controllers:

- FAA JO 7110.65T, Air Traffic Control.
- FAAO 7610.4, Special Operations.
- FAAO 8240.41, Flight Inspection/Air Traffic On-Site Coordination Requirements.
- FAA JO 7220.1B, Air Traffic Control Certification Procedures.
- FAA JO 7340.2, Contractions.
- FAAO 8200.1, United States Standard Flight Inspection Manual (USSFIM).
- FAAO 8260.15, United States Army Terminal Instrument Procedures Service.
- FAAO 8260.19, Flight Procedures and Airspace.
- FAAO 8260.3, United States Standards for Terminal Instrument Procedures (TERPS).
- AR 95-2, Airspace, Airfields/Heliports, Flight Activities, Air Traffic Control, and NAVAIDs.

Contents

5-2. U.S. Army controllers who augment a facility operated by another branch of the U.S. military will comply with the ATC regulations and procedures of the host service.

INTERNATIONAL CIVIL AVIATION ORGANIZATION IMPLICATIONS

5-3. This TC supplements applicable DA, FAA, and ICAO publications to be used in providing ATS. When the U.S. Army provides ATC services in overseas areas, deviations from these standards may be necessary to conform to foreign government regulations. Deviations will be outlined in an agreement between one of the following:

- Theater commander and the host government.
- Host government military commanders and U.S. Army commanders.
- Host government ATC authorities and the U.S. Army commanders.
- Host government ATC authorities and U.S. Army ATC authorities.

5-4. National regulations or agreements adopted for Army use in overseas areas take precedence over this publication; host nation regulations and procedures apply to U.S. Army controllers who augment a civil or foreign ATC facility. However, every effort should be made to conform to this publication.

5-5. Tactical ATC services performed to support aviation mission requirements may also dictate deviations from established standards. Such deviations will be approved in writing by an O-6 or higher.

NORTH ATLANTIC TREATY ORGANIZATION STANDARD AGREEMENTS IMPLICATIONS

5-6. STANAG is the NATO abbreviation for standardization agreement; these agreements are used for the purpose of standardizing—

- Processes.
- Procedures.
- Terms.
- Common military procedures.
- Common technical procedures.
- Common equipment between the member countries of the alliance.

5-7. Each NATO state ratifies a STANAG and implements it within their military. The purpose is to provide common operational and administrative procedures and logistics, so one member nation's military may use the stores and support of another member's military. STANAGs also form the basis for technical interoperability between a wide variety of communication and information systems (CIS) essential for NATO and allied operations.

5-8. STANAGs are published in English and French, the two official languages of NATO, by the NATO standardization agency in Brussels.

5-9. Among the hundreds of standardization agreements (current total near 1300) are those for calibers of small arms ammunition, map markings, communications procedures, and classification of bridges. The following is a list of STANAGs which may have an effect on air and ATC operations:

- STANAG 2999, Use of Helicopters in Land Operations (ATP-49).
- STANAG 3596, Air Reconnaissance Requesting and Target Reporting Guide.
- STANAG 3680, AAP-6 NATO: Glossary of Terms and Definitions.
- STANAG 3700, NATO Tactical Air Doctrine (ATP-33[B]).
- STANAG 3736, Offensive Air Support Operations (ATP-27[B]).
- STANAG 3805, Doctrine and Procedures for Airspace Control in Time of Crisis and War (ATP-40[A]).
- STANAG 4184, Microwave Landing System (MLS).
- STANAG 4586, Standard Interface of the Unmanned Control System (UCS) for NATO UAS interoperability.
- STANAG 7204, Minimum requirements for personnel providing ATS in NATO lead operations.

EXTENDED TACTICAL OPERATIONS

5-10. The nature of tactical operations and training requires special considerations during extended periods greater than 30 days. Facility management and certification procedures for extended tactical operations require further refinement than initial operations. ATC management should begin the planning of extended operations at the onset when redeployment is unknown or is expected to last longer than 30 days.

FACILITY MANAGEMENT

5-11. Extended or enduring tactical operations lasting 30 days or longer will require facility management to develop training materials and supporting administrative documents to accommodate sustained operations. The following items to be developed include:

- FTMs (see appendix B).

- FTPs (see chapter one).
- LOAs, memorandum of agreement (MOAs), and letter of procedure (LOPs) needed. (See appendix A).
- Handover procedures (transition checklists, controller evaluation assessments).
- Required facility charts and aids (runway and airfield diagrams, VCC, and crash grid maps).

CERTIFICATION PROCEDURES

5-12. Operations with a duration of 30 days or greater require site-specific certification. Controllers arriving at these locations after initial certification require skills evaluation consisting of practical knowledge of the local procedures outlined within the FTM and demonstration of all required controller skills outlined in FAA JO 7220.1B. This skills evaluation will be conducted by certifying officials from the outgoing unit for key personnel during relief in place operations. Incoming certifying officials will assume skill evaluations and rating responsibilities on all other unit personnel after handover. Controllers completing initial ratings during extended deployments will complete a fixed-site FTP as outlined in Part I.

SECTION II – SUPERVISION AND MANAGEMENT

TACTICAL AIR TRAFFIC CONTROL RATINGS

5-13. AR 95-2 and FAA JO 7220.1B detail procedures for the administration of ATC ratings. Contained within these policy documents are leadership and examiner responsibilities, time limitations, and skill requirements for the assessment of controller qualifications. Chapter seven of this TC provides the construct for the development of the tactical training program and progression requirements IAW the policies outlined in AR 95-2 and FAA JO 7220.1B. To meet the commonly accepted objectives of the knowledge and skill requirements outlined in ICAO, NATO, and FAA guidelines initial experience gates are required to supplement training assessments and qualifications.

5-14. Initial rating applicants are required to meet minimum experience gates before the facility rating can be completed. These experience gates are required for initial "type" ratings and are supplemental (additional) to knowledge and skill assessments applied by examiners. The intent of these experience gates are not to negate the judgment of examiners as to the veracity of an applicant's qualifications, but are established to better guide controller proficiency which cannot always be assessed during limited evaluation periods.

5-15. Initial rating applicants are required to complete the minimum position hours indicated below before the facility rating can be conducted. These gates are required for all initial rating applicants and include controllers possessing other type ratings:

- ATCT-80 position hours of which 50 percent of this time may be met using simulation devices, the successful completion of the skills and knowledge evaluation required to receive this rating, and all required/selected tasks of the CTL.
- AIC-80 position hours of which 50 percent of this time may be met using simulation devices, the successful completion of the skills, and knowledge evaluation required to receive this rating, and all required/selected tasks of the CTL.
- GCA-10 unaided live approaches after the applicant has been PQ, the successful completion of the skills and knowledge evaluation required to receive this rating, and all required/selected tasks of the CTL. Live approaches are conducted within radar handoff procedures and include emergency, no-gyro, and surveillance approach criteria when established.

5-16. Accredited simulation devices should be used to maximize proficiency and controller development to reach the required knowledge and skills level required for the GCA rating. Simulation may not be used to meet any part of the 10 live approach requirements or the rating evaluation.

5-17. The initial certification and rating process during the course of normal training is unit specific. Continuous entries indicating ratings beyond the initial qualification are not required unless facility operations exceed 30 days, and a location or site specific FTP and rating process has been developed. Figures 5-1 and 5-2 depict examples of how ratings are annotated on FAA Form 7220.1.

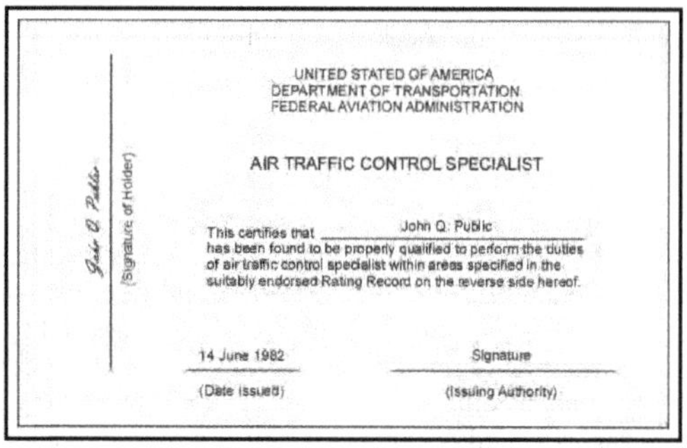

UNITED STATED OF AMERICA
DEPARTMENT OF TRANSPORTATION
FEDERAL AVIATION ADMINISTRATION

AIR TRAFFIC CONTROL SPECIALIST

This certifies that John Q. Public has been found to be properly qualified to perform the duties of air traffic control specialist within areas specified in the suitably endorsed Rating Record on the reverse side hereof.

(Signature of Holder)

14 June 1982 (Date issued)

Signature (Issuing Authority)

Figure 5-1. Sample FAA Form 7220-1, front

RATING RECORD

AREA	RATING	DATE ISSUED	CERTIFYING OFFICIAL
F CO. 3/2 AVN	ATCT	12 Aug 82	Signature
Kandahar, AAF	GCA	13 Apr 08	Signature
Skywatch	AIC	15 Aug 09	Signature

FAA Form 7220-1 (8-76) SUPERSEDES PREVIOUS EDITION

Figure 5-2. Sample FAA Form 7220-1, back

PROFICIENCY REQUIREMENTS

5-18. Controller skills are perishable and require continued use to maintain the appropriate level of proficiency required during rating assessments. The routine exercise of air traffic controllers during aviation training events will help mitigate the loss of perishable skills and more accurately prepare controllers for their wartime mission. To meet the highest readiness levels (RLs) and to better assure controller proficiency the following thresholds must be obtained:

- ATCT-40 position hours for the preceding six months of which no more than 50 percent conducted using simulation devices.
- AIC-40 position hours for the preceding six months of which no more than 50 percent conducted using simulation devices.
- GCA-10 approaches for the preceding six months of which no more than five conducted using simulation devices. Approaches are to be conducted within established radar handoff procedures and include emergency, no-gyro, and surveillance approach criteria.

5-19. Controllers not meeting proficiency requirements outlined above will be reported at a lower RL until position hours can be achieved or a controller evaluation accessing proficiency can be accomplished.

Note. Controller proficiency will be assessed in the reporting period comprised of the preceding six months. T-level ratings will be assigned IAW AR 220-1, Unit Status Report (USR). Rated controllers not meeting the proficiency requirements for the preceding six months will be reported as RL 2 until they meet position hour/approach criteria or a proficiency evaluation has been conducted. Platoon sergeants (PSGs) and controllers assigned to staff positions not requiring ratings are excluded from proficiency requirements and T-level assessments.

COMMUNICATIONS PROCEDURES

5-20. The SL on duty is responsible for all communications emanating from the facility. The facility chief will ensure periodic checks are made to detect and prevent unauthorized transmissions, as discussed below:

- The SL takes action to detect and prevent radio or telephone transmission of false or deceptive communications and obscene, indecent, or profane language. The SL is also responsible for detecting unauthorized or unassigned identifications and preventing willful or malicious interference with other communications.
- Besides normal ATC transmissions, the facility may need to transmit third-party messages about the safety of aircraft operations or the preservation of life or property.
- ATC facilities may relay non-ATC instructions only when no other source of communication is available and the transmissions will not interfere with ATC instructions.

OPERATING INITIALS

5-21. The facility chief will assign controllers, two-letter operating initials. The facility chief will maintain a list of operating initials for all assigned personnel on a facility memorandum. Except where signatures are required, controllers will use the assigned operating initials on all interphone systems and facility forms and records.

MEDICAL RESTRICTIONS TO AIR TRAFFIC CONTROL DUTIES

5-22. Flight physical requirements for soldiers assigned to tactical unit are the same as those required for controllers working at an installation facility as discussed in chapter two of this TC.

5-23. If a supervisor determines a controller's physical or mental health is questionable, he will relieve the controller of ATC duties. The supervisor will refer the controller to a flight surgeon/medical examiner for an evaluation and a ruling. If a controller is receiving a substance or medical procedure that is likely to provoke an adverse systemic reaction, he will be restricted from ATC duties. The controller will not perform ATC duties until declared fit IAW AR 40-501. AR 40-8 addresses the factors to consider and the appropriate medical restrictions to ATC duty.

5-24. Use of all medications will be with the knowledge of a flight surgeon or APA. Personnel ordinarily assigned to an operating position, including those who directly supervise within the facility, will not use the following drugs within a 24-hour period before assumption of duty unless a waiver is obtained:

- Sedatives.
- Tranquilizers.
- Any drug, such as but not limited to, anti-hypertensive agents or duodenal ulcer medications, which has an effect on the central nervous system.
- Any other drug and/or medication likely to affect the alertness, judgment, vision, equilibrium, or state of consciousness.

5-25. Controllers will not be assigned ATC duties for at least 72 hours after donating blood (formal flight surgeon restriction not required). Controllers will coordinate with the facility managers prior to giving blood to minimize impact on the duty schedule.

5-26. Controllers receiving medical or dental treatment or immunizations that could affect duty performance must be cleared by the appropriate medical authority before performing ATC duties.

5-27. Controllers must not perform ATC duties, nor directly supervise other controllers within 12 hours of consuming any amount of alcohol. If alcohol is used during off duty time, it should be conservative so mental alertness and ability to perform is not reduced by the after effects. Abstinence of 12 hours before commencing ATC duties does not guarantee the absence of residual effects.

OPENING AND CLOSING TACTICAL FACILITIES

5-28. The ATC unit commander establishes facility hours of operation per mission requirement. Opening and closing procedures and responsibilities will be coordinated with airfield operations and/or the ATC facility having IFR jurisdiction. When opening and closing, part-time facilities will broadcast the service they are resuming or terminating. These procedures will also be included in a LOA. The facility will publish its hours of operation in the appropriate NOTAM/aviation procedure guide (APG).

STANDARD FACILITY SHIFTS AND WORKWEEKS

5-29. ATC crew endurance is an integral part of the overall risk management program. It is used to control risk due to sleep deprivation or fatigue and prescribe thresholds to trigger command decisions whether to accept the risk. Shift and crew endurance procedures are outlined in AR 95-2. Commanders are required to incorporate fighter management/crew endurance guidance in their safety SOPs IAW AR 95-1and DA Pam 385-90.

SHIFT REQUIREMENTS

5-30. Shift duty and actual shift manning will provide a qualified controller for each operating position in the facility. This does not preclude reducing the actual shift manning to the minimum during periods of limited flying activities.

CONSOLIDATION OF OPERATING POSITIONS

5-31. The facility chief may permit consolidation of operating positions. At least two controllers will be present for duty in the control TWR, GCA, or AIC. One must be facility-rated and the other PQ in at least one position. A facility memorandum will identify those positions applicable to a facility (as designated by the commander or platoon leader [PLT LDR]) and those that cannot be combined with another.

POSITION ASSIGNMENTS

5-32. Only ATC personnel who are qualified to perform the duties as outlined in AR 95-2 and this publication will man operating positions. Controllers will be assigned to positions as required by traffic, equipment, and individual qualifications.

5-33. Trainees will not be assigned to positions to which they are not qualified unless they are under direct supervision of facility-rated controllers.

5-34. Facility-rated controllers providing direct one-on-one supervision are directly responsible for operating the position. Trainees will not be assigned to more than one operating position at a time unless positions are permanently combined within the facility.

5-35. At the discretion of the SL, trainees may conduct precision or surveillance approaches during IFR conditions under certain circumstances.

5-36. They may conduct these approaches if—

- Direct one-on-one supervision is maintained.
- Direct communications override is available at the position of operation.
- Weather conditions are acceptable (not less than a 500-foot ceiling or one-mile visibility).

TRANSFER OF POSITION RESPONSIBILITY

5-37. Position responsibility will be transferred according to FAA JO 7110.65T and appropriate facility directives. Each controller will—

- Read the recent information file, DA Form 3502, and any other operational data, equipment service and maintenance requirements specified.

- Obtain a briefing on communications, traffic and airfield conditions, equipment outages, and current and forecasted weather.
- Accept responsibility for the position only after ensuring the briefing is complete and all questions about the operation of the position have been resolved.

5-38. The relieving controller and the controller being relieved will share equal responsibility for the completeness and accuracy of the position-relief briefing. The facility chief will provide a tailored checklist of the equipment and conditions that will likely be a factor at each position during relief periods.

AIRCRAFT ACCIDENTS AND INCIDENTS

5-39. When a facility, service, or NAVAID has been involved in an aircraft accident or incident, the facility chief must act immediately. The facility chief will obtain accurate and complete information to base a detailed investigation. The responsibilities following an aircraft accident or incident are outlined below.

LEADER RESPONSIBILITIES

5-40. As soon as the facility chief, team leader, SL, or CIC receives notification of an accident or incident, he will—

- Notify the chain of command. When an aircraft accident/incident occurs and any part of a unit is known or suspected to have been involved. The notification will include—
  - Date/time of accident/incident.
  - Number/type aircraft involved.
  - Number of injuries/fatalities.
  - Brief synopsis of events to include ATC involvement.
  - Actions taken.
  - A point of contact by name, position, and telephone number to obtain additional information.
- Request a local weather observation, if weather support is available, unless there has been an intervening METAR or SPECI.
- Record all appropriate details, including the local weather observation, on DA Form 3502.
- Mark and safeguard the recording media that is pertinent to the accident in the same manor described in chapter three of this publication. In the case of an incident, emergency or complaint about ATC service removal of recorded media before normal rotation time is unnecessary.
- Obtain a written statement about the incident or accident from all controllers and supervisory personnel involved. Written records pertaining to an aircraft accident will be retained for a minimum of 6 months. Written records pertaining to an aircraft incident will be retained for a minimum of 30 days.
- Relieve the controller for physical and psychological evaluation by the local medical officer or flight surgeon if there is any indication the controller contributed to the accident or incident. The controller will obtain a clearance from the local medical officer or flight surgeon before returning to duty. The controller will be transported to the local medical facility according to AR 385-10.
- Examine the condition of the equipment, along with technically certified maintenance personnel, to determine whether it could have contributed to the accident or incident.

Note. Additional instruction pertaining to facility actions will be contained in the facility position binder.

INFORMATION RELEASE

5-41. No personnel may give interviews, make statements, or release any written or recorded information to news agencies or unauthorized personnel or organizations. Information on an aircraft accident, incident, or alleged violation of any kind will not be released outside official Army channels without approval from the commander, USAASA. The identity of personnel involved will be treated as restricted information. The installation commander may approve the release of information to Army organizations and Army press releases after consultation with the PAO and the SJA.

ACCIDENTS OR INCIDENTS INVOLVING RADAR FACILITIES

5-42. When an accident or incident involves, or is suspected to have involved radar equipment, the facility will discontinue radar service until a flight inspection is performed.

SECTION III – PERSONNEL TITLES, QUALIFICATIONS, RESPONSIBILITIES, AND RESTRICTIONS

AIR TRAFFIC CONTROL PLATOON LEADER

5-43. The PLT LDR is an MOS 150A air traffic and airspace management technician warrant officer. He supervises the employment of platoon personnel and equipment. The PLT LDR also—

- Establishes policy within platoon.
- Is thoroughly knowledgeable of procedures and standards for separation and control of manned and unmanned systems, airports, and airspace.
- Integrates collective, leader, and Soldier training to accomplish mission.
- Ensures resources are available for training.
- Develops short and long term training strategies ensuring Soldiers are trained and proficient controllers and maintainers.
- Reviews and revises TERPS packets and assists in the certification process of associated NAVAIDs and facilities.
- Assists in development and revision of controlled and Special Use Airspace (SUA).
- Provides technical expertise on employment and use of ATC assets.
- Enforces standards, time limitations, and policies for issuing controller qualification, certification, and facility ratings to ATC personnel.
- Applies procedures for cancellation, suspension or reissuance, and withdrawal of certificates and facility ratings.
- May serve as ATCS/CTO examiner IAW AR 95-2 and FAA JO 7220.1B.
- Provides ATS input for the development and revision of APGs.

PLATOON SERGEANT

5-44. The PSG supervises and manages all ATC facilities under his control at an airfield, heliport, or field site. He also—

- Provides liaison on matters of ATC and airspace to the PLT LDR, unit commander, and representatives of other units, agencies, or commands.
- Ensures ATS systems are maintained, operational and meet all safety standards.
- Ensures training is executed to standard.
- Ensures Soldiers are trained to prepare, cope, and operate in joint, interagency, and multinational scenarios.
- Ensures standards are met and maintains discipline.
- Ensures assigned ATS personnel maintain physical and medical standards.
- Ensures facility personnel conduct training and rating programs according to this publication and prescribed regulations.
- Ensures TERPS packages are complete and accurate.
- May serve as ATCS/CTO examiner IAW AR 95-2 and FAA JO 7220.1B.

- Administers annual written exams and conducts skill evaluations.
- Serves as trainer, mentor, and advisor to the PLT LDR, subordinate noncommissioned officers (NCOs), and Soldiers.

AIR TRAFFIC CONTROL CHIEF

5-45. The ATC Chief position is only found in the airfield operations battalion (AOB). The ATC chief's responsibilities include—

- Supervising and managing all facilities under his control at an airfield, heliport, or tactical site.
- Serving as a liaison on matters of ATC and airspace.
- Assisting with the development of local airfield SOPs.
- Serving as a member of airfield advisory council.
- Coordinating expansion and acquisition efforts for the airfield.
- Developing the pre-accident plan.
- Interfacing with the airspace command and control (AC2) system and the combined air operations center's crash rescue center.
- Overseeing the development of facility training manuals and programs used during extended operations.
- Coordinating LOAs and LOPs.
- Ensuring ATC systems are operationally acceptable and statuses are reported.
- Ensuring facilities collect and safeguard data on aircraft mishaps, emergencies, and violations.
- Ensuring personnel maintain proficiency and training and rating programs are executed IAW prescribed policies.

FACILITY CHIEF/TEAM LEADER

5-46. The facility chief/team leader—

- Ensures the facility operates according to military and FAA, ICAO, and host nation rules and regulations.
- Prepares TERPS packet IAW appendix D of this publication.
- Ensures all controllers meet the physical standards of AR 40-501 and/or local/host nation requirements.
- Ensures the operational readiness of facility equipment and associated NAVAIDs.
- Maintains a current file of pertinent regulations, manuals, charts, maps, and training material IAW appendix A.
- Ensures assigned personnel maintain currency.
- Maintains custodial control of all facility forms, records, and publications and ensures their accuracy, completeness, and distribution.
- Initiates and maintains a facility duty schedule.
- Conducts position qualification evaluations.
- May serve as ATCS/CTO examiner IAW AR 95-2 and FAA JO 7220.1B.
- Administers annual written exams and conducts skill evaluations.
- Must be facility rated and have completed facility management and administration training prior to assuming the position.

5-47. The facility chief has specific duties dependent of the facility of assignment (see FM 3-04.120 for these duties).

SHIFT LEADER

5-48. During the SL's tour of duty, he is responsible to the facility chief for the efficiency of facility operations. He also performs his normal ATC duties in addition to those of the SL. The SL—

- Assigns and directs all phases of the subordinates work.

- Ensures personnel receive OJT and conducts assessments of training through the administration of controller evaluations (DA Form 3479-1).
- Conducts position qualification evaluations when directed by the facility chief but are restricted from conducting annual skill evaluations.
- Assists and advises controllers during emergencies.
- Maintains facility records.
- Ensures personnel are current and proficient.
- Notifies search and rescue facilities of aircraft in distress and provides assistance and advice.
- Delegates responsibility to subordinates and assists the facility chief.
- Evaluates the operational effectiveness of facility systems, subsystems, and equipment.
- Records and reports outages and takes action to correct discrepancies.
- Must be facility rated and have completed facility management and administration training prior to assuming the duties of this position.

CONTROLLER-IN-CHARGE

5-49. A CIC will be designated to assume the duties of the SL under the following conditions:

- When supervisory personnel leave the facility or are off duty, the facility chief will designate a CIC for the period the supervisor is absent. Assigning a CIC assures coordination and cooperation will continue when the SL is not available.
- The CIC will assume duties and responsibilities of the SL. He also performs his normal ATC duties in addition to those of the SL.
- CICs may conduct controller evaluations but are restricted from conducting position qualification assessments and annual skill evaluations.

5-50. Prior to being designated as a CIC, controllers will meet the following prerequisites:
- Be operationally current in the facilities CIC duties are to be preformed.
- Be selected by the ATC/facility chief.
- Successfully complete administration and management training.

5-51. The facility chief will appoint the CIC assignment from the facility's potential supervisors. The facility chief may designate more than one CIC per shift to ensure coverage is achieved during leaves, illnesses, or temporary groundings. The CIC duties should be rotated to expose the controller to supervisory duties and responsibilities. All eligible controllers who meet these prerequisites will be considered for selection as CIC.

5-52. Facility chiefs will determine facility requirements for CICs considering—
- Facility operational needs.
- Scheduling concerns.
- Staffing concerns.
- Special events.
- Other issues.

5-53. Facility chiefs will evaluate controllers based on their knowledge, skills and abilities. Included in these three areas are—
- Problem solving and analytical ability.
- Planning and organizing.
- Decisiveness.
- Judgment.
- Communication skill.
- Interpersonal skill.

CONTROL TOWER OPERATOR AND AIR TRAFFIC CONTROL SPECIALIST EXAMINERS

5-54. CTO and ATCS examiners will be designated and assume duties as outlined below:

- Military CTO and ATCS examiners will be designated according to AR 95-2, FAA JO 7220.1B, and this publication. AR 95-2 explains how to request examiner designations. The facility-rated controllers meeting the requirements of AR 95-2 may be recommended for designation as examiners.
- Primary and alternate ATCS examiners may be appointed per tactical facility as long as not more than two examiners are appointed.
- During the planning stages, leaders must consider the possibility that issuance of temporary FAA CTO certificates will be required for temporary locations.
- Examiners will administer CTO and ATCS facility rating tests according to 14 CFR, Part 65, and this publication. They conduct the tests properly and complete, maintain, and submit the related forms and records according to procedures in FAA JO 7220.1B.
- CTO and ATCS examiners—
  - Maintain test security.
  - Develop and maintain the facility rating tests.
  - Make sure applicants meet eligibility requirements.
  - Issue temporary CTO certificates and sign ATCS certificates.
  - Administer all prescribed written and practical tests for the facility-rating exam.
  - Maintain a record of ratings issued (by name, date, and type) and retain the record in files.
  - Report testing or certification irregularities or problems, as appropriate, to the PSG/facility chief.
  - Conduct annual skill evaluations.

AIR TRAFFIC CONTROL SYSYTEM MAINTENANCE SUPERVISOR

5-55. The ATC Systems Maintenance Supervisor is responsible for all ATS equipment maintenance. Duties include, but are not limited to, the following:

- Coordinate maintenance-related issues, such as LOA, on-call rosters, and NAVAID scheduled maintenance with the PSG or facility chief.
- Ensure maintenance facilities are maintained according to applicable military and FAA publications and standards.
- Ensure the qualifications of maintenance personnel.
- Coordinate ATC equipment maintenance with support and supported units.
- Establish a maintenance training and certification program for the local facility.
- Coordinate facility configuration changes with the PLT LDR/PSG and higher headquarters.
- Maintain, "As built" diagrams and drawings for equipment IAW AR 95-2.
- Maintain a current file of pertinent regulations, manuals, and training material IAW appendix A.

SECTION IV – TACTICAL EQUIPMENT

COORDINATED UNIVERSAL/LOCAL TIME

5-56. All ATC facilities will use UTC and date in all operational activities. Local time will be used for facility duty schedules, daily traffic counts, and other administrative forms and correspondence.

5-57. A reliable clock will be visible from each operating position in all ATC facilities. Clocks will be checked at the beginning of each shift. The results of time checks will be logged on DA Form 3502. Time checks will be performed according to FAA JO 7210.3. In a tactical environment, ATC facilities will obtain a time check from the next higher control facility or from Global Positioning System (GPS).

LIGHT GUNS

5-58. ATC light gun color codes and meanings will be attached to the back or side of the light guns. ATC light guns will be adjusted to provide a red light when activated.

EQUIPMENT CHECKS/CHECKLIST

5-59. The facility chief will establish an equipment checklist to be completed at the beginning of the day. If radio checks cannot be completed during the facility's duty day this will be annotated on the DA Form 3502 in the closing statement. DA Form 3502 will be used to record the results of equipment checks.

5-60. The equipment checklist will be a locally produced form; the checklist may be a separate form, or it may be placed on the back of DA Form 3502. This form is not intended to circumvent the Army maintenance system but only to serve as a list of equipment that must be checked. Controllers must complete standard Army maintenance forms on equipment requiring them. The equipment checklist will be initiated at opening of the facility and reviewed at the beginning of each shift. Completed checklists will be filed with and retained the same as DA Form 3502.

5-61. If all equipment is operational, the entry on the form may be limited to "checklist complete." If outages occur, the entry must identify those outages, the name of the agency notified, and their operating initials, for example, "checklist complete; LIGHT GUNS OTS MAINT/CB NTFYD."

5-62. On DA Form 3502, a capital "E" (equipment) will be placed in the time (UTC) column to the left of entries showing equipment out-of-service time and return-to-service time. The "E" for a specific equipment outage need not be repeated each day thereafter unless the equipment returns to service. Examples of these are, "E 0800, checklist complete, 126.2T OTS MAINT/CB NTFYD" and "E 0810, 126.2T return to service (RTS), radio and recorder checks complete."

TACTICAL ALTIMETER-SETTING INDICATORS

5-63. Tactical ATC facilities not equipped with calibrated altimeter-setting indicators will obtain settings from supporting Air Force weather teams.

RADIO EQUIPMENT

5-64. During the hours of operation, ATC facilities will continuously monitor all assigned radio frequencies to include emergency frequencies VHF 121.5 and UHF 243.0.

RECORDED MEDIA

RECORDER CHECKS AND TAPE CHANGES

5-65. If recorded media equipment is available a facility memorandum will be developed outlining the procedures for changing, marking, loading, and securing recorded media, and for controller/maintenance responsibilities. It is imperative that all controllers and maintenance personnel are properly trained to check the recorder, change the recorded media, and perform PMCS. This training will be noted in section II of DA Form 3479.

5-66. At the beginning of each shift, the SL or CIC will ensure all recording channels are operating properly. Controllers will monitor the quality of recording during their assigned shift.

5-67. The facility chief and the maintenance chief will establish written procedures to ensure the recording quality is checked after all radio, recorder, or telephone equipment maintenance. These checks will be noted on DA Form 3502.

Recording Equipment Labels

5-68. An identification number will be assigned/attached to each recorded media. At the beginning of each day, the number of the recorded media and the device number used to record will be entered on DA Form 3502. If it is necessary to change the recorded media during the shift, the reason for the change, the number of the recorded media removed, and the number of the recorded media and the device used to record will be entered on DA Form 3502 and the initials of the individual making the change.

NAVIGATIONAL AIDS

5-69. All NAVAIDs must pass a flight inspection before IFR operations are conducted. The procedures contained in FAAO 8260 Series will be used to construct a precision or non-precision approach that will service the terminal area. The en route criteria will be established by the Airspace Control Authority (ACA). Critical information about tactical approach procedures at instrumented heliports and airfields must be developed by the sector responsible for the approach. This information must be disseminated to the aviation units, AICs, and the appropriate AC2 elements for inclusion in the airspace control order (ACO), Airspace Procedures Guide, and other related airspace information documents. The following actions will be accomplished to prepare for a flight inspection:

- Ensure all personnel are familiar with FAAO 8200.1.
- Provide accurate facility data for new or relocated facilities.
- Develop an LOA concerning the airspace used for the approach procedure.
- Assign the best-qualified controller available.
- Establish communications on a single dedicated frequency.
- Ensure all facility equipment is calibrated IAW applicable manuals.
- Ensure personnel will be available to make corrections and adjustments.
- Provide transportation to move flight inspection equipment and personnel.

5-70. The approach control facility is normally designated the primary NAVAID monitoring facility. At locations without an approach control, the TWR is designated the primary NAVAID monitoring facility.

UNITED STATES ARMY RADAR FLIGHT INSPECTIONS

5-71. Standard radar instrument approach procedures are as follows:

- Bearings, headings, courses, and radials are magnetic.
- Elevations and altitudes are in feet, mean sea level (MSL), except height above touchdown (HAT), height above airport (HAA), threshold crossing height (TCH), and RA.
- Altitudes are minimum altitudes unless otherwise indicated.
- Ceilings are in feet above airport elevation.
- Distances are in nautical miles unless otherwise indicated, except visibilities in statute miles or in feet RVR.

5-72. Initial approach minimum altitudes will correspond with those established for en route operations in the particular area or as set forth below. Positive identification must be established with the radar controller. The instructions of the radar controller are mandatory from initial contact to final authorized landing minimums, except when:

- Visual contact is established on final approach at or before descent to the authorized landing minimums.
- At pilot's discretion if it appears desirable to discontinue the approach.

5-73. Unless otherwise directed prior to final approach, a missed approach will be executed when—

- Communications on final approach are lost for more than 5 seconds during a precision approach, or for more than 30 seconds during a surveillance approach.
- Directed by radar controllers.
- Visual contact is not established upon descent to authorized landing minimums.
- Landing is not accomplished.

Chapter 5

MONITORS

5-74. Monitors that do not provide an automatic visual or aural alarm will be checked at least once an hour. When an ATC facility is responsible for monitoring NAVAIDs, the facility chief will include monitoring instructions in the FTM. If a NAVAID monitor alarm is received, the identification feature will be checked aurally and the responsible maintenance authority notified immediately. If the alarm cannot be silenced and the identification feature cannot be heard, the NAVAID is considered inoperative.

5-75. If personnel suspect a control line or monitor failure rather than a malfunction of the NAVAID causes an alarm, they must take the appropriate action per local SOPs and the FTM. If a malfunction is confirmed, use of the NAVAID will be discontinued. A NOTAM will be published showing NAVAIDs with inoperative monitors as unmonitored.

Interruptions and Malfunctions

5-76. The facility chief establishes procedures for reporting interruptions to NAVAIDs and malfunctions in communications and radar equipment. They ensure the timely response of maintenance personnel to a report of an interruption or a malfunction.

5-77. The on-duty SL or CIC will report any known or reported malfunction in equipment or interruption to a NAVAID to the appropriate office; for example, maintenance personnel, ARTCC, approach control facility, and any other facility that may be affected. He then reports the malfunction or interruption to the airfield commander.

WIND INDICATOR EQUIPMENT

5-78. Wind indicators should be located at the landing and takeoff area. Because of terrain, distance, and local operational requirements, wind equipment may be located at various sites on the airfield. Readout values derived from transmitters not located at the landing and takeoff area will be used as an aid to determine estimated wind conditions. Estimated wind values transmitted to other facilities and to pilots will be reported as wind estimated (for example, "WIND ESTIMATED TWO ONE ZERO AT FIVE").

NIGHT VISION DEVICES

TRAINING

5-79. Controllers will be trained in the operational use of NVDs at required locations. All NVD training will be entered on DA Form 3479, section II. ATC facilities or units using NVDs will establish a training program for their use.

OPERATION AND CARE

5-80. Orientation and briefing on NVD operation and care consists of a class on the characteristics, function, and maintenance of NVDs IAW the applicable TMs, to include the—
- Removal of NVDs from the receptacle, ensuring pressure is released.
- Removal of the front lens covers.
- Insertion of the battery.
- Adjustments of short gauge for FD and adjustments of infinite for local and GC.

Preparation of the Control Tower

5-81. This instruction includes—
- Use of minimum lighting.
- Covering the console to prevent reflection.

Hands-On Training

5-82. Hands-on training consists of an orientation after dark, to include—
- Instruction on distinguishing prominent terrain and other objects in the area.
- Unimpaired vision of traffic areas.
- Adjustment of devices, as required.
- Distinguishing an aircraft with minimum lighting.
- Difference between participating and nonparticipating aircraft.
- Strict observation of aircraft at all times.
- Control of airfield and landing area lighting.

Visual Contact Loss

5-83. To reestablish contact, the controller must—
- Know the altitude of the aircraft.
- Request aircraft position reports.
- Use known landmarks.
- Have the observation confirmed by another controller.

Night Vision Device Procedures

5-84. To establish local NVD procedures, the PSG/facility chief will coordinate with the airfield commander or the senior field aviation commander supported. These procedures should include—
- NVD routes.
- Traffic density.
- Airfield lighting.
- Hours of operation.
- Traffic restrictions.
- Emergency procedures.
- Weather requirements.
- Nonparticipating traffic.
- Aircraft lighting (lights out or dim mode).
- Publication of a NOTAM, if required.

5-85. Air traffic controllers will be familiar with any exemptions or waivers, which may grant relief to the requirement of CFR 14, Part 91.209 concerning aircraft lighting requirements.

This page intentionally left blank.

Chapter 6

Air Traffic Services

ATS units promote safe, flexible, and efficient use of airspace while enhancing air operations for ground force initiatives through airspace information, terminal air traffic control, and navigational support services.

SECTION I – TERMINAL TOWER OPERATIONS

6-1. Terminal tower operations are executed by either the control tower team or the tactical team (TACT). Each of these teams is responsible for control of aircraft operating within terminal airspace. The teams are also responsible for air and vehicular traffic operating on runways, taxiways, and other designated areas of the airfield. Responsibilities include—

- Coordinating the development of specific terminal airspace procedures peculiar to the airfield.
- Interfacing with military/civilian agencies to ensure tower ATC services are coordinated within the ATS plan for the theater of operations.
- Understanding the ACO and the airspace control plan (ACP).
- Resolving airspace conflicts within the terminal control area.
- Developing standard ingress/egress procedures for UAS operations.
- Dissemination of current and forecasted weather information.
- Establishing electronic data links to Army Battle Command Systems (ABCSs) for terminal facilities.

Contents

6-2. Control tower teams and TACTs may be employed at tactical landing sites or main operating bases where high density air traffic exists. These teams are responsible for controlling transitioning, landing, and departing aircraft. Aircraft movements in, out, and through the terminal area are closely coordinated to ensure deconfliction of airspace and fratricide avoidance.

WEATHER TRAINING

6-3. All controllers should complete initial qualification (Q) weather training before starting phase II but must have completed this weather training prior to being rated. Weather training is valid for a 12-month period and must be renewed by or prior to the anniversary month of their previous training. As part of these certifications, the ATC chief/facility chief will ensure comprehensive training is given to controllers by weather personnel on tower (prevailing) visibility. Tower visibility training will include—

- Definitions.
- Visibility determination criteria and procedures.
- Reporting procedures.
- METARS training includes—
  - Reading aviation weather reports.
  - Abbreviations.

6-4. The results of initial (Q) and annual training (P) will be entered on DA Form 3479 in section II. Required entries in section II include the date training was completed, total training time, and test results if applicable. If remedial training is required, it will be completed as previously outlined, except an "R" will indicate the type of training given. Figure 2-1, page 2-3, provides an example of a remedial training entry.

WEATHER DATA

6-5. The airfield weather status (IFR or VFR) will be posted to DA Form 3502 when daily operations begin. As it changes during the day, the status is again posted to the form.

6-6. Weather support for Army tactical operations is based on the following principles:

- Tactical units must consider weather effects during all planning and operational phases, including deployment and employment.
- Commanders must consider favorable and unfavorable weather conditions to determine the best course of action to accomplish the mission.
- Accuracy of weather forecasts depends on the density and timeliness of weather observations.

6-7. The Air Force provides the weather support required by the Army. AR 115-10 specify each service's functions and responsibilities associated with that support. The USAF weather service provides—

- Weather personnel with the technical training and skills necessary to support the Army.
- Direct weather support for theater, divisions, separate brigades, aviation brigades, regiments, and groups according to jointly agreed upon tactical doctrine and operational support concepts.
- Weather training for Army personnel assigned to take limited surface weather observations in support of Air Force forecasting operations or Army ATC operations.
- Possible effects of weather on systems, tactics, and operations based on critical threshold values identified by the Army.
- Weather observations, forecasts, staff support, and timely warnings of expected weather that may adversely affect operations or that could be a hazard to personnel or materiel.
- Weather support products for use in soil trafficability and hydrographical prediction.
- Unique and specialized meteorological observations and forecasts of data elements not included in standard surface weather observations or critical values on request.
- Weather support for tactical missions, intelligence, and tactical decision aids.

Visibility Checkpoint Charts

6-8. During extended tactical operations, control tower facility chiefs will prepare visibility checkpoint charts in conjunction with the combat weather teams. The weather specialty teams will have range-finding equipment, which can accurately measure objects to be used as reference points. Facility chiefs will use these charts to report tower visibility and to observe changes in the reported visibility. When the official report and the tower observation differ, the tower will report the tower visibility to the weather station and the terminal radar facility. The lesser of the surface (official) and tower visibility will be used for aircraft operations. Tower visibility may include the entire surface area or any portion of the area. For example, "Tower visibility is two and one-half miles" or "Tower visibility to the south is one-half mile." When tower visibility is less than four miles and differs from the reported values, it should be included in the remarks section of an official weather observation. Tower visibility is also transmitted to all arriving and departing aircraft.

SECTION II – RADAR OPERATIONS

6-9. The GCA team provides IIMC recovery capability through ASR and PAR approaches. The GCA team normally operates in conjunction with a control TWR team, with an NDB to form a fully instrumented airfield. The GCA team is responsible for—

- Conducting site surveys and collecting data used to initiate TERPS.
- Coordinating and assisting with flight inspection procedures/flyability checks.
- Developing specific GCA procedures particular to the airfield.

* Coordinating with other military/civilian agencies to ensure radar ATC services are coordinated within the ACP for theater of operations.

RADAR SERVICE

6-10. Radar service will be provided only when the controller has a suitable target and is satisfied that the presentation and the equipment performance are adequate for the service provided.

DAILY PERFORMANCE CHECKS

6-11. The daily radar performance check will be part of equipment checks. Controllers will accomplish this check once each shift, unless lack of traffic makes it impossible. For radar performance checks, ASR systems will have a usable target return maintained along the entire airway/route or arrival/ departure control route for which service is provided. Tracking accuracy along these routes will be within the fix/map accuracy (as described in part I, chapter 2 of this publication). Radar services for arrival or departure routes exist between the normal handoff point and a point one-half mile from the end of the runway.

SECTION III – AIRSPACE INFORMATION CENTER OPERATIONS

6-12. The AIC team provides FF services to aircraft operating within assigned airspace. The actual airspace assigned is dictated by the assigned mission and communications capabilities. Additionally, the AIC team displays the common operating picture (COP) on the Tactical Airspace Integration System (TAIS) as received from feeds from ABCS and battle command enablers system of systems. The AIC team provides en route control of airspace users outside of terminal areas and ensures aircraft operate within the parameters of the ACO. The team coordinates emerging airspace requirements for current operations, broadcasts air and ground threats to participating aircraft, and maintains situational awareness of unmanned aerial systems within their area of responsibility.

6-13. The AIC is responsible for—

* Developing specific airspace information and flight coordination procedures specific to the assigned area of operations (AO).
* Coordinating with other military/civilian agencies to ensure AIC services are coordinated within the ACP.
* Ensuring data and communication links are established for connectivity to other ABCSs and ATC facilities.
* Developing an immediate airspace alert plan.

6-14. AICs, with a staff of qualified ATC personnel, will provide communication and control of corridor feeder-route systems, chokepoints, crossing corridors, and transition areas in cantonment areas, training areas, and ranges. When required, these facilities provide altitude or other means of separation. In addition, they will—

* Issue advisories allowing pilots to separate their aircraft from other aircraft and activities or adverse weather that may endanger the aircraft.
* Monitor the flight progress of all participating aircraft within the facility area of responsibility.
* Advise other area users of aircraft activity that may impact on, or conflict with, the mission or activity.
* Provide assistance during emergencies.
* Assist with search and rescue efforts, as needed.

PROCEDURES

6-15. The procedures developed for conducting day-to-day operation of an AIC depend on a number of circumstances. Local requirements often govern exact operational procedures. The procedures and requirements below establish a minimum standard and will apply to all Army AICs.

6-16. Each facility will have an up-to-date map of its area of responsibility. Each map will depict the following areas and routes:

- EOD/hazardous cargo route.
- Ranges.
- NAVAIDs.
- ADIZs and no-fly areas.
- Prominent obstructions.
- Mandatory reporting points.
- Radio and radar blind spots.
- Airfields and landing areas.
- Restricted/prohibited areas.
- Aircraft entry and exit points.
- Changeover points.
- Corridors, transition areas, training areas, and ranges.
- The same grid system as other area ATC and search and rescue facilities.

6-17. The flight progress of participating aircraft will be monitored, and the maximum time between position reports will be 30 minutes. Less time may be required depending on the type, length, and area of routes (such as an NOE route).

6-18. The facility's area of responsibility will be divided into as many subareas as necessary to simplify recognition and reporting. Each area will be lettered, numbered, or named. The boundaries of these subareas; such as rivers, roads, and power lines, should be easily recognized from the air.

6-19. Procedures will be developed to ensure the timely receipt and dissemination of area weather information. Each facility should be electronically connected to the same weather dissemination equipment as other area ATC facilities.

6-20. Procedures will be developed between the FF facility and other area ATC facilities to ensure timely control information is passed. LOAs will establish procedures concerning hand-offs, control transfers, flight plans, and arrival and departure times.

6-21. The facility should have the capability of communicating with other ATC facilities and agencies using or operating within the facility area of responsibility. Standard ATC radio and interphone phraseology will be used in all facility communications.

6-22. The facility area and airspace is determined by the airspace control authority. The area and airspace may or may not contain a restricted or prohibited area, overlap, underlay or join another ATC facility area or airspace. FAA JO 7400.2 and FAAO 7610.4 contain additional information on the procedures for handling airspace matters and special military operations for operations within the NAS.

SECTION IV – UNMANNED AIRCRAFT SYSTEMS

6-23. Airspace deconfliction is a major consideration during any UAS operation. Effective airspace control prevents mutual interference for all users of the airspace, facilitates AD identification, and accommodates the safe flow of all air traffic. Although UAS frequently operate from tactical field locations, constant communications with the ATS and airspace agencies in theater is required.

DECONFLICTION TECHNIQUES

6-24. Basic techniques for deconflicting UAS operations are—

- Altitude separation.
- Geographical separation, typically by keeping the UAS to one side of a feature such as a road or river.
- Time separation or moving the UAS out of the objective area before aircraft or ordnance arrives.

- A restricted operating zone (ROZ) or track that confines the UAS to a specific region of the airspace.

6-25. Some UAS are equipped with a communications relay package that enables direct communication between the UAS operator and the controlling airspace agency.

6-26. UAS missions, changes in L/R site locations, UAS altitudes; operating areas, identification friend or foe (IFF) squawks, and check-in frequencies are reflected in the daily ATO, ACO, or special instructions (SPINS) and disseminated to appropriate ATS, aviation, and ground units.

6-27. Planners monitor current UAS airspace requirements to anticipate future airspace requirements based on the emerging tactical situation. Changes in allocation of close air support, artillery, Army aviation, and the dynamic re-tasking of UAS will cause conflicts in airspace use. To address these changes, the supported unit should have a periodic AC2 meeting with all the key players (brigade aviation element, S-3 air, air liaison officer, and ATS) to address these issues. A comprehensive LOA is required between the UAS operators, airfield management, and affected ATC facilities.

AIR TRAFFIC CONTROL SEPARATION AND PHRASEOLOGY

6-28. The following are the standards for use of phraseology and separation when controlling UAS in a terminal area:
- Treat UAS as category A aircraft.
- Radar facilities will apply category A separation standards to UAS operations outside of established active restricted areas.
- The restricted area-using agency will establish separation criteria to ensure safe operations within their restricted areas.
- U.S. Army ATC facilities will utilize standard phraseology as prescribed in FAA JO 7110.65T for communications between ATC and UAS pilot/operators.

AIR TRAFFIC CONTROL PROCEDURES

6-29. ATC will adhere to the following procedures when controlling UAS.
- **Description of aircraft types.** Describe UAS to other aircraft by stating UA.
- **ATIS procedures.** Make a new recording when UAS operations are in effect or have terminated for the day.
- **Sequencing and separation.** UAS pilots cannot be instructed to follow another aircraft.
- **Simultaneous same direction operations.** All UAS will be treated as "other" aircraft.
- **Same runway separation.** All UAS will be treated as category III aircraft.
- **Use of visual separation.** Use of visual separation is not authorized.
- **Preventive control.** May be applied IAW FAA JO 7110.65T.

Transient Aircraft Procedures

6-30. ATC will keep the UAS pilot/operator apprised of any known transient aircraft that may affect operations. The UAS pilot/operator will take necessary actions to maintain lateral and vertical separation. ATC should provide UAS pilot/operator recommended altitudes or direct to pre-determined points (UAS zones) to ensure deconfliction.

Wake Turbulence Advisories

6-31. ATC will apply the following procedures:
- Issue cautionary wake turbulence advisories, and the position, altitude and direction of flight to the UAS pilot/operator landing behind all manned aircraft.
- Wake turbulence rules cannot be waived by UAS.

No Radio Aircraft Procedures

6-32. ATC will—

- Notify UAS pilot/operator of any known NORDO aircraft.
- Broadcast on emergency frequencies when a NORDO aircraft is present to establish two-way radio communications with the NORDO aircraft.

6-33. UAS pilot/operator, assisted by ATC will determine the best method to separate UAS and NORDO aircraft. Examples methods include:

- UAS may proceed to UAS zone and hold.
- Cease operations if it will not aggravate the situation.
- Altitude deconfliction.

Emergency Procedures

6-34. ATC will apply the procedures listed in chapter 10 section 1 of FAA JO 7110.65T. The safety of manned aircraft will take precedence over UA in an emergency.

6-35. If primary radio communications between UAS and ATC are lost, UAS or ATC will be notified immediately via predetermined alternate communications method. Failure to establish and maintain radio communication between UAS and ATC will require termination of UAS operations.

6-36. If lost link occurs, the UAS pilot/operator will immediately notify ATC with the—

- Time of link loss.
- Last known position.
- Altitude.
- Direction of flight.
- Conformation of execution of lost link procedures.
- Conformation of visual contact with UAS.

Note. UAS lost link is an emergency, but may not require crash rescue services.

6-37. In the event of a lost link, lost communications between UAS and ATC or lost communications between UAS pilot/operator and observer, ATC will:

- Cease aircraft launches until status of affected UAS is determined.
- Recover other UAS as appropriate.
- Issue advisories and ATC instructions as appropriate to ensure the safe operation of all aircraft.

Chapter 7

Air Traffic Services Training

Leaders must understand how their unit will operate and fight across the full range of military operations and how to plan and execute training using FM 7-0. Training must be innovative yet doctrinally and technically sound. Leaders must enforce individual, collective, and unit performance standards. ATS unit leaders are responsible for the proficiency of their Soldiers, subordinate leaders, teams/crews, and the unit, as a whole.

SECTION I – TRAINING

7-1. The Army provides component commanders with trained leaders and units ready to perform with joint, interagency, intergovernmental, and multinational team members in a contemporary operating environment against an adaptive enemy. A unit commander has two major training responsibilities: develop Soldiers/leaders for future responsibilities and prepare their unit to accomplish the assigned mission. In the absence of a directed mission, commanders must prepare their unit to

Contents

perform those core missions for which the unit was doctrinally designed to execute across the full range of military operations. This full range of military operations is increasingly performed outside of major combat operations and often includes limited interdictions, irregular warfare tactics, and the ability to enable civil authorities. Paramount to this training will be the qualification and certification of Army air traffic controllers to operate within ICAO agreements and provide ATS to civil and non-military aircraft. As detailed later within this chapter, this civil air traffic environment places several unique training challenges upon ATS leaders.

Note: Air traffic leaders must focus air traffic control training and certification requirements to accommodate all phases of full spectrum operations under varying international agreements, NATO policies, joint doctrine, and Army policies.

AIR TRAFFIC TRAINING IMPLICATIONS

7-2. The combined arms training strategy (CATS) incorporates a series of collective training events throughout the year. These events include monthly team training, quarterly situational training exercise (STX), and an annual field training exercise (FTX). ATS collective training events are developmental in nature and are intended to build upon skills mastered during previous training events. The successive building of experience is critical to the mastery of ATC skills and is not easily replicated in singular short duration assessments due to air traffic volume, density, and variation. The building of ATC experience through multiple training events more accurately develops the skills and knowledge required by ATC credentialing directives. This protracted strategy is not always consistent with progression milestones, readiness reporting goals, and unit deployments. ATS leaders should apply strict adherence to skill assessment standards and make ATC assessments consistent with unit and Soldier proficiency levels.

7-3. Army air traffic controllers complete certification requirements IAW FAA credentialing policies detailed within FAA JO 7220.1B and AR 95-2. These documents detail ATC knowledge and skill requirements that must be demonstrated prior to certification and rating. Air traffic controllers providing services to civil, host nation, contract, and other non-military aircraft are obligated to meet statutory requirements of minimum experience before providing services as a CTO.

Note: Initial experience gates for ATCS-ATCT ratings are detailed in chapter 5. ATCS-ATCT ratings do not satisfy certification requirements for civil, host nation, contract, and other non-military aircraft operations. Controllers performing duties within this construct must obtain a CTO certificate IAW AR 95-2 and FAA JO 7220.1B.

7-4. AR 95-2 details an initial and subsequent training strategy to gain the knowledge and skills required to operate in today's operating environment. This strategy incorporates the use of fixed-site ATC facilities found on many installations across the Army. This environment represents the single most effective training enabler for ATC training due to air traffic density, volume, and variation. ATS leaders should recognize the benefits of this training venue and commit to a strategy that includes the use of these facilities for initial experience ratings and refresher training gates as outlined in AR 95-2. The adoption of fixed-site facilities into a unit's core training concept will increase controller proficiency, minimize risk, and better prepare controllers for full spectrum operations as detailed within FM 7-0.

COMBINED ARMS TRAINING STRATEGY

7-5. ATS leaders accomplish their training responsibilities through a series of collective training events to build air traffic proficiencies and qualifications. The three collective training events for the ATS unit are team, STX, and the FTX. These training events are synchronized with other aviation units within the brigade during live-fly training activities. Figure 7-1 depicts the relationship of aviation training activities and echelons in support of ATS training events.

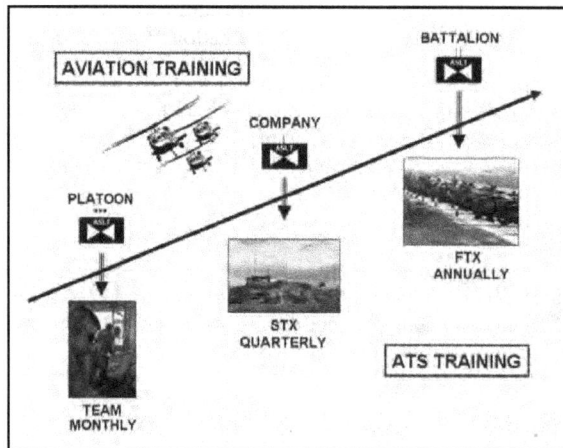

Figure 7-1. ATS training events

TEAM TRAINING

7-6. Team training is designed to exercise all tasks associated with providing ATS to the combat aviation brigade (CAB) and across the division AO. Team training should include hands on performance oriented training to provide airspace information updates to friendly aircraft; control aircraft with a terminal environment; and coordinate and deconflict airspace requirements. The team training should be conducted as part of a higher-level staff exercise (STAFFEX) event while aircraft are conducting aircrew or mission training. The communication navigation maintenance section should participate throughout the team training events to train to maintain ATS equipment.

7-7.   ATS team training events should be accomplished monthly and serve as the primary building block of air traffic skills required for certification. Team training events should be conducted in live traffic environments allowing for the validation of ATS systems emplacement and the conduct of ATC position training.

Terminal Teams (Tower and Ground Control Approach)

7-8.   Team training is focused on training the terminal control platoon providing services to assist in the movement of aircraft. This includes takeoff, landing, separation, and sequencing including full-service radar, TWR communications, NAVAIDs, instrumentation on illuminated airfields, and traffic advisories. Training should be conducted as a scenario driven exercise as part of an ongoing flight company STX using actual aircraft to conduct ATS operations. Prior coordination of airfield site selection and preparation should be conducted to ensure proper airfield conditions are met. Since the GCA team normally operates in conjunction with a control TWR team, the scenario can range from and austere landing site to a fully instrumented airfield. If fully instrumented, the GCA team should practice providing IIMC recovery capability to an AAF, and ASR and PAR within designated airspace.

7-9.   The PLT LDR should structure training to focus the control TWR team and the GCA team on tasks associated with providing terminal ATC services including precision and non-precision approaches to participating military aircraft. The scenario should include operating with aircraft during team training while exercising the GCA team's ability to employ with the TWR team, providing recovery capability and surveillance vectoring to arriving and departing aircraft operating in the terminal area. The platoon should practice to reach proficiency in the following tasks, control TWR operations upon 30 minutes of arrival, operational within 1 hour of arrival, support aircraft recovery operations including personnel recovery, MEDEVAC, and assistance to aircraft in (simulated) distress; and provide navigational assistance to friendly aircraft. If the airfield is operational with ground and air traffic, the control TWR team should train on their responsibility to control air and vehicular traffic operating on runways, taxiways, and other designated areas of the airfield.

Airspace Information Center Team

7-10. AIC team training is designed to exercise all tasks associated with providing FF services to participating aircraft. Team training should include hands on performance oriented training to provide airspace information updates to friendly aircraft; provide near real-time interface for airspace changes; and coordinate and deconflict airspace requirements. AIC team training should be conducted with aircraft that are conducting aircrew or mission training. A comprehensive scenario driven event will exercise the AIC platoon's ATC tasks to include: critical in-flight advisories/updates of airspace deviations within the AO; FF services to friendly aircraft operating within assigned airspace; development of the COP on the TAIS; information updates required for AD and air traffic management operations.

7-11. Team training should also focus on future planning for emerging airspace requirements; development of airspace alert plans; providing input to the ACO/ACP; and assisting in establishing procedures for aircraft operating in uncontrolled airspace. The AIC team should train to—

- Monitor and provide input on hostile aircraft intrusion warnings.
- Provide locations of rapid refueling points (forward arming and refueling points [FARPs]).
- Terminal facilities.
- On call NAVAIDs.
- Terminal airfield status.
- Monitor and assist combat search and rescue operations.
- Plan airspace information including command and control (C2) ROZs or orbit areas for Army airborne C2 system, and air mission planning data and airspace control information for terminal facilities.

7-12. The training scenario should also include the TACT operations providing for services to remote sites landing zones (LZs), pickup zones (PZs), assembly areas (AAs), and FARPs. AIC liaison activities should be reviewed and exercised during team training in preparation for walk and run level events. Liaison training should include coordinating develop of specific airspace information and flight coordination procedures; coordinating procedures with other military/civilian agencies; review of the coordination requirements to ensure data and communication links are established for connectivity to other ABCSs and ATC facilities.

Tactical Teams

7-13. This team training is designed to train TACTs to coordinate aviation operations and provide initial rapid response ATS and command, control, and communication (C3) in support of Army aviation and joint missions. Training should emphasize the mobility of the TACT allowing the commander flexibility during all stages of force projection.

7-14. The training should be scenario driven and conducted in conjunction with aircraft in support of crew progression flight training and other live fly events. The scenario should be tailored to train TACTs to provide aviation units with on-the-spot control and advisory capabilities in any environment. The company commander must incorporate assembly area selection training into the team training and planning should include the various types of assembly areas used by Army aviation units. Headquarters section personnel should review criteria for landing sites and assembly area selection to include, security, concealment, and accessibility to main supply routes, air avenues of approach, location of friendly units, and suitability of ingress and egress routes. The TACTs should be employed during a battalion or flight company event as they train to coordinate/occupy assembly areas, set up LZs/pick up zones, or operate at or near FARPs.

7-15. TACTs should train to be capable of providing a non-precision NAVAID, positive, and procedural ATS and secure UHF, VHF, frequency modulation (FM), satellite communications (SATCOM) and high frequency (HF) radio communications, and limited meteorological information to aircraft participating in assigned airspace. In addition to this event, TACT training can be conducted during other team training exercises (airfield and landing site planning, and AIS) and should train to provide terminal and airspace information services where air assets require coordinated movement. These teams should train to employ man pack NDB (pathfinder mode) and secure data/voice communications packages, providing low probability of interception. Team members should be proficient on the automated systems for which they have responsibility.

SITUATIONAL TRAINING EXERCISE

7-16. The ATS STX training is designed to refine the capabilities of the ATS company by building upon previous team training exercises that trained tasks associated with the AIC, terminal services, forward area support services and airfield and landing site planning and preparation. The STX is a 24-hour event conducted in a field environment and focused on the tasks associated with providing ATS to the CAB across the division AO.

7-17. The STX should be conducted in conjunction with a battalion/brigade command post exercise (CPX), the CAB subordinate battalion's STAFFEX events, or a flight company tactical training exercise. It should be scenario driven from the higher echelon event using the ATS commander's planning process to drive the exercise. Commanders must train to consider specific capabilities when planning ATS operations. STX training should include planning mission support that includes airspace and air traffic management, automated airspace planning and en route, terminal, and precision recovery throughout the brigade combat team and division AO. ATS teams should train to provide air traffic management and airspace information support using TAIS. Airfield and landing site planning should consider the physical geography of the site and the related activities in or around the main operating base and landing areas. The scenario should allow the commander to identify functional site considerations for fuel points and fuel storage areas, ordnance storage areas, arming/de-arming areas, MEDEVAC areas, weather support services, field of view and natural and manmade obstructions.

7-18. The training should include providing airspace information updates to friendly aircraft; coordinating between aircraft and the CAB/division; providing near real-time interface for airspace changes; and coordinating and deconflicting airspace requirements. It should be scenario driven from the higher echelon event using the ATS commander's planning process to drive the exercise. Commanders must train to consider specific capabilities when planning ATS operations.

7-19. The training should include providing airspace information updates to friendly aircraft; near real-time interfaces for airspace changes; and the coordination and deconfliction of airspace requirements. The scenario driven training should also focus on terminal services to assist in the movement of aircraft. This includes takeoff, landing, separation, and sequencing, including full-service radar, TWR communications, NAVAIDs, instrumentation on illuminated airfields, and traffic advisories. During one of the STX events training, the TACTs should be utilized to provide coordination of aviation operations at simulated remote and austere locations. TACTs should be exercised during initial entry and rapid response operations training such as occupying AAs, LZ/PZ and FARPs. Training is in preparation for the company internal FTX.

7-20. STXs should be accomplished quarterly and serve as gate qualifications to advanced air traffic tasks under complex traffic environments. ATS STX training events should incorporate company size aviation formations to stress air traffic skill requirements.

FIELD TRAINING EXERCISE

7-21. The ATS FTX is designed to evaluate the ATS Company's ability to perform its mission essential tasks. The event exercises core and ATS mission task selections, and incorporates general mission tasks to include move to and occupy; establish an AO; protect; and sustainment. The FTX validates all company planning and coordination cells, teams and sections, validating all unit standing operating processes and procedures during tactical operations. The field scenario should support 24-hour continuous operations, exercise TOC configurations, shifts, and the need for displacement of the company headquarters and ATS teams during combat operations. The FTX should focus on stressing the company leadership and C2 while providing ATS support operations across the operational environment.

7-22. The FTX is conducted with higher headquarters oversight to ensure training participation with aircraft operating under similar conditions providing a realistic environment. The FTX should include planning mission support that includes airspace and air traffic management, automated airspace planning and en route, terminal, and precision recovery throughout the division AO. ATS teams should provide air traffic management and airspace information support using TAIS. Airfield and landing site planning should consider the physical geography of the site, and the related activities in or around the main operating base and landing areas. The scenario should allow the commander to identify functional site considerations. Liaison activities should occur during the exercise with AC2 cells organic to division and corps to assist ATS elements in deconflicting, synchronizing, and integrating airspace/landing site requirements.

7-23. The exercise should include providing airspace information updates to friendly aircraft, with near real-time interface for airspace changes, and coordinating and deconflicting airspace. The event should evaluate terminal services to assist in the movement of aircraft including, takeoff, landing, separation, and sequencing including full-service radar, TWR communications, NAVAIDs, instrumentation on illuminated airfields, and traffic advisories. The TACTs should be employed to provide coordination of aviation operations at simulated remote and austere locations.

7-24. The FTX must be resourced and fully supported with assets external to the company. External resources may include training areas, opposing forces, and higher headquarters staff. The FTX is conducted with the supported units deployed in a field environment under tactical training conditions. Operations are conducted continuously (day and night) for the duration of the exercise. The company commander should use the results of the evaluation to gauge readiness, to identify doctrinal, operational or tactical weakness, and to structure future training prior to deployment into an operational environment. Company personnel must maintain proficiency on those automated tactical systems for which they have primary operational responsibility or may employ.

SECTION II – AIR TRAFFIC TRAINING PROGRAM

7-25. The air traffic training program (ATTP) is the ATS commander's program designed to train combat-ready certified air traffic controllers. This training ranges from task proficiency at the individual level, to team proficiency, and finally to unit proficiency in the execution of mission essential tasks necessary for the accomplishment of combined operations as defined in the Army universal task list and the CTL.

APPLICABILITY

7-26. The ATTP is comprised of individual ATC skill training events exercised throughout the year within the combined arms training strategy. Figure 7-2 depicts the parallel relationship of controller training and RL progression. In this figure, controller training, knowledge and skill assessments outlined within the ATC rating program construct of FAA JO 7220.1B parallel the RL progression guidelines and unit proficiency assessments outlined within FM 7-0. It is important to note that these efforts are not separate initiatives undertaken by unit personnel. Controller training conducted IAW the ATC rating program and RL progression are interlinked to form the basis of unit and soldier proficiency. Sustainment training after the qualification event to maintain controller task proficiency at the highest levels of unit readiness is also indicated in the graphic.

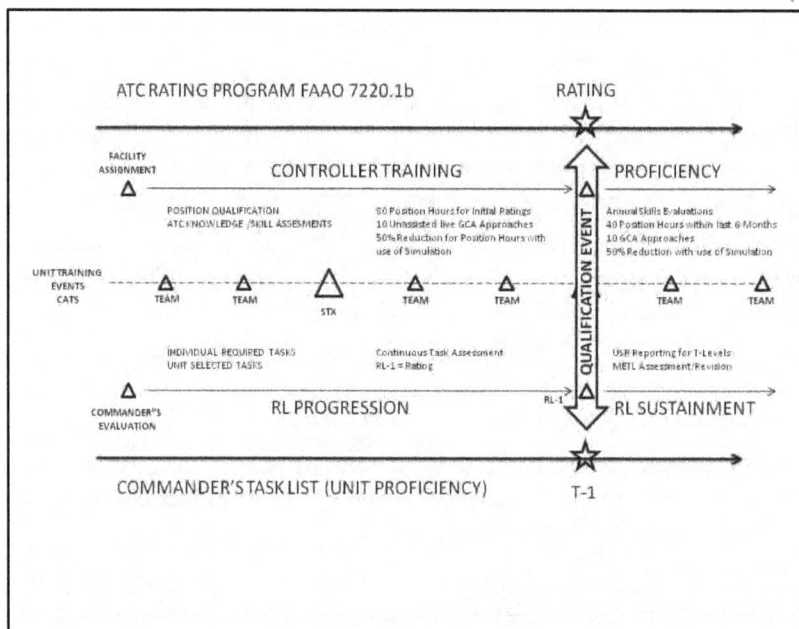

Figure 7-2. ATTP relationship

7-27. The ATTP consists of three types of training; qualification, proficiency, and remedial contained within two training phases; qualification phase, and position and certification phase. The goal of the ATTP is to produce proficient and mission-ready air traffic controllers and ATS units. The ATTP applies to all controllers that perform ATC duties and the critical tasks associated with the installation, operation, and maintenance of their team's mission equipment. Each PLT LDR, PSG, and team chief is responsible to the commander for the development of the ATTP. The ATTP will be developed and executed to meet training time limits established in AR 95-2.

7-28. Commanders and subordinate leaders use publications such as soldier training publications, FM 3-04.series; FM 7-0, unit task lists, and the CATS to develop the unit's ATTP. The first step in this process is to evaluate the unit's METL to determine training requirements.

DEVELOPMENT

7-29. The ATTP is the commander's training program, and he is responsible for its effectiveness and content. The PLT LDRs, PSGs, and team chiefs are the primary unit trainers tasked with the development and implementation of the ATTP at the individual and team training levels.

7-30. Individual and team tasks are the foundation on which the ATTP is built. Unit implementers advise the commander on required tasks, applicability of team tasks to unit roles and METL based missions, geographical factors affecting training and operational employment, training assets, and recurring training issues.

7-31. After analysis of unit METL, unit leaders' input, and higher commander's guidance, commanders develop supporting individual task lists (CTL) for each team. Commanders will then establish a short-range, long-range, and near-term training plan to ensure crews gain and maintain proficiency in unit collective tasks. Implementers must be familiar with the commander's training intent and with the three training plans to implement the ATTP.

TYPES OF TRAINING

QUALIFICATION

7-32. Newly assigned personnel will complete all required qualification training before they can obtain a rating. This training is also given to facility rated controllers when new procedures are instituted, new ATC equipment is fielded, or existing ATC systems are upgraded. This training will be annotated in section II and III (as applicable) of DA Form 3479.

PROFICIENCY

7-33. Facility-rated or PQ controllers are given proficiency training to remain current and proficient on ATC policies, procedures, and equipment. This type of training includes but is not limited to weather certification, changes to ARs, FMs, handbooks, and operational procedures. Proficiency training will be annotated in sections II and III (as applicable) of DA Form 3479.

REMEDIAL

7-34. Remedial training will be given only to personnel who have shown that they are no longer qualified to perform satisfactorily in a control position at which they previously qualified. This training is given to correct a demonstrated weakness and consists of classroom instruction or additional time on the position under direct supervision, or both. The PSG/team chief determines the time limits for the controllers' remedial training. This training will be annotated in sections II and III of DA Form 3479.

TRAINING PHASES

PHASE I - QUALIFICATION

7-35. Phase I training consists of the knowledge and skills requirements to successfully complete all individual and team training in the following areas:
- Air traffic system and subsystems (install, operate, and prepare for movement).
- ATC policy and administration (AR 95-2, AR 40-501, AR 40-8).
- Airspace C2 procedures.
- ATC procedures (FAA JOs: 7110.65 and 7220.1).
- FLIPs, charts, maps.
- Prime mover (vehicle) operations.
- Radio communications/operation.
- Communications security equipment.
- Power generation/alternative power requirements.
- Initial weather training.
- Operations orders and overlays.
- Airfield design (landing, movement, and parking areas).

Phase II – Rating

7-36. This phase measures the ability of trainees to control air traffic in a tactical environment. The trainee receives hands-on training at each operating position and completes examinations on the ATTP requirements that apply to the control procedures. Phase II rating is comprised of knowledge and skills specific to each facility. The trainee is evaluated on each operating position, and the results are recorded on DA Form 3479-1 and annotated in section II of the DA Form 3479.

7-37. The following knowledge and skill sets will be trained and evaluated during Phase II rating:

- **Tower Tasks:**
  - Separation or air traffic ensured.
  - Makes necessary transmissions.
  - Safety alerts are provided.
  - Uses appropriate communication methods.
  - Required coordination is performed.
  - Conducts relief briefings.
  - Control judgment applied.
  - Uses light gun signals.
  - Priority of duties is understood.
  - Conducts FD duties.
  - Positive control is provided.
  - Conducts ground controller duties.
  - Effective traffic flow is maintained.
  - Conducts local controller duties.
  - Aircraft identity is maintained.
  - Scans entire control environment.
  - Knowledge of equipment capabilities and operation.
  - Communications are clear and concise.
  - Uses prescribed phraseology.
  - Provides traffic advisories.
  - Strip postings and FD entries are accurate.
  - LOAs/SOPs/directives are adhered to.
  - Additional ATC services provided.
  - Recovers from equipment failures and emergencies.
- **GCA Tasks:**
  - Separation or air traffic ensured.
  - Makes necessary transmissions.
  - Safety alerts are provided.
  - Uses appropriate communication methods.
  - Required coordination is performed.
  - Conducts relief briefings.
  - Control judgment is applied.
  - Priority of duties is understood.
  - Conducts FD duties.
  - Positive control is provided.
  - Conducts feeder controller duties.
  - Effective traffic flow is maintained.
  - Conducts final controller duties.
  - Aircraft identity is maintained.

- Knowledge of equipment capabilities and operation.
- Communications are clear and concise.
- Uses prescribed phraseology.
- Provides traffic advisories.
- Strip postings and FD entries are accurate.
- LOAs/SOPs/directives are adhered to.
- Additional ATC services provided.
- Recovers from equipment failures and emergencies.
- **AIC Tasks:**
  - Makes necessary transmissions.
  - Safety alerts are provided.
  - Uses appropriate communication methods.
  - Required coordination is performed.
  - Conducts relief briefings.
  - Control judgment applied.
  - Priority of duties is understood.
  - Conducts FD duties.
  - Conducts FF controller duties.
  - Effective traffic flow is maintained.
  - Recovers from equipment failures and emergencies.
  - Aircraft identity is maintained.
  - Knowledge of equipment capabilities and operation.
  - Communications are clear and concise.
  - Uses prescribed phraseology.
  - Provides traffic advisories.
  - Strip postings and FD entries are accurate.
  - LOAs/SOPs/directives are adhered to.
  - Additional ATC services are provided.

7-38. Upon completion of position qualification on all operating positions, the controller will be given a pre-FAA/ATCS facility rating examination. This written examination will consist of 50 to 100 questions covering the skills and knowledge requirements of FAA JO 7220.1B for the rating desired. These questions will focus primarily on the topics the trainee must know to operate as a controller at the facility assigned. A failed examination returns the trainee to classroom study, re-examination, and is annotated on DA Form 3479, sections II and III.

7-39. Once the pre-FAA exam is complete, the controller will be given a final FAA/ATCS facility rating examination and a practical evaluation by the ATCS examiner. The written, oral, and practical evaluation for facility rating will be annotated on DA Form 3479, section II. The results of the practical evaluation will be recorded on DA Form 3479-1. This evaluation will be maintained on DA Form 3479 for one calendar year. The written examination will consist of 50 to 100 questions on topics as outlined in FAA JO 7220.1B and other areas deemed appropriate by the examiner for the facility rating being sought. A failure of this examination, returns the trainee to classroom study and rescheduling of the examination. This failure is annotated on DA Form 3479, sections II, III.

ADMINISTRATION AND MANAGEMENT TRAINING

7-40. Management training is an ongoing program wherein supervisors continuously train subordinates to assume supervisory positions. Administration and management training will culminate in a written examination of at least 25 questions. As a minimum, this training will include—
- Chapter 13 of the FTM (when applicable during extended operations).

- AR 95-2 chapter 14 and 15 Para 14-6, 14-8, 14-9, 15-2, 15-3, 15-4.
- 14 CFR parts 65.31 to 65.50.
- FAA JO 7220.1B (chapter 5 Para. 9, chapter 6, Para 3 and 5).
- Chapters 5, 6, and 7 of this TC.

7-41. The administrative management exam will be administered prior to assuming the duties of CIC, SL, ATC training supervisor, or facility chief. All training and test results will be entered into sections II, III, (as appropriate), of DA Form 3479.

PROGRESSION

7-42. AR 95-2 establishes procedures, policy, responsibilities, and standardization requirements for ATC training programs. The status of ATS unit training depends upon the status of individual/team/collective training. Individual, team, and collective proficiency must be balanced by ensuring training resources are used to train both at the individual and collective proficiency level. RLs correlate a Soldier's proficiency level and mission readiness.

7-43. RL training begins with development of proficiency at the individual level and progress through team to collective proficiency. This process follows the crawl-walk-run model of training. Tasks required for air traffic controllers to progress from various levels are contained within the Soldier's CTL. CTL requirements are battle-focused, tasked-based requirements derived from the unit's METL and appropriate ATTP for the air traffic system the Soldier is assigned to or training on. In some cases, air traffic controllers may have more than one RL. For example, controllers who are RL 1 in their assigned ATS system may be RL 3 or RL 2 in other ATS systems within the unit.

READINESS LEVELS

LEVEL 1

7-44. Air traffic controllers are awarded RL 1 upon completion of all ATTP training requirements. This phase culminates with an ATC rating and controller evaluation IAW AR 95-2 and appropriate FAA orders. A controller awarded this RL has been determined to possess the necessary tactical and technical skills to perform duties at the full performance level and has demonstrated task proficiency on all tasks of the CTL. Controllers should be removed from RL 1 and identified RL 2 when additional training is required, the controller does not meet proficiency requirements, or annual skills evaluations have exceeded mandatory completion intervals.

LEVEL 2

7-45. Air traffic controllers are awarded RL 2 when undergoing advanced ATS system training at the team level and the required CTLs for RL 1 have not yet been met, when controllers have not met currency thresholds, or have demonstrated a weakness after obtaining RL 1 status and require additional training. This RL is characterized with proficiency in collective tasks and team tasks associated with the advanced operation of ATS systems. Tasks are performed in complex varying environments and require successful coordination and integration of combined arms operations. Advanced ATC procedures for the safe operation and handling of aircraft during all phases of tactical operations are a critical element of this level. Controllers possessing a previous ATC rating of the same type may be awarded this level through the commander's evaluation processes. Controllers will remain at RL 2 until all RL 1 level provisions have been met and ATC certification has been successfully completed.

LEVEL 3

7-46. Air traffic controllers are awarded RL 3 when they have completed an MOS awarding ATC school and/or are assigned to an ATS system for which they have not previously obtained an ATC rating. This RL is characterized with the individual task proficiency in the installation, operation, and operator's maintenance of air traffic systems. This phase reinforces basic ATC procedures in controlled training and limited aircraft traffic environments. A controller assigned this RL is under the direct supervision of leaders and trainers of the ATS unit.

LEVEL 4

7-47. Air traffic controllers are awarded RL 4 when ATTP progression is not required or has been temporarily suspended due to the following:

- Controller is assigned as a platoon sergeant or ATC chief.
- Controller is assigned to a staff position not requiring ATTP progression and/or development.
- Controller is medically grounded/pending medical disqualification.
- Controller is pending MOS reclassification/chapter actions.
- Controller is assigned to a National Guard position without being a graduate of an approved ATC school.

Note. For the Soldier described in bullet five above, training records may be opened, but the CTL is not established until completion of an approved ATC school.

EVALUATIONS

COMMANDER'S EVALUATION

7-48. The commander's evaluation provides an opportunity to assess newly assigned air traffic controllers and allows the association of a higher RL due to previous ratings. This evaluation consists of a records review by the commander or his designated representative within 30 days after the controller is assigned to the unit for the active component. The reserve component commander or his designated representative must conduct this evaluation within 45 days of the controller's assignment to the unit.

7-49. The controller may initially be designated RL 2 if he/she successfully completed all phases of an ATTP in the same type rating. The following guidelines apply:

- Graduates of an ATC school who are on their first unit of assignment may not be awarded RL 2 based solely on a commander's evaluation.
- Previously certified air traffic controllers may not be awarded RL 2 if more that 12 months have passed since completion of that type rating or 12 months has passed since the last successful skills evaluation of that type rating.
- Controllers may not be assigned RL 1 based upon a commander's evaluation. RL 1 will only be awarded after the successful completion of CTL and training requirements contained within the unit's ATTP. RL 1 may only be awarded upon successful completion of a rating or skills evaluation by the examiner.

NO-NOTICE EVALUATIONS

7-50. A comprehensive no-notice evaluation program is a valuable tool allowing commanders to monitor training effectiveness at all levels. Each command must establish, in writing, a no-notice proficiency evaluation program to be executed by the unit's ATCS/CTO examiners. No-notice evaluations may be written, oral, and practical or any combination thereof in a live or simulated environment. This program measures the effectiveness of individual, team, and collective training. Commanders use the results of no-notice evaluations to ensure unit standardization, readiness, and to tailor the unit's individual, crew, and collective training programs. The results of no-notice evaluations will be recorded on DA Form 3479-1 and retained in the controller's records until completion of the annual skill's evaluation.

TRAINEE/CONTROLLER EVALUATIONS

7-51. The use of DA Form 3479-1 for trainee/controller evaluations serves as a valuable instrument within the ATTP. These evaluations provide the trainee with the required feedback necessary to keep them on track in the training program and provide for them areas of weakness requiring more emphasis.

7-52. DA Form 3479-1 is used in conjunction with all simulation training sessions. Supervisors in tactical units will use DA Form 3479-1 during simulation training events to provide trainee feedback and identify areas requiring additional simulation training sessions, as well as use the form to document proficiency hour requirements IAW paragraph 5-18.

7-53. Supervisors will determine when to conduct trainee/controller evaluations based upon trainee performance. The supervisor should conduct evaluations based upon observed trends during training and to emphasize and reinforce training points. Evaluations will be conducted IAW appendix F.

ANNUAL SKILLS EVALUATIONS

7-54. Annual skills evaluations are required for RL 1 controllers and will consist of the following requirements to maintain proficiency:

- Individual and crew task iterations on the ATC system/subsystem of assignment as designated by the commander on the CTL.
- Annual proficiency evaluation on all positions of the facility of assignment during the control of live air traffic.
- Annual written examination consisting of 50-100 questions on the subject matter pertaining to the rating held all of which may be administered open book.

7-55. The annual examination and skills evaluation will be administered by the commander's designated representative. The operating position evaluations will be recorded on DA Form 3479-1 and the results of both the written exam and the position evaluation will be entered in section II of DA Form 3479. The skills evaluation and written exam will be maintained on the right side of the controller's training records folder and removed when the next evaluation is complete.

7-56. Failure of the written (less than 70 percent overall) or unsatisfactory performance on the evaluation portion of the annual skills requirement will result in assignment of RL 2 status and remedial training. The content and duration of this training will be determined by the facility chief. Remedial training will be noted on DA Form 3479 section III. Individuals unable to regain proficiency will be processed IAW AR 95-2.

7-57. Annual skills evaluations must be completed within 12 calendar months of rating or last skills evaluation. Annual skills evaluations not completed within the designated 12-month period will result in assignment of RL 2 status until an annual skills evaluation can be completed. Improper planning and scheduling of annual skill evaluations during live-fly training events may result in lower unit readiness levels. Unit leaders are encouraged to maximize all live-fly training events to ensure completion of skill evaluations before the annual period concludes.

Note. Platoon leaders, examiners, or platoon sergeants are responsible for reviewing written examinations to ensure they are current, relevant, and adequate to assess the knowledge required to perform all duties associated with the rating held.

SECTION III – AIR TRAFFIC TRAINING PROGRAM REQUIREMENTS

COMMANDER'S TASK LIST

7-58. The CTL is the base document from which the RL progression program is developed. It is incumbent on the facility chief to define the sub tasks associated with those identified tasks of the CTL and any additional tasks required for the rating. The tasks, sub tasks, and academic subjects required within the RL progression program are identified in paragraphs 7-35 through 7-37 of this chapter.

7-59. The commander and unit leaders develop a task list to support each rating. The CTL is a written agreement between the commander and the team member. The requirements established by the CTL are tailored to the proficiency training needs of the individual team member. It specifies the tasks the team member must accomplish during the training year.

7-60. An individual task is defined as a task primarily performed by the individual team member, though assistance may be sought from any team members, in completion of the task by the team member. Individual tasks cover baseline skills, knowledge, and procedures necessary to operate the ATS system and selected team equipment.

7-61. Team tasks are selected by the commander to support the performance of the unit METL. A team task is primarily performed by multiple team members during the performance of a mission. It requires a combination of specific actions by various team members to perform the task to standard. Individual team members are responsible for performing specific roles during performance of the task. These tasks cover skills, knowledge, and procedures to operate the system during the performance of tactical or special missions.

7-62. Commanders may develop additional tasks for inclusion on the CTL, as needed, to accomplish the unit's mission. The commander lists them separately on the CTL when an additional task is developed by the unit. The commander must perform a risk analysis for performance of the task and determine training required for personnel to attain proficiency in the task. The additional tasks must include—

- Task number (if applicable).
- Title of the task.
- Conditions under which the task is performed.
- Standards for performance of the task.
- Description of how the task is performed.
- Considerations for performance of the task such as environmental and safety.
- Training/evaluation requirements.

COMMANDER'S TASK LIST FORMS

7-63. Figures 7-3 and 7-4, pages 7-14 and 7-15, depict DA Form 3479-11 (Commander's Task List [ATS]-Tower Operator). Not illustrated are DA Form 3479-12 (Commander's Task List [ATS] GCA Operator) and DA Form 3479-13 (Commander's Task List [ATS] AIC Operator). These forms are completed in the same manner as the Tower Operator CTL example provided.

COMMANDER'S TASK LIST (ATS)			
TOWER OPERATOR			
For use of this form see TC 3-04.81; the proponent agency is TRADOC.			

PART I.   CONTROLLER PERSONAL DATA

NAME *(last, first, MI)*			RANK	ATCS
PUBLIC, JOHN Q.			PV2	1234
DUTY POSITION	DATE ASSIGNED	OPERATING INITIALS	RL ASSESSMENT	BIRTH MONTH
TOWER OPERATOR	25 JUL 1998	JP	☐ RL 2 ☒ RL 3	FEBRUARY

PART II.   REQUIRED TASKS   *(Part II tasks must be evaluated during progression and annual skills evaluations)*

TASK	TITLE	COMPLETION DATE
011-143-0012	Process Pilot Reports (PIREPS)	8 FEB 99
011-143-0014	Process Flight Progress Strips	20 NOV 98
011-143-0015	Control Aircraft, Vehicles And Personnel By ATC Light Gun Signals	7 JAN 99
011-143-0017	Control The Flight Of SVFR Arrival/Departure Aircraft	8 FEB 99
011-143-0018	Provide Traffic Information/Advisories	7 JAN 99
011-143-0019	Select Runway For Use	
011-143-0021	Identify Data In DOD Flight Information Publications (FLIPS)	20 NOV 98
011-143-0022	Provide Emergency Assistance	
011-143-0023	Issue Airport Condition/Information	7 JAN 99
011-143-0024	Perform Assumption Of Duty Requirements	20 NOV 98
011-143-0028	Control the Flight or IFR Arrival/Departure Aircraft	
011-143-0038	Control the Flight of VFR Arrival/Departure Aircraft	7 JAN 99
011-143-0039	Identify Basic Airspace Command And Control Procedures	7 JAN 99
011-143-1021	Communicate Using Interphone Procedures	7 JAN 99
011-143-1022	Decode Military Aircraft Designation Symbols, Service, And Mission Prefixes	20 NOV 98
011-143-5055	Record ATC Facility Daily Activities	20 NOV 98
011-143-5057	Communicate Using Radio Communication Procedures	7 JAN 99
011-143-5060	Control Aircraft Taxi	8 FEB 99
011-143-5063	Decode METAR Weather Reports	8 FEB 99

PART III.   SELECTED TASKS   *(Selectable tasks IAW duty assignment and equipment available)*

TASK	TITLE	SELECTED	COMPLETION DATE
011-141-0001	Locate a Geographical Coordinate on JOG-A	☒ Yes	20 NOV 98
011-143-7003	Install assigned ATS System	☒ Yes	20 OCT 98
011-143-7004	Operate assigned ATS System	☒ Yes	20 OCT 98
011-143-7002	Prepare assigned ATS System for Movement	☒ Yes	20 OCT 98
011-143-0067	Extract Information from Airspace Command and Control Documents, Air Tasking Order (ATO), Airspace Control Order (ACO) and Special Instructions (SPINS)	☒ Yes	
011-143-0068	Install Non-Directional Radio Beacon Set	☒ Yes	7 JAN 99
011-143-0069	Operate Non-Directional Radio Beacon Set	☒ Yes	7 JAN 99
011-143-0070	Prepare Non-Directional Radio Beacon Set for Movement	☒ Yes	7 JAN 99
071-329-1019	Use a Map Overlay	☒ Yes	

DA FORM 3479-11, OCT 2010

Page 1 of 2
APD PE v1.00ES

Figure 7-3. Tower operator CTL (front side)

PART III.	SELECTED TASKS	(Selectable tasks IAW duty assignment and equipment available)	(Continued)	
TASK	**TITLE**		**SELECTED**	**COMPLETION DATE**
071-334-4002	Establish A Helicopter Landing Point		☒ Yes	20 NOV 98
113-573-6001	Recognize Electronic Attack (EA) and Implement Electronic Protection (EP)		☒ Yes	20 NOV 98
113-587-2070	Operate SINCGARS Single-Channel (SC)		☒ Yes	7 JAN 99
113-587-2071	Operate SINCGARS Frequency Hopping (FH) (Net Members)		☒ Yes	7 JAN 99
113-596-1068	Install Antenna Group OE-254/GRC		☒ Yes	7 JAN 99
113-609-2053	Operate the Automated Net Control Device (ANCD)		☒ Yes	
113-609-4000	Restore the Simple Key Loader (SKL) AN/PYQ-10		☒ Yes	
113-610-2005	Navigate Using the Defense Advanced Global Positioning System Receiver (DAGR)		☒ Yes	7 JAN 99
113-610-2006	Program the Defense Advanced Global Positioning System Receiver (DAGR)		☒ Yes	7 JAN 99
113-610-2044	Navigate Using the AN/PSN-11		☒ Yes	7 JAN 99

PART IV.	GENERAL COMMENTS	(List unit METL tasks or skill level 2/3/4 MOS tasks and other comments)

011-143-2007   Retain Records, Logs, and Recorded Media _____

011-143-2010   Process Airspace Coordination Measures _____

Conduct NVD Operations _____

Conduct Sling-Load Operations _____ 7 JAN 99

PART V.	ACKNOWLEDGEMENT	
Facility Chief Printed Name	Signature	Date
SMITH, JOHN L.	*John L Smith*	12 OCT 98
Air Traffic Controller Printed Name	Signature	Date
PUBLIC, JOHN Q.	*John Q. Public*	12 OCT 98
Commander/Platoon Leader Printed Name	Signature	Date
JONES, FRANK E.	*Frank Jones*	18 OCT 98

DA FORM 3479-11, OCT 2010

Page 2 of 2
APD PE v1.00ES

Figure 7-4. Tower operator CTL (back side)

AIR TRAFFIC CONTROL SIMULATION EQUIPMENT

7-64. When available, ATS unit leaders should incorporate ATC simulation into there over all training strategy. The simulation systems used should provide commonality and adherence with established DOD policy for simulation systems. To achieve system effectiveness, the capabilities of the system must be measured against required skill performance standards.

7-65. Simulation exercises should ensure controllers have the means to meet training requirements and maintain a competent level of proficiency. The system should provide timely controller information and support. This is necessary to accomplish safe separation requirements between aircraft and obstacles, provide visually verifiable weather conditions, and accomplish expeditions and positive control of air traffic in a simulated terminal environment.

TRAINING SCENARIOS AND DATABASES

7-66. Scenarios and databases will be tailored to include specific task coverage to ensure satisfactory performance for each facility operating and control position. Position instructional blocks should include tasks controllers are not routinely required to perform. Development of position scenarios will measure all standards for that position as dictated by the CTL and those tasks depicted on DA Form 3479-1 used during evaluations. Scenarios and databases will be designed to aid in the task performance during live traffic conditions used for position qualifications, ratings, annual proficiency evaluations, and pre-deployment training.

Note: Simulation may be used during all training phases but is excluded from use during position qualifications, ratings, and annual skill evaluations. These events require the controller to demonstrate successful performance of knowledge and skills required during live-traffic conditions.

7-67. The ATC/facility chief is responsible for—

- Developing a training plan and documenting controller's progress of basic ATC fundamentals. DA Form 3479-1 trainee/controller evaluations used to evaluate controllers in a simulated environment should indicate "Simulator" in block 1 of the evaluation.
- Incorporating simulation into the appropriate CTL. The simulation training plan will adhere, to the existent possible, to chapter six and seven.
- Overseeing the scenario development to ensure a realistic training environment.
- Ensuring training is provided, as needed, to primary trainers to operate stand-alone simulation.
- Ensuring a sufficient number of realistic scenarios meet or exceed normal traffic levels and complexity.
- Ensuring scenarios are designed to prepare controllers to work effectively in a live environment.
- Ensuring minimum standards are met for each operating/control position during evaluations.
- Ensuring training provides airspace/procedural requirements.

SECTION IV – UNIT STATUS REPORTING

7-68. The two primary ARs governing readiness reporting are AR 220-1 and AR 700-138. The current master maintenance data file (MMDF) for all reportable system/subsystem/equipment is available at https://www.logsa.army.mil. The logistics support activity (LOGSA) site requires registration for access. Although this guide deals primarily with training, a commander must be intimately familiar with both of these regulations. The USR gives the commander a snapshot of the unit's overall training and equipment status, and aviation logistical readiness directly affects the unit's ability to conduct aviation training.

COMMANDER RESPONSIBILITIES

7-69. Commanders determine their unit's overall status based on an assessment of the unit's capability to accomplish its assigned mission. The commander's responsibilities listed in AR 220-1 include—

- Maintaining the highest unit status level possible with given resources.
- Reviewing subordinate unit reports for accuracy and compliance with applicable requirements.
- Distributing unit equipment and resources against mission essential requirements on a priority basis.
- Training to the highest level possible with the resources that are available.
- Submitting unit status between regular reports, as required.

- Ensuring unit has computer hardware/software to process and submit the USR and related Army Status of Resources and Training System reports.

7-70. A unit's C-level indicates the degree to which the unit has achieved prescribed levels of fill for personnel and equipment, the training status of those personnel, and the maintenance status of the unit's equipment. AR 220-1 C-level definitions include—

- **C-1.** The unit possesses the required resources and is trained to undertake the full wartime mission(s) for which it is organized or designed.
- **C-2.** The unit possesses the required resources and is trained to undertake most wartime mission(s) for which it is organized or designed.
- **C-3.** The unit possesses the required resources and is trained to undertake many, but not all, portions of the wartime mission(s) for which it is organized or designed.
- **C-4.** The unit requires additional resources or training to undertake its wartime mission(s), but it may be directed to undertake portions of its wartime mission(s) with resources on hand.
- **C-5.** The unit is undergoing a service-directed resource action and is not prepared, at this time, to undertake the wartime mission(s) for which it is organized or designed.

7-71. Resourcing factors for commanders to consider include morale, discipline, availability of critical equipment, and availability of qualified key person.

ASSESSING AND REPORTING UNIT PROFICIENCY IN MISSION ESSENTIAL TASKS

7-72. A unit's METL is derived from an analysis of the assigned wartime missions and is approved by the next higher headquarters in the unit's reporting chain of command. The commander, at all levels, assesses the unit's ability to execute mission essential tasks to standard. Commanders consider the unit's ability to perform in unique operational environments as required by the unit's METL. When assessing unit proficiency, commanders make use of personal observations, records, reports and the assessments of others (internal and external to the unit).

7-73. The commander considers the demonstrated proficiency of subordinate units, leaders, Soldiers, and the availability of critical resources required to support METL training as follows:

7-74. The unit and organic sub-elements demonstrate proficiency during external evaluations, deployments at combat training centers, emergency deployment readiness exercises, FTX, CPXs, operational readiness exercises, and other training events described in the unit's CATS. Proficiency is measured in terms of the units' demonstrated ability to perform the tasks as stated in the approved METL, including supporting tasks not specified in the METL but necessary for performance of METL tasks. Proficiency is judged based on performance of tasks to standard. Full METL proficiency is achieved when a unit has attained a trained (T) level of proficiency in all METL tasks as defined in FM 7-0. Sustainment of proficiency then becomes the commander's challenge.

7-75. Leader qualification includes not only those areas of training required by the base branch of the officer/warrant officer/NCO, but may also include those areas required by professional leadership development programs that support the unit's mission.

7-76. In addition to maintaining a minimum number of qualified individuals (minimum fill described below) to perform most of the critical warfighting tasks to standard, commanders must satisfactorily accomplish collective training events as defined in the appropriate CATS.

7-77. Commanders perform a training events execution review (TEER) IAW AR 220-1 to review and confirm the results of their T-level determinations in light of their units' accomplishment of critical training events.

7-78. The events to be reviewed come directly from the training plan the unit presented at the quarterly training briefing (QTB). This training plan is a direct product of the commander's assessment of those METL tasks in which the unit must attain and sustain proficiency.

7-79. Using unit training records, the commander compares executed training events with planned training events for the previous quarter's QTB or yearly training brief (YTB) for RC commanders. When scheduled training events were not completed to standard, the commander assesses the impact on his T-rating.

7-80. Specific guidance is provided in AR 220-1 on when remarks are necessary on the USR, or when commanders should downgrade T-ratings because of training that was not performed.

CONTROLLER STATUS AND UNIT STATUS RELATIONSHIP

7-81. The status of ATS unit training depends on the status of individual/crew/collective training. Individual, crew, and collective proficiency must be balanced by ensuring training resources are used to train at both the individual and collective proficiency level. Controller proficiency will be reported monthly for the preceding six months. The T-level rating provides meaningful information for the entire chain of command. The unit training T-level is a major factor in determining how many days the unit needs to train to standard on METL tasks. Commanders use the number of days the unit needs to train to standard on METL tasks, along with the information in AR 220-1 to determine the overall training T-level. Table 7-1 explains the ATS T-levels requirements.

Table 7-1. Controller training T-level ratings

T1	Not less than 85 percent of required controllers are RL 1 in the ATS system of assignment.
T2	Not less than 75 percent of required controllers are RL 1 in the ATS system of assignment.
T3	Not less than 65 percent of required controllers are RL 1 in the ATS system of assignment.
T4	Does not meet minimum criteria for T3.

Note. Unit controller strengths used to determine T-level ratings are derived from the required controller strength necessary for the operation of air traffic facilities. Platoon sergeants and air traffic personnel not assigned to ATS systems are not used in the calculation of T-levels.

Chapter 8

Air Traffic Services Maintenance Training Program

This chapter specifies the procedures for implementing and maintaining a uniform air traffic services maintenance training program (AMTP) for U.S. Army ATC maintenance technicians. The AMTP establishes the standards for measuring the technical proficiency of ATC maintenance technicians. It also ensures the technical competence of all maintenance personnel having direct responsibility for the safe operation of systems/subsystems/equipment critical to air navigation and ATC. The program establishes the procedures for documenting the technicians' proficiency, granting authority, and assigning certification responsibility.

PROGRAM DEVELOPMENT

8-1. The AMTP consists of six steps containing three phases of training. The AMTP is designed to administer a certification program with the goal of providing qualified technicians that meet the stringent requirements for properly maintaining ATC equipment. The technician must satisfy the theory and performance requirements specified in this chapter to meet qualification requirements of the assigned position. After completing qualification requirements, the technician may be assigned the responsibility of certifying specific systems/subsystems/equipment.

8-2. The responsibility for the certification program is shared by the ATS unit commanders and AMTP examiners. The examiners assist with the development of comprehensive examinations used as part of the certification process for maintenance technicians. This certification applies only for the specified ATC system/subsystem/equipment. The examiner must possess certification for the entire system on which he examines another technician.

8-3. Designated examiners will—

- Provide overall direction to, and guidance on, the AMTP.
- Identify and specify the theory and performance requirements.
- Standardize and continually evaluate and update all phases of the AMTP.
- Develop, validate, review, and revise theory and performance examinations.
- Determine the systems to be added or deleted from the AMTP.
- Resolve comments, questions, and disputes about the examinations.
- Maintain database files containing complete verification records.

8-4. AMTP examiners will be designated in writing by commanders directly responsible for ATS maintenance personnel. These examiners will exercise control over the AMTP for their unit of assignment.

8-5. AMTP examiners may certify technicians from other units if the requesting unit commander does not have a qualified examiner. AMTP examiners for ATSCOM, ACOMs or Theater Airfield Operations Group (TAOG) will maintain training certification and related training records for ATS maintenance personnel assigned to the headquarters staff element and provide command guidance to subordinate units. Examiners will—

- Maintain files containing complete technician certification and related training records on each technician.
- Provide the technician with the training materials needed to accomplish comprehensive training on the systems/subsystems/equipment.
- Administer and monitor the theory and performance examinations.

- Develop and document OJT on the site-specific systems/subsystems to support the certification program.
- Advise the commander on the status of ATS maintenance certification.
- Coordinate with the maintenance chief for NOTAM if training is required on any in-use operational system/subsystem/equipment.
- Conduct and record the annual review on DA Form 3479.
- Conduct the annual review of the certification records documenting that the technician—
  - Has maintained the certification proficiency level.
  - Is assigned only those certification responsibilities supported by valid certification authority.

8-6.   The flow chart in figure 8-1, page 8-3, depicts the ATS maintenance technician certification process, which begins after the technician is assigned to the unit.

Note. If certified on a particular system/subsystem, the maintenance chief reviews the technician's training records and conducts a practical evaluation. Upon successful demonstration of tasks indicated on the CTL the technician is awarded RL 1. If not previously certified continue with step 3.

- **Step 1.** The technician enters the maintenance training program; technician is either RL 2 or RL 3. This step includes—
  - Establishing training records.
  - Orientation on equipment.
  - Orientation on facilities and their locations.
  - Initial counseling on maintenance and shop operations.
  - Statement of performance expectations.
  - Orientation on safety.
  - Overview of classes.
  - SOP requirements.
- **Step 2.** The technician enters a phased training program (RL 3) on individual systems or equipment (for example, AN/TSQ-221 and Army-Navy/very high frequency radio communication [AN/VRC]-103). This step consists of—
  - **Phase I.** The technician is trained on the theory of operation, system/subsystem/equipment operational characteristics, power requirements, frequency spectrum, and normal operating standards. Also covered in this phase are the required reference material, forms and records, maintenance allocation charts, PMCS and TMDE procedures and requirements, and local SOP requirements.
  - **Phase II.** The technician is trained on alignment systems and subsystems, sequential and system interface alignment procedures, and TMDE requirements and settings. This training also includes reference material and local SOP requirements, forms, and records completion.
  - **Phase III.** The technician is trained on system and subsystem fault localization, schematic use, maintenance allocation charts, and major and minor component installation/removal procedures. This training also includes tool requirements and usage, safety and quality control requirements, supply procedures, and reference material and local SOP requirements.
- **Step 3.** When the technician has satisfactorily completed the three phases above, the examiner will request the examination from ATSCOM (in writing).
- **Step 4.** The examiner administers the examination to the technician in two parts. All theory examinations are "open book."
  - **Part 1.** The technician completes the comprehensive written examination, which consists of questions on Phases I, II, and III.
  - **Part 2.** The technician is given the hands-on performance examination on Phases II and III.

- **Step 5**. The examiner grades the examination and sends the results to Commander, ATSCOM, AFAT-ATS-CT, 2805 Division Road, Fort Rucker, Alabama 36362-5265. If the technician passes the examination, the technician is issued a certification on that system/subsystem/equipment and awarded RL 1 if all requirements have been met. If the technician fails the examination, the examiner identifies the specific areas in which the technician had problems. The technician is reentered in the phased training program.
- **Step 6**. The technician is now certified on the applicable system or subsystem and is designated RL 1. The flow process is continued when the technician encounters a new system or new equipment.

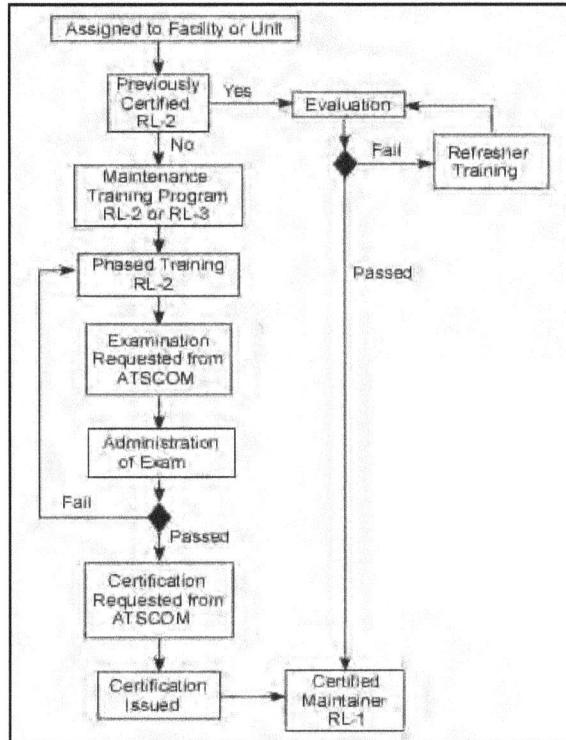

Figure 8-1. ATS maintenance certification process

THEORY OF OPERATION AND PERFORMANCE EXAMINATIONS

8-7.   All theory and performance examinations used in the certification program will be used to determine whether the examinee knows the theory and practical techniques required to perform maintenance, and diagnose and correct deficiencies on ATC systems/subsystems/ equipment. Comprehensive examinations are developed using TMs, FMs, TCs, handbooks, manufacturer manuals, joint acceptance standards, and senior maintenance personnel. Equipment examinations are comprehensive in scope, covering not only the equipment within the system but also the auxiliary equipment considered part of the system.

8-8.   The written examination will test the technician's understanding and knowledge of a wide range of information. The questions will cover system oriented theory, operational characteristics, subsystems, power requirements, frequency spectrum, and normal operating standards. Some questions require calculations and analytical reasoning.

Administration of Theory Examinations

8-9. When administering the theory examinations, the examiners will—
- Understand and apply mandatory secure-handling requirements to protect program integrity.
- Not discuss or disclose the contents of examinations.
- Prepare an appropriate area for administering examinations and give the examinee required instructions and materials.
- Caution the examinee on the official nature of the examinations and the penalties involved for disclosure of the contents.
- Allow examinees the use of reference material (personal or supplied) during the examinations.
- Control and time examinations as prescribed and process completed examinations as instructed.
- Store examination papers in a secure file.

8-10. If the technician fails the theory examination, he is ineligible to take the performance examination. If a technician passes the theory examination but fails the performance examination, he is not required to take another theory examination. The examiner will ensure he uses a different version of the examination each time a technician retakes the examination. A technician may not take a theory or performance examination more than three times in a 12-month period.

Security in Handling Theory Examinations

8-11. Everyone in the examination chain concerned with the certification process must maintain security in the handling of written examinations. Compromise of examinations in any form is a serious violation of the rules of conduct and discipline. Any violation will require the appropriate official to take disciplinary action. Any person having personal knowledge of a compromise on any segment of the written examination will advise the unit commander of the details. The security requirements of theory examinations include but are not limited to—
- Placement of documents in locked storage (secured with a combination lock or the equivalent).
- Accountability for all examinations after their completion.
- Refusal to discuss or transfer examination content.

Performance Examinations

8-12. Performance examinations are used to demonstrate a technician's proficiency. These examinations vary in length according to the complexity and scope of the system/subsystem/equipment. The use of reference material is encouraged during the examination. The examinee makes the actual adjustments, alignments, or software program changes; evaluates system performance; and corrects equipment maladjustments. The examiner observes the results and verifies the accuracy of the adjustments, alignments, or changes.

8-13. The examiner may deviate from the printed examination to ensure the examinee has the required proficiency. The examinee should be told of any deviations before taking the examination.

8-14. If there is a published OJT course, the performance examination may be incorporated as an integral part of OJT. When there is no published OJT course, the examination may be used as a study outline. When the examination is so used, the individual who provides OJT should not be the examiner.

8-15. The examiner may make only minor changes to the performance examination to make it compatible with the system used. Operations and questions other than those given on the performance examination may be used to assure the examinee's total system knowledge. When maintenance procedures or system configurations change, facilities will recommend changes be made to the examinations.

Administration of Performance Examinations

8-16. The distribution of the performance examination prior to the examination is encouraged. The technician will be made thoroughly familiar with the examination requirements and related test equipment during OJT. The examinee will complete the examination unassisted, except in instances requiring two people to make a particular adjustment or alignment.

8-17. Once the examinee has completed an operation, the examiner grades the performance. Failure of one operation constitutes failure of the entire examination.

8-18. If a technician requiring certification authority fails an examination, the supervisor will return the technician to the phased training program. The improvement program will be documented in the technician's official certification and related training record. The program will contain the—

- Training for the deficient areas identified.
- Recommended study material.
- Method for measuring progress.
- Time schedule for improvement program completion.
- Name of instructors and method of documenting training.

8-19. Certification examinations will be reviewed and updated by unit examiners regularly. Examinations are combined when redundancy is discovered or revised when found to be obsolete. Examiners detecting questions that are not correct or relevant to the system/subsystem/equipment for which the technician is being tested will delete or correct the questions when found.

COMMANDER'S EVALUATION

8-20. The commander's evaluation provides an opportunity to assess newly assigned ATS maintenance personnel and allows the association of a higher RL due to previous air traffic system certifications. This evaluation consists of a records review by the commander or his designated representative within 30 days after the maintainer is assigned to the unit. If the maintainer successfully completed all phases of an AMTP in the same ATS system and demonstrates the appropriate skill level on all tasks of the CTL he may be initially designated RL 1. Commanders should utilize practical hands-on assessments to confirm proficiency levels of maintainers. The following guidelines apply:

- Graduates of MOS 94D school who are on their first unit of assignment may only be awarded RL 3 until they have successfully completed maintenance certification on at least one ATS system.
- Previously certified ATS maintenance personnel may not be awarded RL 1 if more than 12 months have passed since direct maintenance actions have been performed on the ATS systems of the present unit.

COMMANDER'S TASK LIST

8-21. The CTL is a written agreement between the commander and the team member. The requirements established by the CTL are tailored to the proficiency training needs of the individual team member. It specifies the tasks the team member must accomplish during the training year.

8-22. All maintenance specific tasks will be selected by the commander and incorporated into the CTL for team members who perform maintainer duties. These maintenance tasks cover procedures, knowledge, and skills required to perform maintenance on ATS systems and sub systems.

8-23. Commanders may develop additional tasks for inclusion on the CTL, as needed, to accomplish the unit's mission. The commander lists them separately on the CTL when an additional task is developed by the unit, the commander must perform a risk analysis for performance of the task, and determine training required for personnel to attain proficiency in the task. The additional tasks must include—

- Task number.
- Title of the task.
- Conditions under which the task is performed.
- Standards for performance of the task.
- Description of how the task is performed.
- Considerations for performance of the task such as environmental and safety.
- Training/evaluation requirements.

8-24. Figures 8-2 and 8-3, page 8-7, illustrate DA Form 3479-14 (Commander's Task List [ATS] ATS Maintainer).

COMMANDER'S TASK LIST (ATS)				
ATS MAINTAINER				
For use of this form see TC 3-04.81; the proponent agency is TRADOC.				

PART I. ATS MAINTAINER PERSONAL DATA

NAME (last, first, MI)				RANK
JONES, JOHN H.				PFC

DUTY POSITION	DATE ASSIGNED	OPERATING INITIALS	RL ASSESSMENT	
ATC EQUIPMENT REPAIRER	25 OCT 1998	JJ	☐ RL 2 ☒ RL 3	

PART II. SELECTED TASKS   *(Selected tasks must be evaluated during progression and annual skills evaluations, on the systems and sub-systems the soldier is certified to maintain, as designated on DA Form 3479-10-R.)*

TASK	TITLE	SELECTED	COMPLETION DATE
093-94D-0060	Perform PMCS on ATNAVICS	☒ Yes	16 MAR 99
093-94D-1000	Prepare Radar Set (AN/TPN-18A) for Flight Check	☐ Yes	
093-94D-1006	Perform Preliminary Checks and Alignments of Radar Set	☐ Yes	
093-94D-1010	Perform PMCS on Landing Control Central (AN-TSQ-71B)	☐ Yes	
093-94D-1016	Troubleshoot Radar Set (AN/TPN-18A)	☐ Yes	
093-94D-1019	Perform PMCS on Interrogator Set (AN/TPX-44)	☐ Yes	
093-94D-1020	Troubleshoot Landing Control Central (AN-TSQ-71B)	☐ Yes	
093-94D-1029	Troubleshoot Interrogator Set (AN/TPX-44)	☐ Yes	
093-94D-1030	Repair Landing Control Central (AN/TSQ-71B)	☐ Yes	
093-94D-1036	Repair Radar Set (AN/TPN-18A)	☐ Yes	
093-94D-1039	Repair Interrogator Set (AN/TPX-44)	☐ Yes	
093-94D-1050	Prepare ATNAVICS (AN/TPN-31) for Flight Check	☒ Yes	16 MAR 99
093-94D-1069	Perform PMCS on Interrogator Set (AN/TPX-56)	☐ Yes	
093-94D-1070	Troubleshoot ATNAVICS	☐ Yes	
093-94D-1079	Troubleshoot Interrogator Set (AN/TPX-56)	☐ Yes	
093-94D-1080	Repair ATNAVICS	☒ Yes	16 MAR 99
093-94D-1089	Repair Interrogator Set (AN/TPX-56)	☐ Yes	
093-94D-1160	Perform PMCS on ATC Central (AN/TSW-7A)	☐ Yes	
093-94D-1170	Troubleshoot ATC Central (AN/TSW-7A)	☐ Yes	
093-94D-1180	Repair ATC Central (AN/TSW-7A)	☐ Yes	
093-94D-1260	Perform PMCS on TTCS (AN/TSQ-198)	☒ Yes	28 NOV 98
093-94D-1270	Troubleshoot TTCS (AN/TSQ-198)	☒ Yes	28 NOV 98
093-94D-1280	Repair TTCS (AN/TSQ-198)	☒ Yes	28 NOV 98
093-94D-1360	Perform PMCS on TAIS (AN/TSQ-221)	☐ Yes	
093-94D-1370	Troubleshoot TAIS (AN/TSQ-221)	☐ Yes	
093-94D-1380	Repair TAIS (AN/TSQ-221)	☐ Yes	
093-94D-1420	Troubleshoot Radio Beacon Set (AN/TRN-30 (V))	☒ Yes	16 NOV 98
093-94D-1430	Repair Radio Beacon Set (AN/TRN-30(V))	☒ Yes	16 NOV 98
093-94D-1460	Perform PMCS on Electronic Shop (AN/ASM-146B)	☒ Yes	4 DEC 98

DA FORM 3479-14, OCT 2010

Page 1 of 2
APD PE v1.00ES

Figure 8-2. Sample ATS maintenance CTL (front side)

PART II.	SELECTED TASKS	*(Selected tasks must be evaluated during progression and annual skills evaluations, on the systems and sub-systems the soldier is certified to maintain, as designated on DA Form 3479-10-R. (Continued)*		

TASK	TITLE	SELECTED	COMPLETION DATE
093-94D-2450	Operate Electronic Shop (AN/ASM-146B)	☒ Yes	16 MAR 99

SKILL LEVEL 2-4 TASKS

TASK	TITLE	SELECTED	COMPLETION DATE
093-94D-2901	Maintain Calibration Program	☐ Yes	
093-94D-3000	Supervise Preparation of Radar Set (AN/TPN-18A) for Flight Check	☐ Yes	
093-94D-3910	Determine ATC Maintenance and Operation Test Procedures Requirements	☐ Yes	
093-94D-4040	Verify Preparation of AN/TSQ-71B for Flight Inspection	☐ Yes	

PART III.	GENERAL COMMENTS	*(List unit METL tasks or skill level 2/3/4 MOS tasks and other comments)*

PART IV.	ACKNOWLEDGEMENT

This form, air traffic control maintenance Soldier training publications, mission training plans, and TC 3-04.81 establish Air Traffic Services Maintenance training program requirements.

ATS Maintenance NCOIC Printed Name	Signature	Date
SMITH, WILLIAM A.	*William Smith*	26 OCT 98
ATS Maintainer Printed Name	Signature	Date
JONES, JOHN H.	*John Jones*	26 OCT 98
Commander/Platoon Leader Printed Name	Signature	Date
JONES, FRANK E.	*Frank Jones*	26 OCT 98

DA FORM 3479-14, OCT 2010

Page 2 of 2
APD PE v1.00ES

Figure 8-3. Sample ATS maintenance CTL (back side)

PROGRAM PROGRESSION

8-25. Maintenance personnel assigned to an ATS unit will be certified within the time limits specified in AR 95-2.

8-26. The commander should consider unit RLs and mission requirements when training is initiated for the particular system or sub system. Training time begins the first duty day after an individual is formally assigned to the maintenance section and will be annotated on DA Form 3479-9.

> *Note.* AR 95-2 establishes training time limitations and authorized reasons to stop maintenance training.

8-27. RL training begins with development of proficiency at the individual level and progress through team to collective proficiency. This process follows the crawl-walk-run model of training. Tasks required for air traffic maintenance personnel to progress from various levels are contained within the Soldier's CTL. CTL requirements are battle-focused, tasked-based requirements derived from the unit's METL. The following guidelines should be utilized when assigning RLs to air traffic maintenance personnel and assessing AMTP progression.

READINESS LEVEL-1

8-28. Air traffic maintenance personnel are awarded RL 1 upon completion of AMTP training requirements. An ATS maintainer awarded RL 1 has been determined to possess the tactical and technical skills needed to perform maintenance duties on the ATS system and subsystems. ATS maintainers should be removed from RL 1 and identified RL 2 when additional training is warranted due to a lack of proficiency.

READINESS LEVEL-2

8-29. ATS maintenance personnel are awarded RL 2 when undergoing advanced ATS system training at the team level and the required CTLs for RL 1 have not yet been met. This RL is characterized with proficiency in collective tasks and team tasks associated with the advanced maintenance of ATS systems. ATS maintenance personnel are awarded this RL when they have achieved certification on at least one ATS system of the unit. Tasks are performed in complex varying environments and require successful coordination and integration of combined arms operations. Advanced maintenance procedures during all phases of tactical operations are a critical element of this level.

READINESS LEVEL-3

8-30. ATS maintenance personnel are awarded RL 3 when they have completed an MOS awarding school and/or are on initial assignment to an ATS unit and have not achieved maintenance certification on any ATS systems of the unit. This RL is characterized with the individual task proficiency in the installation, operation, and unit level maintenance of air traffic systems. This phase reinforces basic maintenance procedures and theories. A maintainer assigned this RL is under the direct supervision of leaders and trainers of the ATS unit when performing maintenance actions.

READINESS LEVEL-4

8-31. ATS maintenance personnel are awarded RL 4 when AMTP progression is not required or has been temporarily suspended due to the following:
- Maintainer is assigned to a staff position not requiring AMTP progression and/or development.
- Maintainer is pending MOS reclassification/chapter actions.
- Maintainer is assigned to a National Guard position without being a graduate of the 94D School.

MAINTAINER STATUS AND UNIT STATUS RELATIONSHIP

8-32. The status of ATS unit training depends on the status of individual/crew/collective training. Individual, crew, and collective proficiency must be balanced by ensuring training resources are used to train at the individual and collective proficiency level. The T-level rating provides meaningful information for the entire chain of command. The unit training T-level is a major factor in determining how many days the unit needs to train to standard on METL tasks. Commanders use the number of days the unit needs to train to standard on METL tasks, along with the information in AR 220-1 to determine the overall training T-level. Table 8-1, page 8-9, reflects T-levels requirements.

Table 8-1. Maintainer training T-Level ratings

Level	Requirements
T1	Not less than 85 percent of required maintainers are RL 1.
T2	Not less than 75 percent of required maintainers are RL 1.
T3	Not less than 65 percent of required maintainers are RL 1.
T4	Does not meet minimum criteria for T-3.

This page intentionally left blank.

Appendix A

Reference Material

The ATC chief/facility chief will maintain a current set of facility directives, LOAs, FAA handbooks and orders, ARs, FMs, and TMs. All references will be immediately available to facility personnel for operations, reference, training, and study.

REFERENCE FILES, CHARTS, DIAGRAMS, AND MAPS

AIR TRAFFIC CONTROL ADMINISTRATION AND CONTROLLER REFERENCE FILES

A-1. The ATC administration and controller reference files will include the publications listed in this appendix. This file should also contain copies of FTMs, SOPs, operating manuals, and other materials of value to controllers and facility operations. Advances in technology and the accessibility of digital publications have made the need for multiple files unnecessary. An ATC administration reference file will be maintained in the office of the ATC chief/PSG/facility chief/maintenance chief and the controller reference file will be maintained in all ATC facilities. Digital copies may be used as long as computer access is readily available to controller in the ATC facilities. Table A-1 lists the publications required for the ATC administration and controller reference file. Table A-2, page A-3, lists the required maintenance publications.

Table A-1. Required ATC administration and controller reference files

Publications	ATC Administration Reference File		Controller Reference File	
	Installation	Tactical	Installation	Tactical
Army Regulations				
AR 25-400-2	X	X		
AR 25-50	X	X		
AR 40-8	X	X	X	
AR 40-501	X	X		
AR 95-2	X	X	X	
AR 115-10	X	X		
AR 115-11	X	X		
AR 385-10	X	X		
AR 420-1	X	X		
DA Pamphlets				
DA Pam 25-30		X		
DA Pam 25-403	X	X		
DA Pam 385-10	X	X		
DA Pam 385-30	X	X		
DA Pam 385-90	X	X		
DA Pam 750-8	X	X		
FAA Publications				
Approach Procedures	X	X	X	X

Table A-1. Required ATC administration and controller reference files

Publications	ATC Administration Reference File		Controller Reference File	
	Installation	Tactical	Installation	Tactical
Sectional Charts	X	X	X	X
IFR Supplement	X	X	X	X
VFR Supplement	X	X	X	X
FAA JO 7110.65T	X	X	X	X
FAA JO 7210.3	X	X		
FAA JO 7220.1B	X	X	X	
FAAO 7900.5	X	X		
FAAO 8200.1	X	X		
FAAO 8260.3	X	X		
FAAO 8260.19	X	X		
FAAO 8260.15	X	X		
14 CFR Part 65	X	X		
14 CFR Part 91	X	X		
14 CFR Part 99	X			
14 CFR Part 105	X	X		
32 CFR Part 245	X			
FAAO 8020.11	X	X		
Doctrinal Publications				
FM 3-04.120		X		X
TC 3.04.81	X	X	X	X
FM 3-21.38		X		
FM 3-52		X		X
FM 3-52.1		X		X
FM 3-52.3		X		X
FM 3-52.2		X		
Unified Facilities Criteria				
UFC 3-260-1	X	X		
UFC 3-535-01	X	X		
FAA Joint Publications				
JP 3-52		X		X
ICAO				
ICAO Manual 7910	X	X		

Table A-2. Required ATC maintenance reference files

Publications	Maintenance			
	Installation	Tactical Sections		
Army Regulations				
AR 25-400-2	X	X		
AR 70-1	X	X		
AR 95-1	X	X		
AR 95-2	X	X		
AR 385-10	X	X		
AR 420-1	X	X		
AR 700-138	X	X		
AR 710-2	X	X		
AR 725-50	X	X		
AR 735-5	X	X		
AR 750-1	X	X		
AR 750-43	X	X		
DA Pamphlets				
DA Pam 25-30	X	X		
DA Pam 710-2-1	X	X		
DA Pam 710-2-2	X	X		
Supply support pamphlet (SS Pam) 750-8	X	X		
DA Pam 750-3	X	X		
FAA Publications				
FAAO 6000.6	X	X		
FAAO 6000.15	X			
FAAO 6130.3	X			
FAAO 6190.16	X			
FAAO 6191.3	X			
FAAO 6310.9	X			
FAAO 6310.19*	X			
FAAO 6310.30	X			
FAA JO 6360.1*	X			
FAA JO 6360.14	X			
FAAO 6410.18	X			
FAAO 6480.6	X			
FAAO 6740.2	X			
FAA JO 6770.2*	X			
FAAO 6820.7*	X			
FAAO 8020.11	X	X		
FAAO 8200.1	X	X		
* Required only at installations with systems listed in chapter four.				

Table A-2. Required ATC maintenance reference files

Publications	Maintenance			
	Installation	Tactical Sections		
Doctrinal Publications				
FM 3-04.120		X		
TC 3.04.81	X	X		
TC 11-6		X		
FM 4-30.3	X	X		
FM 10-27-4	X	X		
FM 4-25.11	X	X		
FMI 6-02.70	X	X		
International Civil Aviation Organization				
Annex 11	X	X		
Supply Bulletin				
SB 11-573	X	X		
Technical Bulletins				
TB 11-6625-3263-25	X	X		
TB 43-0118	X	X		
TB 43-0129	X	X		
TB 43-0133	X	X		
TB 43-180	X	X		
TB 385-4	X	X		
TB 750-25	X	X		
TB Med 523	X	X		
TB Sig 222	X	X		
Technical Manuals				
TM 5-811-3	X	X		
TM 9-6140-200-14	X	X		
TM 43-0139	X	X		
Unified Facilities Criteria				
UFC 3-260-01	X	X		
UFC 3-535-01	X	X		
UFC 3-260-05A	X	X		

RECENT INFORMATION FILE

A-2. The ATC chief/facility chief will maintain an information file in a folder, binder, or clipboard. The file will be used to post shift schedules and new information about facility operations. This file is temporary. Items are removed and filed IAW AR 25-400-2 after all personnel have initialed the document. It will be readily available to controllers in facility operating positions. Each controller will read and initial new directives, changes, or other materials before assuming a control position. Items may be removed from the file when all controllers have initialed them.

OPERATING POSITION FILES

A-3. Each facility will maintain operating position files in a loose-leaf binder or some other suitable display file. These files will be available for each operating position so all controllers have an immediate source for confirming data or obtaining information.

A-4. All local procedures and instruction handbook materials pertaining to a certain operating position will be identified, defined, and maintained. For example, an arrival control position file should include LOAs, memorandums, and other documents pertaining to arrival control procedures.

A-5. Mandatory items for operating position files include—

- Instructions dealing with airfield emergencies (such as in flight/ground emergencies, hijacking, bomb threats, facility evacuation, and position specific responsibilities).
- A list of suitable airports, as determined by the facility chief, showing runways, type of surface lighting, and distance and bearing from the facility.
- Suggested items for operating position files include—
  - Instrument DP diagrams.
  - Photographs or exact depictions of a radarscope adjusted to optimum.
  - Extracts from LOAs, LOPs, and facility memorandums.
  - A photograph or exact depiction of a video map superimposed over radar-ground returns to aid in determining the accuracy of the scope alignment.

CHARTS, DIAGRAMS, AND MAPS

A-6. Each ATC facility, control TWR, radar facility, and flight-following facility will maintain certain charts, diagrams, and maps for reference. The requirements for these materials are—

- **ATC facility.** Each ATC facility will maintain current crash grid maps, sunrise and sunset tables, and FLIPs.
- **Control tower**. Each control TWR will develop and maintain the following diagrams and charts.
  - **Airfield diagram.** The airfield diagram will depict runways, ramps, blind spots, ILS-critical areas, helipads, wind equipment, and RT groups. The facility chief will review the chart annually and post the date of review to the chart.
  - **Intersection-takeoff diagram.** The intersection-takeoff diagram will depict distances remaining rounded down to the nearest 50 feet (for example, 4,075 would be rounded down to 4,050 and 10,045 to 10,000). The intersection-take-off diagram maybe incorporated into the airfield diagram provided no information is omitted and the diagram remains legible.
  - **Visibility charts.** The facility chief and weather support personnel will prepare a chart of day and night visibility markers. They may use panoramic photographs marked with distances and cardinal compass points. Each marker will be identified and its distance from the TWR noted. The height of the marker also will be noted if used for estimating heights of clouds and obscuring phenomena. The facility chief and weather personnel will review these charts annually; both personnel conducting the review will annotate their name and the date on the chart.
- **Radar facility**. Each radar facility will keep a runway diagram of each airfield it services and a map of the facility's jurisdiction area. The map will depict airfields, NAVAIDs, Class D airspace, area and section boundaries, MOA restricted and prohibited areas, airways, and prominent objects. The facility will also maintain a video map, if the capability exists, and an MVA chart. Appendix D contains details about video maps and MVA charts.
- **Airspace Information Center.** Each airspace information (flight-following) facility will keep an up-to-date map of its area of responsibility. Chapter two contains additional information about flight-following procedures.

ADMINISTRATIVE CORRESPONDENCE

A-7. The ATC facility will maintain a file of administrative correspondence. This correspondence should include LOAs, LOPs, and facility memorandums.

LETTERS OF AGREEMENT

A-8. ATC Leaders will negotiate a LOA when operational or procedural needs require the cooperation and concurrence of other persons, facilities, or organizations outside of the facility.

A-9. Conditions requiring the creation of an LOA and examples are found in FAA JO 7210.3. The process for development and coordination of a LOA may be found in FAA JO 7210.3 with the following exceptions:

- Army facilities and deployed units will coordinate LOAs affecting aircraft operations or pilot procedures with resident and supported aviation unit commanders.
- Army facilities and deployed units (when practical) will forward LOAs as applicable to the FAA service area DAR as identified for that location in AR 95-2, the U.S. Aeronautical Services Detachment-Europe, or the Eight Army ATC coordinator.
- LOAs between Army units or other Army elements on the same airfield are coordinated with the airfield division chief/commander/manager in lieu of the DAR. LOAs between Army units or other Army elements not on the same airfield, but on the same installation, will be coordinated with the installation AT&AO in lieu of the DAR.
- LOAs will not be used to describe procedures for the joint use of restricted or prohibited airspace.
- LOA describing procedures for issuance of NOTAMs.

A-10. LOAs will not be used to standardize internal facility administrative procedures. The process for approval and distribution of an LOA can be found in FAA JO 7210.3 and AR 95-2. Coordinate all letters with the appropriate DAR during the development stage or upon modification. Provide copies of the final version of these letters to the appropriate DAR. Units operating in host countries will coordinate each LOA with the appropriate office in theater, with USAASD–E for its area of responsibility, the Eighth United States Army (EUSA) ATC coordinator's office for Korea, or with the appropriate AT&A officer.

A-11. Each LOA will be reviewed annually by all signatories and documentation of the review will be kept on file in the facility. The DAR; the Commander, United States Army Aeronautical Services Detachment-Europe (USAASD–E); the EUSA ATC coordinator's office (Korea); or the ACOM/ASCC/DRU/ARNG/installation AT&A officer will participate in these reviews.

A-12. LOAs will be stored and maintained IAW the requirements for Army Records Information Management System (ARIMS) file 95-1f. Figure A-1, page A-7, provides an example of the LOA format.

```
┌─────────────────────────────────────────────────────────────────────────┐
│                                                                           │
│   (Name) Air Route Traffic Control Center and (Name)  FAA   (Name)  Approach │
│   Control and ___(Name)__                                                  │
│                                                                           │
│                          Letter of Agreement                              │
│                                                                           │
│                                          Effective:_ (Date)_               │
│                                                                           │
│   Subject: Special VFR Operations Within ___(Name)___ Airport Surface Are  │
│                                                                           │
│   1. Purpose: (List responsibilities, and describe necessary coordination.)│
│                                                                           │
│   2. Cancellation: (Use as required.)                                     │
│                                                                           │
│   3. Scope: (Specify areas having ATC responsibility and names and types of facilities.)│
│                                                                           │
│   4. Responsibilities:  (Specify responsibilities.)                       │
│                                                                           │
│   5. Procedures:                                                          │
│                                                                           │
│      a. ATC assigned airspace. (List the procedures for requesting and authorizing airspace,│
│   handling aircraft to and from airspace, and notifying ATC when the airspace is no longer│
│   required.)                                                              │
│                                                                           │
│      b. Transfer of control. (Specify transfer procedures.)              │
│                                                                           │
│      c. Departures. (Specify the required advance time for filing flight plans, and outline additional│
│   items required in the flight plan. For example, list the type of departure and the control transfer│
│   points.)                                                               │
│                                                                           │
│      d. En route. (Include in this information that ATC is responsible for effecting separation in assigned│
│   airspace when nonparticipating aircraft are cleared to operate within that airspace.)│
│                                                                           │
│      e. Arrivals. (Outline handoff procedures and special instructions.)  │
│                                                                           │
│      f. General. (Include, if appropriate, missed-approach procedures, special VFR operations, and│
│   provisions for handling movement of national-defense aircraft in emergencies.)│
│                                                                           │
│   6. Attachments: (List, as required, items such as a chart of ATC-assigned airspace areas and common│
│   reference or handoff points.)                                          │
│                                                                           │
│   Airfield Commander, ___(Name)___ AAF        Chief, ____(Name)____ ARTCC  │
│                                                                           │
│   Chief, ___(Name)_____ ATC Facility         Director, ___(Name)___ Region│
│                                                                           │
│   (Name and title of appropriate authority)                               │
│                                                                           │
└─────────────────────────────────────────────────────────────────────────┘
```

Figure A-1. Sample format for an FAA or a U.S. Army LOA

LETTERS OF PROCEDURE

A-13. ATC leaders will prepare a LOP for stating specific terms regarding the joint use of restricted or prohibited airspace as defined in 14 CFR Part 73 or local theater equivalents.

A-14. ATS leaders responsible for developing LOP will ensure LOPs are worded so the Army maintains the greatest degree of mission flexibility within limits prescribed by law or regulation and that each will address, at a minimum:

- Scheduling procedures and updates, to include requirement and time parameters for providing updates to the schedule.
- Activation/deactivation procedures.
- Activation/deactivation times.
- Transfer of the airspace during emergency conditions.
- Transfer of the airspace for situations caused by weather.

A-15. Example process steps for development, coordination, approval, and distribution of a LOP may be found in FAA JO 7210.3 except:

- Army facilities will format LOPs using the guidance and examples in AR 25-50 for memorandums of agreement. The term "letter of procedure" will be substituted for "memorandum of agreement". Additional paragraphs such as "cancellation" and "attachments" may be added as needed. LOPs originated by other agencies (FAA, USAF) which the Army will sign may follow the format of the originating agency.
- In addition to the requirements in FAA JO 7210.3, Army facilities and deployed units (when practical) will coordinate LOPs with the installation AT&A officer.
- Army facilities and deployed units (when practical) will forward LOPs as applicable to the FAA service area DAR as identified for that location in AR 95-2, the U.S Aeronautical Services Detachment-Europe, or the Eight Army ATC Coordinator. A cover memorandum will accompany the LOP and must include any changes to an existing LOP, along with background information for each change. If the LOP is new, a brief description of the operations to be accommodated should be outlined. The unit commander will approve/sign the memorandum.

A-16. To ensure timeliness and conformance to current policies and directives, the LOP will be reviewed annually no later than the anniversary month of the original document. A memorandum or cover letter documenting the review will be posted to the LOP. A single document may be used to record the annual review of more than one LOP provided each LOP is specifically listed on the document.

A-17. LOPs will be stored and maintained IAW the requirements for ARIMS file 95-2f.

OPERATIONS LETTERS

A-18. Effective with publication of this publication, all existing operations letters will be converted to LOA no later than the anniversary month of the original letter. No further operations letters will be developed.

FACILITY MEMORANDUMS

A-19. The ATC chief/facility chief will issue facility memorandums when internal facility operations must be regulated and standardized. Memorandums will contain instructions on the administrative or operational practices and procedures within the facility. The ATC chief may issue a memorandum as a combined facility document when it applies to two or more ATC facilities under his jurisdiction.

A-20. Facility memorandums will follow the standard Army memorandum format IAW AR 25-50 and be numbered in sequence (10-1, 10-2 meaning the first/second memorandum for 2010). They will be limited to one subject, operation, or procedure; enclosures and attachments may be included. Facility memorandums will be reviewed for currency annually no later than the anniversary month of the original document. The ATC chief/facility chief will date and sign the annual review.

OPERATING RECORDS AND FORMS

A-21. Facility records will be managed according to the procedures in AR 25-400-2 and as directed by the servicing adjutant general. They are a part of the facility's permanent records and subject to review by authorized personnel or agencies. Entries on all facility operating forms will be neat and accurate. When practical, entries should be typewritten (computer generated forms may be used); however, entries may be printed in ink. Incorrect entries will not be erased or struck over. When an entry must be corrected, a line will be typed or drawn through the incorrect portion and the correct entry made. The controller correcting the error will initial the correction.

OPERATIONAL HAZARD REPORT

A-22. Controllers witnessing procedural or material operational hazards or unsafe ATC practices or procedures will submit DA Form 2696 (Operational Hazard Report) to their supervisors. Procedures covering the completion and disposition of DA Form 2696 are covered in DA Pam 385-90. The ATC chief/facility chief will ensure blank copies of this form are available. He will also ensure completed forms are correct and submitted through the appropriate commander to the local aviation safety officer or airfield operations officer. The FTM will include instructions for preparing and submitting DA Form 2696.

A-23. Operational hazard reports are not to be used to report alleged flight violations for punitive action. AR 95-1 provides guidance for processing alleged flight violations.

AIR TRAFFIC CONTROL FACILITY PERSONNEL STATUS REPORT

A-24. All facilities will prepare and submit DA Form 3479-6 (ATC Facility and Personnel Status Report) or an automated version of the form within the first 15 workdays of the succeeding calendar month. All Army National Guard and Army Reserve units will submit DA Form 3479-6 quarterly based on a calendar year. The units will forward this completed unclassified form to the ACOM headquarters through the normal chain of command. They also will send a copy directly to Commander, ATSCOM, AFAT-ATS-CT, 2805 Division Road, Fort Rucker, Alabama 36362-5265. All installation ATC facilities will provide the local airfield division chief/commander/manager with a copy of the monthly traffic record (block 11 of the form). The responsible commander or his designated representative will verify the accuracy of the report. Instructions for completing the manual DA Form 3479-6 are listed in table A-3.

Note. If there is an advantage in doing so, this form or data may be transmitted by electronic means.

Table A-3. Instructions for completing DA Form 3479-6

Block 1. Unit.	Enter the agency, battalion, company, platoon, or detachment having command of the ATC facility, branch, division, element, or section identified in the report. Include the mailing address of the city, post, or station.
Block 2. Facility, Branch, Division, Element, Section.	Enter the name, title, or number of the section to which ATC personnel being reported are assigned (for example, Forney AAF, Hanchey Army Heliport (AHP), 1st Platoon, or 3rd Platoon).
Block 3. Date.	Enter the month and year the report covers in the following format: MM YY (Dec 02).
Block 4. Hours of Operation.	Enter the number of hours per day and days per week that each facility or staff element operates. More than one entry may be required to indicate different hours of operation. (For example, Monday through Friday/16 hours [M-F/16] or Saturday, Sunday, and Holidays/8 hours [S-S-H/8].)
Block 5. Manned Positions.	Enter an X under each position normally manned by an individual dedicated to that position during each shift. If an individual is normally responsible for more than one position during a given shift, show position responsibility by entering C1 under each position. (For example, show the normally combined positions of GC and LC by placing C1 under each position for that shift). If more positions are combined and assigned to a second individual, enter C2 under these positions. Shift A will be the first shift of the day (for example, 0600-1400 or 0700-1500). Shift B will be the second shift of the day, and shift C will be the third shift of the day. The facilities that do not operate on weekends and holidays will use shift D for those periods.
Block 6. TDA Authorizations (by MOS).	Enter both controller and maintenance ATC personnel by MOS (or job series for civilians); follow with the authorized total and on-hand total (for example, 15Q 5/4, 2152-2/2, 94D-2/1, or 0856-1/2). Do not indicate skill levels. DA Form 3479-6 reporting is for the status of the facility/section on the last day of the month. All personnel on SD or temporary duty (TDY) are considered on-hand at the losing facility/section for reporting purposes. Any person that has PCS, transferred, end term of service (ETS), terminated employment, or is on terminal leave during the course of the month (to include the last day) is no longer on-hand at the end of the month.
Block 7. TOE Authorizations (by MOS).	Enter totals the same way as in block 6.
Block 8. Aircraft Activity (by Shift).	Enter the total aircraft activity for each shift. Using the installation facility criteria (see instructions in block 11), report the aircraft activity for tactical ATC

Table A-3. Instructions for completing DA Form 3479-6

	exercises by shift only. For installation facilities, the totals in block 8 will be the same as the totals in block 11.
Block 9. Remarks.	Use this block to explain any entry in blocks 1 through 8.
Block 10. Personnel.	Enter alphabetically, by facility or section, all assigned military and civilian controller, and maintenance personnel. Complete block 10 as shown below:

Block 10. Personnel. (continued):

Column (a) Name. Enter the individual's last name, first name, and middle initial.

Column (b) Rank. Enter the rank for military and pay grade for civilian employees (for example, SSG, GS 11, or WG 10).

Column (c) MOS. Enter the individuals primary MOS. For civilians, enter 2152 or 0856, as appropriate.

Column (d) ETS. Enter the individual's current ETS/retention control point (RCP) date (military only).

Column (e) ATCS No. Enter the individual's assigned ATCS certificate number.

Column (f) Date Assigned. Enter the date the individual was assigned to a tactical section or facility for training. Enter a new assigned date each time an individual is moved geographically or is moved from one facility to another within the same facility complex (for example, Heidelberg to Wiesbaden or TWR to GCA). If dual rated, the date assigned will be the facility/section of primary assignment.

Column (g) Date Rated. Enter the letter T for trainee. Enter the date the individual was issued a facility rating for that facility. This date will correspond to the date entered on the back of the ATCS certificate. If, for example, an individual is rated in TWR and working in GCA, make no entry in this column until he becomes rated in GCA. Annotate the TWR rating, however, in the Remarks column.

Column (h) Remarks. Enter the following information, as applicable:

- The gaining unit will list SD personnel or personnel not working in the MOS and indicate the primary unit.

- The primary unit will list SD personnel and indicate the location of the SD.

- Indicate when an individual is a 90, 60, and 30-day loss for ETS or PCS loss. Units reporting their DA Form 3479-6 electronically will ensure surrendered ATCS certificates are mailed IAW the standards associated with the paper-filed format.

- Enter REQ if making a request for reissuance of an ATCS certificate. State the reason for the request, such as lost, worn, or name change; indicate the date the individual completed ATC School. These entries will remain in the remarks column until the individual receives a new ATCS certificate.

- Enter primary and additional ATC duty assignments (for example, facility chief, training supervisor, or examiner).

- Enter the number of calendar months an individual is extended with a TTE and the expiration date of the extension. An approved TTE starts the day after the initial rating period ends. The TTE expires the same day on a later calendar month. Include the reason the individual did not become rated, qualified, or certified in the prescribed time.

- Enter groundings, and include the estimated date for return to duty. List the reason for grounding using one of the following terms: positive urinalysis, medical, administrative, or disciplinary.

- Enter reclassification actions. An individual being reclassified remains on report with no ATCS number until reclassified.

Table A-3. Instructions for completing DA Form 3479-6

	• State the reason for suspension (or example, apathy, lack of ability, or pending medical evaluation). • Enter the social security number of newly assigned individuals. • Enter the dual rating (for example, TWR/GCA). • Enter any other data (for example, maintenance certified [AN/TSQ71B, FPN-40], pathfinder, tactical certification, or additional skill identifiers as appropriate).
Block 11. Monthly Traffic Record.	In addition to the data in block 8, ATC facilities will maintain a monthly traffic count in the following categories:
Block 11a.	Enter the name of the AAF/AHP.

Block 11b and 11c.	TWR–IFR and TWR–VFR. Movement by (1) local and (2) transient aircraft. Use the following criteria to count control TWR activity:
	    Count a single aircraft arrival, departure, or overflight as one.
	    Count a single aircraft touch-and-go, stop-and-go, low approach, missed approach, or wave-off/go-around below the traffic pattern altitude as two.
	    Count formation flights according to the number of aircraft in the formation. (For example, count a flight of two aircraft flying a low approach as four and a flight of two aircraft making a full stop as two.)
	    Count helicopters remaining within the ATA while on air taxi to or from working or alert areas the same as departures or arrivals. Enter the count in the TWR VFR local column.
	    Count UAS traffic the same as manned aircraft. TWR–VFR movement by (1) local and (2) transient aircraft.

Block 11d. ARAC (not to include final) by (1) IFR and (2) VFR.	Use the following criteria to count approach control activity:
	    ARTS/STARS (TOWER DISPLAY WORKSTATIONS) have the capability for automated traffic count and should be used fully. Unique traffic that cannot be programmed into the automation system will be counted and added to the automated count manually.
	    Count aircraft operations the same as TWR operations. However, count formation flights as only one operation.
	    Count aircraft as instrument operations when they are provided separation regardless of existing weather conditions or type of flight plan.
	    Count VFR operations, and enter them in the same format and category as instrument operations (for example, military, air carrier, and general aviation).
	    Count UAS the same as manned aircraft.

Block 11e. GCA radar vector (pattern).	Count each GCA pattern (vector) to the final approach course/fix as one or when radar vectors are provided as part of a missed approach. When GCA/ASR radar is used for range monitoring/flight-following of UAS aircraft, the provisions established for flight-following facilities will be used. If active separation for IFR UAS from other UAS or manned aircraft is applied, IFR count will apply.
Block 11f. GCA/ARAC (1) final ASR and (2) final PAR.	Count each GCA ASR final, and PAR final as one.

Block 11g.	AIC/TWR FF (total count). Use the following criteria to count total FF activity:
	    Count the initial contact with an aircraft as one.
	    Count formation flights as a single operation.
	    Count each position report made while the aircraft is en route as one. (To be counted, the position report must be posted to the flight progress strip.)
	    Count each aircraft entering or departing an unmanned area (restricted area, range and NOE, NVD route) as one. (To be counted, this data must be posted to the flight progress strip.)

Table A-3. Instructions for completing DA Form 3479-6

	Count UAS traffic the same as manned aircraft.
Block 12. Date.	Enter the date the form was completed.
Block 13. Prepared by.	Enter the name of the individual who completed the form and the telephone numbers (commercial, including the area code, and DSN). A signature is not required.
Block 14. Last TB received.	Enter the last TB message received.
Block 15a.	Authentication officer. Enter the name, title, office symbol, and telephone numbers (commercial, including the area code, and DSN) of the commander or civilian equivalent.
Block 15b.	Signature of authentication officer. The commander or civilian equivalent signs this block.
Note. The appropriate acronyms will be used for position titles. If the appropriate acronyms are not listed in the glossary of this publication, local acronyms will be used in block 5 and defined in block 9, Remarks.	

SYSTEM OUTAGE REPORTING

A-25. System outages involving ATC installation equipment will be reported to ATSCOM on a monthly basis as an attachment to DA Form 3479-6. Outages include all out-of-service conditions (for example: one channel of a dual-channel system out-of-service condition). The attachment will contain the following:

- Unit/organization.
- Facility/airfield.
- System/subsystem.
- Serial number.
- Date out of service (DD MM YY).
- Date returned to service (DD MM YY).
- Not mission capable maintenance hours.
- Not mission capable supply hours.
- Reason for outage.
- Restore method. (Action[s] taken to return system to fully mission capable status).

GROUND-CONTROLLED APPROACH OPERATIONS LOG

A-26. Flight strips or DA Form 3501 (GCA Operations Log) (figure A-2, page A-13) may be used to record air traffic in GCA facilities. When used, DA Form 3501 is initiated at the beginning of each calendar day (0000 local time or whenever the facility begins operations for the day). Time entries will be in UTC. The ATC chief/PSG/facility chief will review each completed DA Form 3501 and sign the authentication block (block 2). If more than one form is required to log daily activities, the pages will be numbered consecutively and stapled together. Daily totals will be entered on the final form.

GCA OPERATIONS LOG
For use of this form, see TC 3-04.81; the proponent agency is TRADOC.

1. FACILITY		2. FACILITY CHIEF'S SIGNATURE	3. DATE
PINBALL GCA, FORT ORD, CA		Jno Q. Public	8 AUG 2009

4. OPERATIONS – S/S = Supervised or simulated   LV = Live Unsupervised/Non-simulated

FLIGHT PLAN IFR (a)	VFR (b)	AIRCRAFT IDENT (c)	TYPE (d)	RADAR ID TIME (UTC) (e)	TYPE APRCH (f)	ASR PATTERN S/S (g)	ASR PATTERN LV (h)	ASR FINAL S/S (i)	ASR FINAL LV (j)	PAR FINAL S/S (k)	PAR FINAL LV (l)	EMER NO GYRO (m)	RELEASE TIME (UTC) (n)	REMARKS (o)
X		R12345	UH-60	0615	PS	MN/CB				MN/CB		X	0628	SMOKE IN COCKPIT
X		R23456	AH-64	0810	LA		CB				CB		0823	N/A
	X	R54321	CH-47	0924	TG		NC		NC			X	0936	NO GYRO
	X	R53124	OH-58	1005	SG	AR		AR					1022	RADAR SIMULATOR
X		R23244	C-12	1034	FS								1047	CB ILS MONITOR
3	2	ENTER TOTALS IN COLUMNS AT LEFT. (TOTAL NUMBER OF IFR OPERATIONS)/(TOTAL NUMBER OF VFR OPERATIONS)		TOTAL IFR TOTAL VFR		1	1	1	1	1	0	0	1	0

DA FORM 3501, OCT 2010   PREVIOUS EDITIONS ARE OBSOLETE.   Page _____ of _____   APD PE v1.00ES

Figure A-2. Sample DA Form 3501

A-27. DA Form 3501 will be completed as follows:

- **Item 1.** Enter the name of the GCA facility.
- **Item 2.** The facility chief signature is required.
- **Item 3.** Enter date.
- **Item 4a and 4b.** Insert an X for the aircraft of a VFR or IFR flight plan in the applicable column.
- **Item 4c.** Enter aircraft identification or call sign (R12345).

- **Item 4d**. Enter aircraft type (UH60).
- **Item 4e**. Enter the time of radar contact in UTC.
- **Item 4f**. Enter LA (low approach), FS (full stop), TG (touch-and-go), or other type of approach.
- **Item 4g**. Enter the operating initials of the controller conducting the supervised or simulated (S/S) ASR pattern portion of the approach and the initials of the controller who is signed on behind a trainee or controller on remedial training. An example would be BR/CB.
- **Item 4h**. Enter the operating initials of the controller conducting the live unsupervised and non-simulated ASR pattern portion of the approach.
- **Item 4i**. Enter the operating initials of the controller conducting the S/S ASR final portion of the approach and the initials of the controller who is signed on behind a trainee or controller on remedial training. An example would be BR/CB.
- **Item 4j**. Enter the operating initials of the controller conducting the live unsupervised and non-simulated ASR final portion of the approach.
- **Item 4k**. Enter the operating initials of the controller conducting the S/S final portion of the precision approach and the initials of the controller who is signed on behind a trainee or controller on remedial training. An example would be BR/CB.
- **Item 4l**. Enter the operating initials of the controller conducting the live unsupervised and non-simulated final portion of the precision approach.
- **Item 4m**. Enter an X if the approach is an emergency or No Gyro simulated or live.
- **Item 4n**. Enter the time the aircraft was released to another agency, TWR, or ARAC.
- **Item 4o**. Enter remarks such as missed approach the controller's initials followed by ILS MON if the controller monitored a NAVAID approach or departure (CB ILS MON) or any other control instructions.

A-28. Add up all approaches for VFR and IFR aircraft in columns 4g through 4l at the bottom of DA Form 3501 and write the cumulative total is written in the bottom left corner of DA Form 3501.

A-29. DA Form 3501 will be filed daily with DA Form 3502 and retained for a minimum of six calendar months. For example, all logs in June 2009 may not be destroyed until 1 January 2010. ARAC facilities may use flight progress strips to record traffic movements instead of DA Form 3501. Flight progress strips will be maintained for six calendar months.

DAILY REPORT OF AIR TRAFFIC CONTROL FACILITY

A-30. All Army ATC facilities will use DA Form 3502 (an electronic version may be used) to record daily activities. This form will be initiated at the beginning of each calendar day (0000 local time or when facility operations begin for the day). Entries will be in UTC. The logs will be closed at midnight local for facilities operating on a 24-hour basis. Facilities operating less than 24 hours a day will open the log when the facility opens for daily operations and close the logs when the facility officially ends operations for the day.

A-31. Only authorized Army, FAA, and ICAO abbreviations and phrase contractions will be used for entries. The entries will describe all abnormal conditions, unusual occurrences, or items of interest. Examples of entries are equipment checks, outages or restorations, emergencies, accidents and unsafe conditions. The operating initials of the individual making the entry will follow all entries in the remarks section of the form.

A-32. Supervisory responsibility will be indicated in the remarks section using assigned operating initials (for example, "CB ASSUMED DUTIES AS SL"; "CB DEPARTED FACILITY, WS ASSUMED DUTIES AS CIC").

A-33. The facility chief will review each DA Form 3502 for accuracy and sign in the authentication block. This form will be filed daily and retained for a minimum of six calendar months. (For example, June 2009 logs may be destroyed 1 January 2010.)

AIR TRAFFIC CONTROL POSITION LOG

A-34. DA Form 3503 (Air Traffic Control Position Log) provides a record of personnel assigned to each operating position within an ATC facility. Controllers assigned responsibility for an operating position initiate the DA Form 3503 at the beginning of each calendar day. (This would be 0000 local time or when facility operations begin for the day). Entries will be in UTC. Pages will be added as necessary to complete the day. The logs will be closed at midnight local for facilities operating on a 24-hour basis. Facilities operating less than 24 hours a day will open the log when the facility opens for daily operations and close the logs when the facility officially ends operations for the day.

A-35. Controllers requiring direct supervision will use their operating initials followed by a slant mark (/) and the facility-rated controller's initials. Those under direct supervision include—

- Controller trainees who are not positioned qualified.
- Controllers being evaluated for facility rating by ATCS/CTO examiners.
- Rated controllers who are not current.
- Rated controllers who are receiving remedial training.

A-36. DA Form 3503 is filed daily with DA Form 3502 and retained for a minimum of six calendar months (for example all the logs in June 2009 may not be destroyed until 1 January 2010.)

A-37. Electronic methods used to track position of assignment may be used. Printed copies of position assignments must be produced daily and retained for six calendar months. Voice recordings of position assignments will not be used to satisfy facility record keeping requirements.

Note. When correcting the DA Form 3503 a line will be drawn through all blocks, with the operating initials of the controller making the correction at the end of the line.

FLIGHT PROGRESS STRIPS

A-38. When FAA Form 7230-7.2 (Flight Progress Strip: Terminal Continuous Without Center Perforation) or FAA Form 7230-8 (Flight Progress Strip: Terminal-Cut) are utilized in lieu of DA Form 3501, they shall be prepared IAW guidance contained in FAA JO 7110.65T and retained for a minimum of six calendar months (for example, June 2009 logs may be destroyed 1 January 2010).

A-39. FAA Form 7230-21 (Flight Progress Strip: FSS) will be used to record all flight-following movements.

A-40. TWR facilities may use VFR logs or notepads instead of flight strips to record all VFR operations except flight-following movements, if there is an advantage in doing so. All other facilities will record IFR and VFR operations on appropriate flight strips.

A-41. FAA Form 7230-21 (NSN 7530 01 449 4244) and the flight strip holder (NSN 6605-00-485-6649, Type 5) may be ordered through the normal supply channels.

A-42. Standard ATC control information symbols will be used, and completed strips maintained in the same manner as other ATC flight strips.

A-43. Instructions for completing FAA Form 7230-21 (figure A-3, page A-16) are as follows:

- Block 1. Aircraft identification.
- Block 2. Aircraft and equipment suffix used for special equipment such as the DME transponder.
- Block 3. Altitude.
- Block 4. Beacon code.
- Block 5. Route or area of flight.
- Block 6. Radio or radar contact time in UTC.
  Block 7. Destination (the training area or intended landing area.
- Block 8. ETA at the destination in UTC.
- Block 9. Coordination effected (Control Reporting Center, AIC, range control, and ADIZs).

- Block 10. Type mission (for example, NOE, NVD, and administrative).
- Block 11. Time of last radio contact and handoff information.
- Block 12. Time at reporting points.
- Blocks 13 & 14. Reporting points, amendments, clearances, that correspond to block 12. Blocks 13 and 14 can be changed or modified by the facility as necessary.

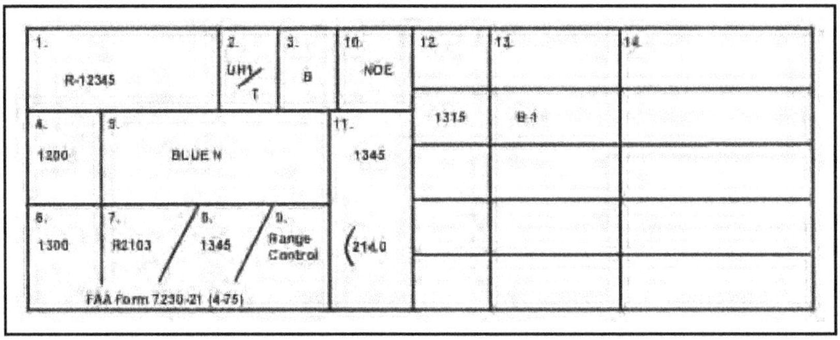

Figure A-3. Sample completed progress strip

Appendix B

Facility Training Manuals

This appendix provides outlines for installation and tactical FTMs. These outlines cover indoctrination, equipment, responsibilities, and emergency equipment and notification procedures. They also cover local area information, reference material, coordination procedures, and facility administration and management. Facilities will use only the portions of these outlines pertaining to that specific facility.

B-1.   Table B-1 is a detailed outline for an installation FTM.

Table B-1. Installation facility training manuals outline

Chapter 1 Installation Facility Indoctrination	
1-1.Mission.	

1-2. Air Traffic Control Facility.	a. Operating hours and reporting time.
	b. Duty schedule.
	c. Pre-duty requirements.
	d. Duty requirements.
	    (1) Briefings.
	    (2) Facility cleanup.
	e. Training program.
	    (1) Description.
	    (2) Type (classroom, hands-on, and so forth).
	    (3) Written, oral, and practical exams.
	    (4) Training time limitation (AR 95-2).
	    (5) Facility training schedule.
	f. Controller reference file.
	    (1) Contents.
	    (2) Location.
	g. Facility reference file.
	    (1) Contents.
	    (2) Location.

1-3. General Description of Associated Facilities.	a. Weather. b. Base operations. c. Dispatch. d. Other ATC facilities. e. Range control. f. Fire station. g. Alert sections.
1-4. Training Records.	a. Use. b. Location. c. Access.
1-5. Electronic Warfare Training.	a. Threat briefing. b. Equipment vulnerabilities. c. Electronic countermeasures. d. Recognition of electronic countermeasures and appropriate electronic counter countermeasures. e. Meaconing, intrusion, jamming, and interference reporting.
1-6. Facility Forms.	

Table B-1. Installation facility training manuals outline

Chapter 2 Air Traffic Control Facility Equipment	

2-1. Radio Communication Equipment.	a. Transmitters.
	    (1) Type.
	    (2) Location.
	b. Receivers.
	    (1) Type.
	    (2) Location.
	c. Frequencies.
	d. Channelization.
	e. Standby communications equipment.
	f. Secure voice operation.
	g. Maintenance and outage.

2-2. Land-Line Communications Equipment.	a. Interphone.
	    (1) Type.
	    (2) Location.
	    (3) Use.
	    (4) Circuit identification.
	    (5) Maintenance and outage.
	b. Telephones.
	c. Intercommunications units.
	    (1) Type.
	    (2) Location.
	    (3) Use.
	    (4) Maintenance and outage.
	d. Weather dissemination.
	    (1) Type.
	    (2) Location.
	    (3) Use.
	    (4) Maintenance.
	e. Automation equipment.
	    (1) Type.
	    (2) Location.
	    (3) Use.
	    (4) Maintenance and outage.

2-3. Recording Equipment.	a. Type. b. Location. c. Positions/frequencies recorded. d. Tape change procedures. e. Playback. f. Maintenance and outage.
2-4. Bright Radar Indicator Tower Equipment.	a. Operation and use. b. Automation procedures.
2-5. Airfield/Heliport Lighting.	a. Control panel. b. Runway and helipad. c. Threshold. d. Boundary. e. Approach. f. Taxiway. g. Rotating beacon. h. Obstruction. i. Wind direction indicator.

Table B-1. Installation facility training manuals outline

	j. Spotlights. m. Maintenance and outage. n. Other.
2-6. Monitoring Equipment.	a. Equipment monitored. b. Operational checks. c. Maintenance checks.
2-7. Automatic Terminal Information Service.	a. Use. b. Operational procedures. c. Message content and sequence. d. Maintenance and outage.

2-8. Miscellaneous Equipment.	a. Light guns.
	b. Traffic counters.
	c. Binoculars.
	d. Wind instruments.
	e. Altimeters.
	f. Clocks.
	   (1) Time check.
	   (2) Setting procedure.
	g. First aid kits.
	h. Fire extinguisher.
	i. Fuse boxes.
	j. Heating and cooling equipment.
	k. Emergency power.
	l. Emergency egress system.
	m. NVDs.
	n. Maintenance and outages.

2-9. Operator Maintenance of Facility Equipment.	
2-10. Notice to Airmen.	a. Responsible agency. b. Equipment outages requiring a NOTAM. c. Controller action.
Chapter 3 Responsibilities	

3-1. Operating Positions.	a. Control TWR.
	   (1) FD.
	   (2) GC.
	   (3) LC.
	   (4) Clearance delivery.
	   (5) Approach control.
	   (6) Combined positions.
	   (7) Others.
	b. GCA.
	   (1) Feeder.
	   (2) FD.
	   (3) Final.
	c. ARAC.
	   (1) FD.
	   (2) Arrival.
	   (3) Departure.
	   (4) PAR.
	   (5) Other.
	d. AIC.
	   (1) FD.
	   (2) Flight-following control.
	   (3) Other.

Table B-1. Installation facility training manuals outline

3-2. Supervisors.	a. Controller in charge. b. SL. c. Training supervisor. d. Facility chief. e. ATC chief/ATC AR SGT.
Chapter 4 Local Airport/Heliport Information	

4-1. Airport/Heliport.	a. Responsible agency.
	b. Layout.
	c. Runways.
	    (1) Width.
	    (2) Length.
	    (3) Weight restrictions.
	    (4) Preferential runway.
	d. Other landing areas.
	    (1) Taxiways.
	    (2) Width.
	    (3) Weight restrictions.
	e. Ramp area.
	    (1) Hangar locations.
	    (2) Parking areas.
	    (3) Taxi restrictions.
	    (4) Servicing areas.
	f. Services available.
	g. Airport boundaries.
	h. Crash standby points.

4-2. Tower Visibility Restrictions.	
4-3. Instrument Landing System-Critical Areas.	
4-4. Radio Blind Spots.	
4-5. Compass Rose.	
4-6. Very High Frequency Omnidirectional Range Receiver Checkpoints.	
4-7. Airport/Heliport Obstructions.	a. Bearing. b. Height. c. Distance.
4-8. Traffic Patterns.	
4-9. VFR Reporting Points.	a. Bearing. b. Distance.
4-10. SVFR.	a. Minimums. b. Routes. c. Reporting points.

4-11. Local Airport/Heliport Rules and Regulations.	a. Taxi regulations.
	b. Terminal procedures.
	    (1) MEDEVAC.
	    (2) Local night vision systems procedures.
	    (3) Very important persons.
	    (4) Hot refueling.
	    (5) Aircraft types and call signs.
	c. Hazardous cargo.
	d. Emergency equipment location.
	e. Restricted aircraft movement.
	f. Airfield security.
	g. Noise abatement.

Table B-1. Installation facility training manuals outline

	h. Launch and recovery procedures.
	i. Autorotation.
	  (1) Procedures.
	  (2) Areas.

4-12. Aircraft Operations.	a. Scheduled air carriers. b. Nonscheduled operations. c. Military operations. d. General aviation operations.

4-13. Weather Reporting Procedures.	a. Responsible agency.
	b. Visibility checkpoints.
	c. Day.
	  (1) Bearing.
	  (2) Distance.
	d. Night.
	  (1) Bearing.
	  (2) Distance.
	e. Nearest weather reporting facilities.
	f. PIREPs.
	g. Weather warnings.
	h. High-wind plan.

4-14. Unauthorized Personnel and Vehicles.	a. Reporting. b. Recording Incidents.
Chapter 5 Emergency Equipment and Notification Procedures	

5-1. Available Equipment.	a. Ambulance.
	b. Firefighting equipment.
	c. Rescue equipment.
	  (1) Helicopter.
	  (2) Other.

5-2. Emergency Notification Procedures.	a. Controllers.
	  (1) Position responsibilities.
	  (2) Closing and opening the airfield.
	  (3) Foaming runways.
	  (4) Required reports.
	b. Firefighting personnel and equipment.
	c. Medical personnel and equipment.
	d. Military police.

5-3. Incidents and Accidents.	a. On-the-airfield. b. Off-the-airfield. c. Information sources. d. Primary reporting procedures. e. Format and recording of reports.
5-4. Emergency Security Control of Air Traffic.	a. Procedures for implementation of ESCAT. b. Civil and military ATC responsibilities. c. Air traffic priority list.
Chapter 6 Local Area Information	
6-1. Class 'C' Airspace (Radar).	a. Boundaries. b. Adjacent areas. c. Altitudes. d. Airways.
6-2. Class 'D/E/G' Airspace.	a. Dimensions and description. b. Adjacent class 'B/C/D/E' airspace.
6-3. Surface Area.	a. Boundaries. b. Users.

Table B-1. Installation facility training manuals outline

6-4. Navigational Aids.	a. Type. b. Location. c. Identification. d. Airways.
6-5. Prominent Objects and Obstructions.	a. Bearing. b. Height. c. Distance.

6-6. Special Use Airspace.	a. Location.
	    (1) Boundaries.
	    (2) Altitudes.
	    (3) Times.
	    (4) Controlling agency.
	b. Use.
	c. Remotely piloted vehicles/unmanned aerial vehicles.
	    (1) Area.
	    (2) Procedure.
	d. Nap-of-the-earth.
	e. NVDs.
	    (1) Area.
	    (2) Procedure.
	f. IFR/VFR corridors.
	g. Airstrips.
	    (1) Location.
	    (2) Use.

6-7. VFR Training Areas.	
6-8. Adjacent Airports/Heliports.	
6-9. Parachute Areas.	
Chapter 7 Letters, Memoranda, Reports, and Forms	
7-1. Letters of Agreement.	a. Agencies. b. General content.
7-2. Facility Memoranda.	
7-3. Operational Hazard Reports.	a. Preparation. b. Submission.
Chapter 8 Flight Plans, Strips, and Markings	

8-1. Flight Plans.	a. Types.
	b. Requirements.
	c. Local filing.
	d. In-flight filing.
	e. Action upon receipt.
	    (1) IFR.
	    (2) VFR.
	    (3) SVFR.
	f. Procedures.
	    (1) Forwarding information.
	    (2) Flight plan changes (IFR to VFR).

8-2. Flight Strips.	a. Marking. b. Retention.
Chapter 9 Instrument Flight Rules and Coordination Procedures	
9-1. Approach Procedures.	a. Initial approach altitudes. b. Holding patterns. (1) Location.

Table B-1. Installation facility training manuals outline

	(2) Description. c. Procedure turns. d. Final approach altitude and heading. e. Release points. f. Missed-approach procedures. g. Weather minimums.
9-2. Departure Procedures.	a. Routes. 　(1) DPs. 　(2) Transitions. b. Altitudes between fixes and intersections. 　(1) Normal assigned frequencies. 　(2) Minimum en route altitudes.
9-3. Coordination Procedures.	a. Interposition. b. Local facilities. c. ARTCC. d. Adjacent airports.
9-4. Inadvertent Instrument Meteorological Conditions.	
9-5. Multiple Emergency Hand-Off Procedures.	a. Frequency management. b. Coordination. c. Abbreviated (short) approaches. d. Sequencing and separation standards.
Chapter 10 Secondary Radar	
10-1. Components.	a. Interrogator. b. Transponder. c. Decoder.
10-2. Type of Equipment (AN/TPX-41 AND ATCBI-3).	
10-3. Presentations.	a. Factors. 　(1) Line-of-sight. 　(2) Aircraft altitude. 　(3) Reflections. 　(4) Resolution. 　(5) Ring-around. 　(6) Slant-range. b. Interface. c. Others.
10-4. Code Assignments.	a. Facility. b. Adjacent facilities. c. Emergency.
Chapter 11 Radar	
11-1. Equipment.	a. Type. b. Display. c. Alignment and adjustment. d. Characteristics. e. Keyboard. f. Computer. g. Radar coverage. h. Simulators.
11-2. Minima.	a. MVA. b. Minimum safe altitude (MSA). c. MRA. d. SVFR.

Table B-1. Installation facility training manuals outline

11-3. Use.	
Note. This paragraph was left blank intentionally. The ATC chief/PSG/facility chief may use it to expound on, or refer to, radar use, services, separation, sequencing, and phraseology contained in FAA JO 7110.65T. All Army radar controllers are required to know and use the applicable radar procedures in the handbook. For purposes of testing, training, proficiency, and record keeping, FAA JO 7110.65T, chapter five will be considered an extension of this manual.	
Chapter 12 Facility Administration	
12-1. Daily Administration.	a. Compiling traffic count. b. Recording traffic count. c. Maintaining facility forms and records. d. Filing facility forms and records.
12-2. Storing of Records.	a. Labels. b. Storage area. c. Retention.
12-3. Dissemination of Information.	a. Accidents and incidents. b. Numbers and types of aircraft. c. Types and capabilities of equipment. d. Personnel. e. Operations. f. Others.
Chapter 13 Air Traffic Control Management Training	
13-1. Administration.	
13-2. Facility Reports.	
13-3. Operational Hazard Reports.	
13-4. Accidents or Incidents.	
13-5. Flight Inspection Procedures.	
13-6. Training Records and Training Programs.	
13-7. Administration of Facility Qualification and Rating Program.	
13-8. Army Regulations.	
13-9. Letters of Agreement, and Facility Memorandum.	

ABBREVIATED OUTLINE FOR A TACTICAL FACILITY TRAINING MANUAL

B-1.   Tactical ATC facilities may follow the abbreviated training manual outlined in table B-2, page B-9. These manuals will be developed when deployments are 30 days or longer so a controller can be trained and receive a rating at an airfield or heliport.

Table B-2. Abbreviated training manual outline

Chapter 1 Tactical Facility Indoctrination
1-1. Mission.
1-2. Facilities.
1-3. General Description of Associated or Supported Units.
1-4. Training Records.
1-5. Electronic Warfare Training.
1-6. DA Form 3501, DA Form 3502, and DA Form 3503.
Chapter 2 Air Traffic Control Facility Equipment
2-1. Radio Communications Equipment.
2-2. Land-Line Communications Equipment.
2-3. Power Generation Equipment.
2-4. Navigational Equipment.
2-5. Airfield/Heliport Lighting.
2-6. Miscellaneous Equipment.
2-7. Equipment Maintenance.
Chapter 3 Responsibilities
3-1. Control Tower (7A OR AN/MSQ-135).
3-2. Tactical Team (Tactical Terminal Control System [TTCS]).
3-3. GCA Team (71B OR Air Traffic Navigation, Integration, and Coordination System [ATNAVICS].
3-4. Airspace Information Centers (TAIS).
3-5. Supervisor.
Chapter 4 Local Airfield/Heliport and Area Information.
4-1. Airfield/Heliport Location.
4-2. Visibility Restrictions.
4-3. Radio Restrictions.
4-4. Airfield/Heliport Obstructions.
4-5. Traffic Patterns.
4-6. VFR Reporting Points.
4-7. Local Rules and Regulations.
4-8. Weather Reporting Procedures.
Chapter 5 Emergency Equipment and Notification Procedures
5-1. Available Equipment.
5-2. Emergency Notification Procedures.
5-3. Facility Actions.
5-4. Incidents and Accidents.
Chapter 6 Local Area Information
6-1. Class B/C/D/E Airspace.
6-2. Adjacent Class B/C/D/E Airspace.
6-3. Navigational Aids.

Table B-2. Abbreviated training manual outline

6-4. Prominent Obstructions.
6-5. Restricted and Prohibited Areas.
6-6. Adjacent Airfields/Heliports.
Chapter 7 Letters, Memoranda, Reports, and Forms
7-1. Letters of Agreements.
7-2. Facility Memoranda.
7-3. Operational Hazard Reports.
Chapter 8 Flight Plans, Strips, and Markings
8-1. Flight Plans.
8-2. Flight Strips and Markings.
Chapter 9 Instrument Flight Rules and Coordination Procedures
9-1. Approach Procedures.
9-2. Departure Procedures.
9-3. Coordination Procedures.
9-4. Vertical Helicopter Instrument Flight Rules Recovery Procedures.
9-5. Multiple Emergencies Handoff Procedures, Frequency Management, Coordination Procedures, Abbreviated (Short) Approaches, and Sequencing and Separation Standards.
Chapter 10 Secondary Radar
10-1. Components.
10-2. Type of Equipment.
10-3. Code Assignment.
Chapter 11 Radar
11-1. Equipment.
11-2. Minima.
11-3. Use.
Chapter 12 Facility Administration
12-1. Facility Operating Forms.
12-2. Storing of Records.
12-3. Dissemination of Information.
Chapter 13 Air Traffic Control Management Training.
13-1. Administration.
13-2. Facility Reports.
13-3. Operational Hazard Reports.
13-4. Accidents and Incidents.
13-5. Flight Inspection Procedures.
13-6. Training Records and Training Programs.
13-7. Administration of Facility Qualification and Rating Program.
13-8. Army Regulations.
13-9. Letters of Agreements, and Facility Memoranda.
13-10. TERPS.

Appendix C

Theodolite Operations

The accuracy of Theodolite measurements depends on the proper care, setup, and adjustment of the instrument. See the TM or manufacturer's publication for the proper setup, leveling, and sighting of the Theodolite. Personnel must be careful when removing the Theodolite from its carrying case and mounting it onto the tripod. This appendix explains the correct procedures for positioning and orienting the Theodolite. It also includes flight inspection commissioning factors and preventive maintenance measures.

POSITIONING

C-1. The Theodolite will be positioned according to the criteria for the PAR. Figure C-1 depicts how to position the Theodolite, while figures C-2 to C-6, pages C-2 to C-4, depict how it is repositioned. If an aircraft equipped with the automatic flight inspection system is not used for the commissioning inspection, a Theodolite will be used to determine glide angles including lower safety limits. For a PAR facility performance evaluation, the Theodolite is placed as close to the runway as possible. However, it must be placed forward of the runway point of intercept (RPI) to minimize or eliminate the elevation difference between the RPI (touchdown) and the Theodolite location; this difference includes the height of the Theodolite eyepiece. The touchdown reflector is usually abeam the RPI but not always. Aircraft operations will dictate how close to the runway the Theodolite can be located.

Note. The elevation and azimuth scales are graduated in whole degrees, whereas the elevation and azimuth tangent screws are accurate in degrees and tenths of a degree.

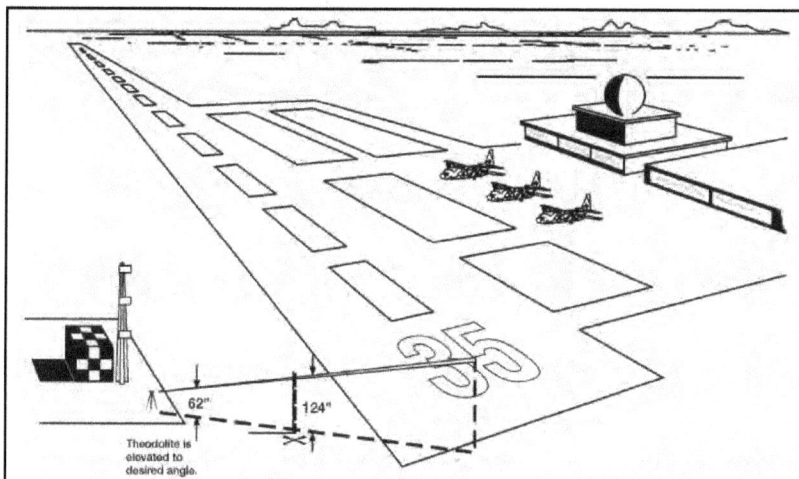

Figure C-1. Theodolite positioned

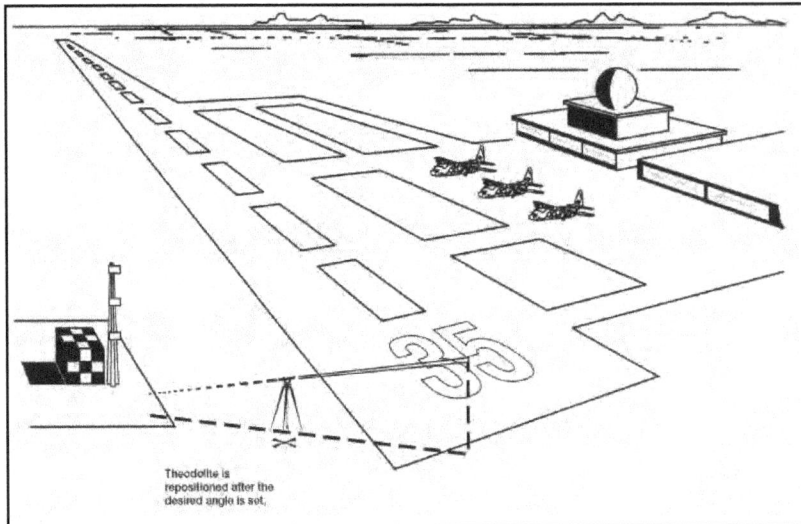

Figure C-2. Desired angle set and a Theodolite repositioned

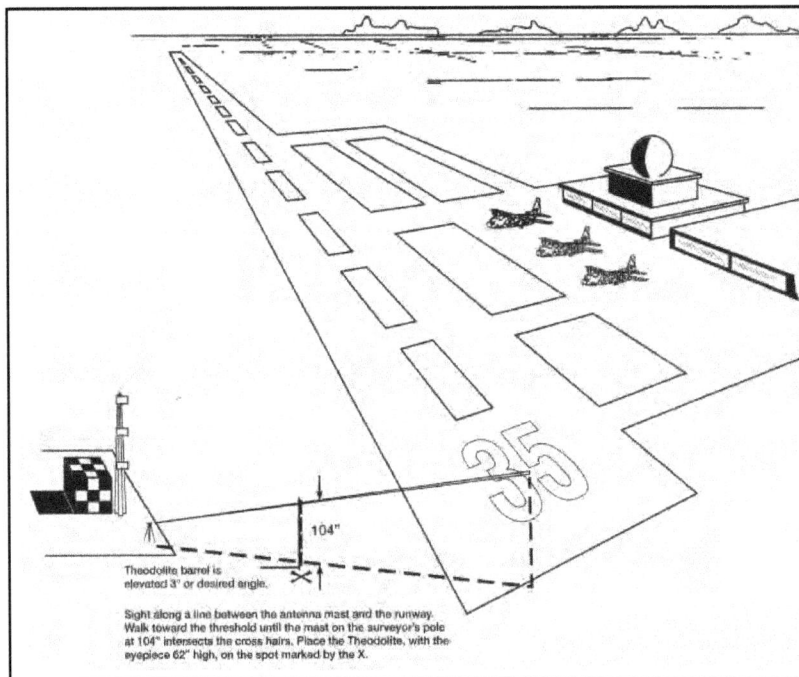

Figure C-3. Theodolite barrel elevated

TC 3-04.81

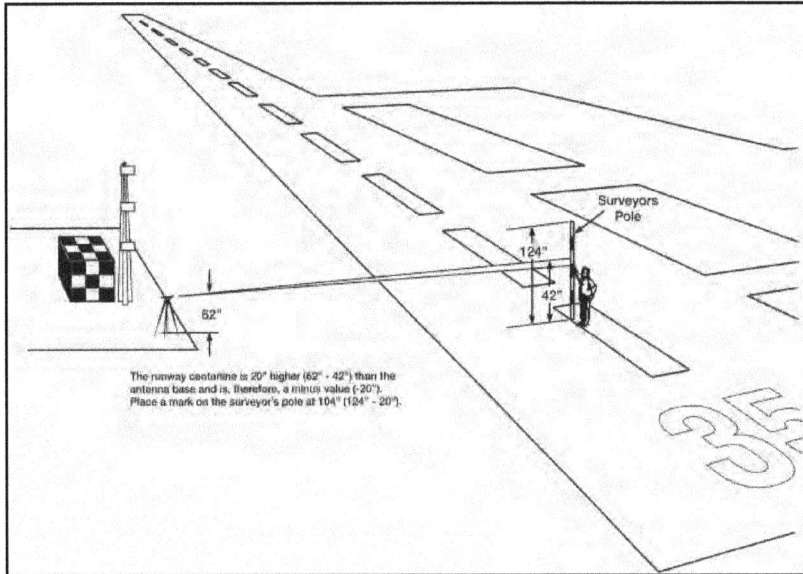

Figure C-4. Adjustment for height differences

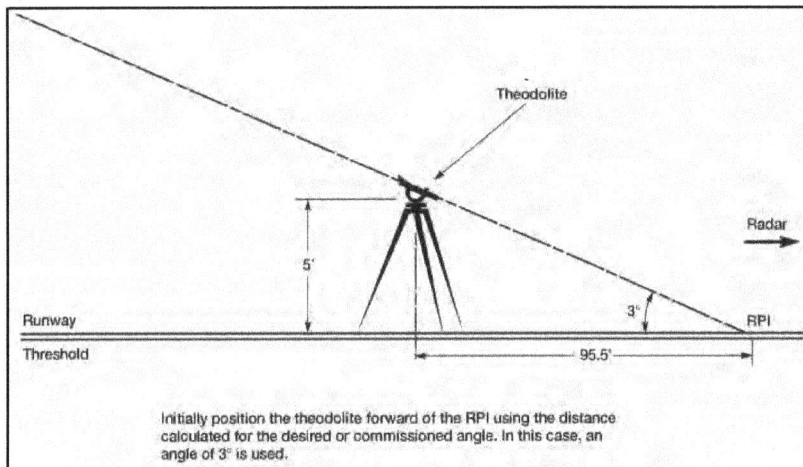

Figure C-5. Theodolite positioned for zero elevation difference

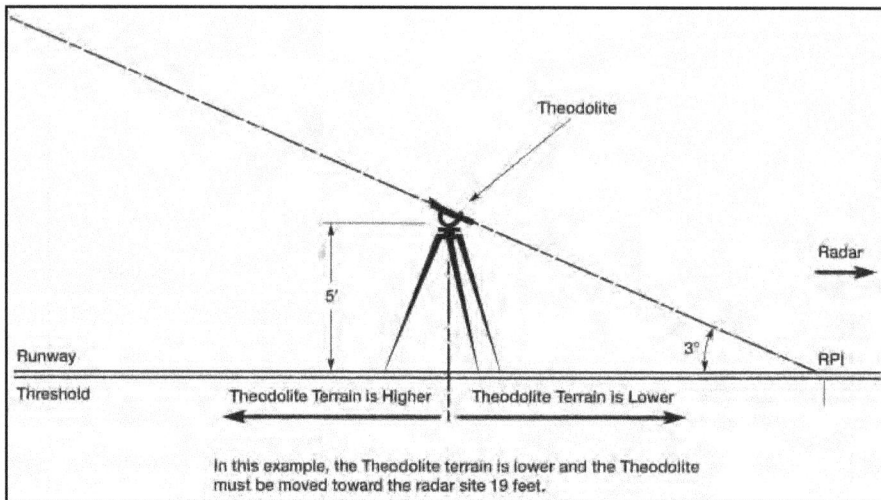

Figure C-6. Theodolite positioned for known elevation difference

ORIENTATION

C-2. The Theodolite is oriented on the actual glide slope angle (for example, 2.5 degrees) on the vertical scale when set up on the observation point and viewing the approach end of the runway. The following steps will orient the Theodolite properly:

- **Step 1.** With a lensatic compass, select a prominent object; record its bearing from the observation point.
- **Step 2.** Place the Theodolite at the observation point.
- **Step 3.** Level the Theodolite.
- **Step 4.** Set the azimuth scale and azimuth scale tangent screw to read the exact azimuth of the established reference point.
- **Step 5.** Loosen the lower clamp and sight the reference point as close to the vertical crosshair as possible.
- **Step 6.** Retighten the lower clamp, and then adjust the slow-motion screw until the vertical crosshair is exactly on the reference point. Make the final adjustment by turning the slow-motion screw clockwise.

Note. Because of the prism arrangement in some Theodolite telescopes, objects viewed through the proper plane may be presented upside down. When the aircraft appears in the bottom half of the scope, it is high. When it appears in the top half, it is low.

FLIGHT CHECK COMMISSIONING FACTORS

C-3. Communications with GCA is essential during a PAR flight inspection. Only on-glide-path calls will be recorded. Calls inside of decision height (DH) will not be recorded. Radar will be capable of detecting an aircraft a minimum of 7.5 nautical miles from touchdown and within the azimuth and elevation sector portrayed on the radarscope.

C-4. The flight inspection is a team effort; therefore, good communications is vital. Aircrew members will continuously advise the Theodolite operator of their intentions. The Theodolite operator should ask questions if there is doubt and request assistance if problems arise.

Note. To evaluate the equipment, it is important to record at least 15 to 20 on-glide-path calls.

C-5. At a minimum two approaches for each runway and one lower safe check are required for commissioning. The lower safe limit is normally 0.5 degree less than the glide path angle (GPA); however, obstacle clearance is all that is required.

C-6. To evaluate bends on the approach, range will be given at least once per mile.

C-7. The Theodolite is placed as close to the runway as possible and forward of the RPI. The locations of the marked reference points are calculated using the formulas shown below. Figure C-7 depicts how to determine zero elevation differences.

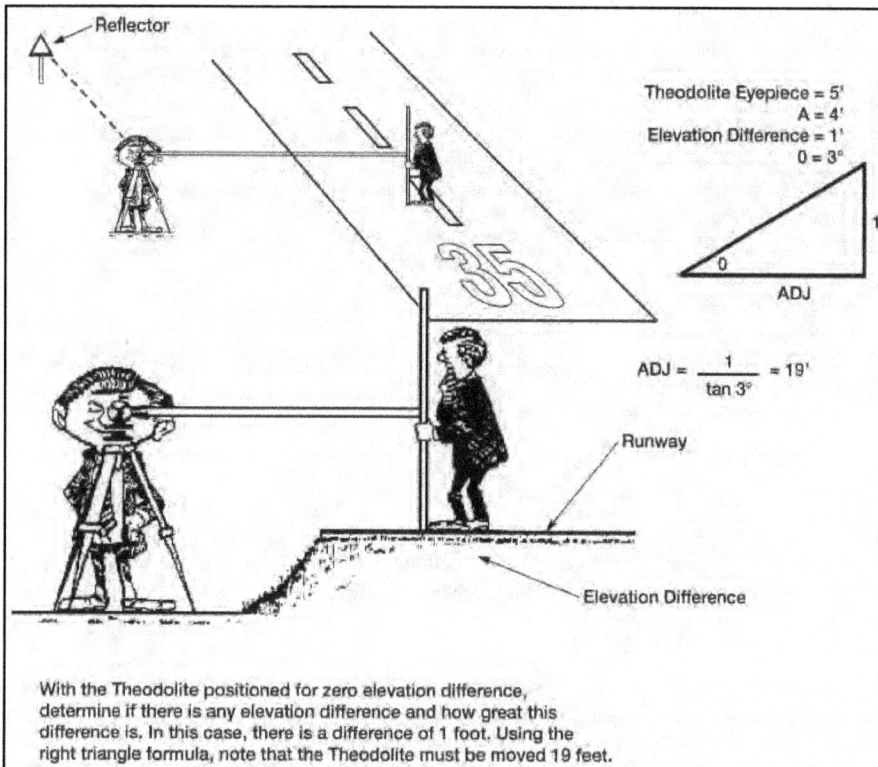

With the Theodolite positioned for zero elevation difference, determine if there is any elevation difference and how great this difference is. In this case, there is a difference of 1 foot. Using the right triangle formula, note that the Theodolite must be moved 19 feet.

Figure C-7. Zero elevation difference calculated

FORMULAS

C-8. The following formulas are used when determining Theodolite positioning:
- Opposite = Adjacent x Tangent; or O = A x T.
- Adjacent = Opposite/Tangent; or A = O/T.
- Tangent = Opposite/Adjacent; or T = O/A.

> ### Example
> 5-foot/3-degree tangent (.0524078) = 95.4 feet. Therefore, the Theodolite would be placed 95.4 feet forward of RPI.

PROBLEMS AND SOLUTIONS

C-9. With a 1,200-foot ceiling and a 3-degree angle, what is the distance? The solution is 1,200/3 degrees (.0524078) = 22897.365/6076.1 = 3.76 nautical miles. This is not acceptable. With a 2,000-foot ceiling and a 3-degree angle, what is the distance? The solution is 2,000/3 degrees (.0524078) = 38162.275/6076.1 = 6.28 nautical miles. This is acceptable.

Radar Course Alignment Check

C-10. At some locations, it may be necessary to use a Theodolite to supplement the pilot's observations, especially when the runway is extremely wide or poorly defined by surrounding terrain. The following steps are performed:

- **Step 1.** Place the Theodolite on the centerline of the runway at a location suitable for operation.

Note. Use optical or mechanical plummets to ensure the Theodolite is precisely placed at the center of the runway.

- **Step 2.** Level the Theodolite.
- **Step 3.** Place a stadia rod on the centerline of the runway at the threshold.

Note. Previously surveyed runways should have a nail/spike installed in the pavement indicating the centerline of the runway at the threshold.

- **Step 4.** Set and calibrate the Theodolite horizontal display for zero degrees with the vertical crosshair centered on the stadia rod and verify horizontal calibration.
- **Step 5.** Have the final controller furnish information as to the aircraft's position relative to the runway centerline.
- **Step 6.** The Theodolite operator will continuously track the aircraft and inform the pilot of the aircraft position relative to the runway centerline.

PREVENTIVE MAINTENANCE

C-11. Theodolite operators must keep the instrument clean and protect it from damage through mishandling or neglect. Listed below are some of the measures operators should take to keep the Theodolite in good condition. Routine care of the instrument includes the following:

- Protect the instrument from dust and foreign matter by covering with the canvas hood while the instrument is left standing unused or packed in the carrying case for transportation.
- Inspect for loose or broken parts after use.
- Take care not to twist off the brass screws when tightening them.
- Occasionally wipe off the instrument (except for the telescope lens) with a soft, clean cloth.
- Clean the telescope lens with a clean, soft-haired brush, and then wipe clean with special lens tissue.
- If lens tissue is not available, use either a soft facial tissue or a linen handkerchief that has been washed several times. Be careful not to wipe the lens because the lens surface is easily ruined by scratches.
- If it is necessary to clean the inside surface of the lens, unscrew the object lens barrel but do not remove the lens from the barrel.

- If it is necessary to clean the lens, unscrew the eyepiece but be careful not to touch the fragile crosshairs that are exposed.
- If the silvered surfaces of the tangent screw drum scales and the elevation scale become tarnished from contact with the operator's hands, remove the oxidation by rubbing the surfaces with bone black or by applying a few drops of clock oil. Leave the oil on the surfaces overnight, and then wipe the surfaces clean with a soft cloth. Leave a very thin film of oil on the surfaces to protect them. (The azimuth scale is covered and does not require routine cleaning.)
- Replace in carrying case when not in use.
- Remove the sunshade from the telescope and place on the baseboard with the long side away from the center of the baseboard. Place the dust cap over the object lens of the telescope. Fold the long sights flat down.
- Disengage the elevation tangent screw, and swing the telescope upside down so the sights are on the bottom of the tube. Do this carefully so that long rear right does not strike the transverse level. Point the object lens up at approximately a 30-degree angle. Leave the tangent screw disengaged.
- Disengage the azimuth tangent screw. Unscrew and remove the Theodolite from the tripod head, keeping one hand on the instrument at all times. Cradle the instrument against the body with the forearm while replacing the baseboard on the Theodolite by turning it clockwise.
- Rotate the Theodolite until the rear end of the baseboard slides into the case and the wood blocks face outward. Reposition the telescope slightly, as necessary, to permit the baseboard to slide all the way in and the door on the carrying case to shut.
- Replace the screw cap protecting the treads of the tripod heads.

This page intentionally left blank.

Appendix D

Approach Procedures

This appendix contains criteria and guidance on TERPS and preparing MVACs.

TERMINAL APPROACH PROCEDURES

D-1. TERPS is the process of developing approach procedures based on location, obstacles, airspace, air traffic flow, procedures desired, and aircraft performance IAW FAAO 8200.1, FAAO 8260.15, FAAO 8260.3, and this publication.

D-2. Under national agreement (NAT) 127, the FAA provides worldwide TERPS service for the U.S. Army. This service will include original procedure development and amendments as necessary (to include procedures for contingency/exercise operations), facility and procedure flight inspection service, site evaluation of proposed NAVAIDs (reimbursable service), and procedure processing. Request for procedure development will be forwarded to the FAA through USAASA, United States Army Aeronautical Services Detachment-Europe (USAASD-E).

REQUIRED INFORMATION FOR PROCEDURE DEVELOPMENT

D-3. In order to construct instrument approach procedures, accurate coordinates are required. As a minimum, the plans or drawings must contain survey data required for design of instrument approach procedures all distances (in feet) and elevations (in mean sea level) in hundredths of a foot; all latitude and longitude are in hundredths of a second and assumed to be in world grid system–84/North American Datum–83 unless otherwise noted. Do not round values. Data requirements should be compiled in memorandum format to accompany the TERPS packet airfield/heliport. Data requirements are:

- For all runway/helicopter pad/landing zone instrument procedures:
  - Data contained in the airfield obstruction chart survey (if one has been conducted).
  - Airport MAGVAR and year.
  - Type of runway/pad/zone surface and condition.
  - Type of runway/pad/zone markings and condition.
  - Type of runway/pad/zone lights.
  - Type and length of approach lights. If displaced runway threshold operations are in effect, do the approach lights extend to the displaced runway threshold?
- Identify which agency provides the airport weather and state whether the weather station operates 24 hours. If not, identify who will provide airport weather and how it will be reported to ATC facilities:
  - Altimeter source for the approach.
  - Category (A/B/C/D/E) and type of aircraft/helicopter to fly the procedure (critical design aircraft) and FAAO 8260.3 wheel height group classification for procedure.
  - Type of procedure(s) required.
  - Circling authorized? If yes, list any circling area restrictions.
  - Suggested missed approach routes and altitudes.
  - MVAC required when vectoring is provided by the facility.
  - Suggested FAF altitude.
  - SUA near airfield.
  - Suggested final approach courses.
  - Airspace for the approach control facility and other nearby ATC facilities.
- For ground-base non-precision instrument procedures:

- Data contained on DA Form 3501-1 (Precision Approach Radar [GCA] Data).
- Type of radar.
- Desired GPA/glideslope.
- Facility identifier (ICAO).
- Remote monitor location (radar facility, tower, base operations, police station, and so on).
- Facility operating hours (times in Zulu); if fewer than 24 hours, what are the operating hours?
- For PAR:
  - Data contained in the PAR (GC approach) data.
  - Desired GPA.
- For ASR:
  - Type of radar.
  - Data contained on DA Form 3501-1.
- Any obstacle data available.
- The following general TERPS information:
  - Category (A/B/C/D/E) and type of aircraft/helicopter to fly the procedure.
  - Type of procedure required.
  - Circling authorized? If yes, list any circling area restrictions.
  - Suggested missed approach routes and altitudes.
  - MVAC required when vectoring is provided by the facility.
  - Suggested FAF altitude.
  - SUA near the airport.
  - Suggested final approach courses.
  - Airspace for the approach control facility and other nearby ATC facilities.

D-4. Table D-1 provides information on developing procedures for aircraft categories based on minimum runway length:

Table D-1. Aircraft category procedures

Category	Length
E	As coordinated with Commander, USAASA/USAASD-E
D	4,000 ft or greater
A,B,&C	Less than 4,000 ft
Copter	Any Length

Note. Restrict the minimum height above landing (HAL)/HAT of copter PAR procedures to 200 ft. HAT/HAL values less than 200 ft require Commander, USAASA approval.

D-5. Are any photographs of airport (surface, air or satellite); maps (scale 1:24000 through 1:500000); airport layout plans; or civil engineering master tabs available? If so, provide copies. If required information is not provided, the best decision for the design of the procedure will be made with the available survey information provided.

Contingency/Exercise Operations

D-6. Commander, USAASA/USAASD-E must provide appendix one data requirements to the flight inspection central operations team, AJW-335. Emergency, contingency, and exercise procedures are intended for loose-leaf publication and documented on FAA Form 8260-7 (Special Instrument Approach Procedures). HQ, USAASA is responsible for coordinating charting requirements.

D-7. Any photographs of the airport (surface, air, or satellite), maps (scale 1:24,000 through 1:500,000), airport layout plans or civil engineering master tabs must also be provided if available.

D-8. If required information is not provided, the National Flight Procedures Office (NFPO) will determine the best procedure design based on the airfield/heliport data requirements for instrument approach procedures.

TERMINAL INSTRUMENT PROCEDURES PACKETS

D-9. A TERPS packet will be completed each time a NAVAID is installed for operational use. Instructions for completing each form in the packet are provided for clarification and guidance.

D-10. When the radar system is deployed (VFR training/military use only), the packet sent to the DAR/USAASD-E/ATSCOM will include the following documents:
- MVAC drawn on two copies of the appropriate sectionals.
- FAA Form 7210-9 (En Route Minimum IFR Altitude/Minimum Vectoring Altitude Obstruction Document).
- DA Form 3501-1.

D-11. DA Form 3501-1 is used to distribute information on tactical NAVAIDs to supported units. The form should be completed and distributed early enough in the mission that it is included in the aviation unit's APG.

D-12. DA Form 3501-1 (figure D-1, page D-4) contains all the information required by USAASA/USAASD-E to have a terminal instrument approach procedure developed. When ASR approaches are requested, the information contained in the PAR data sheet for the specific radar will be used to develop the procedure.

D-13. Instructions for completing DA Form 3501-1 are as follows:
- **Item 1.** List the name of the airport/airfield/facility.
- **Item 2 through 5.** Self-explanatory.
- **Item 6a through 6d.** Provide the coordinates (6b and 6c) to the 1/100 second, and elevation (6d) to the 1/100 foot for the items listed in 6a. Numbered items correspond to the diagram in item 9.
- **Item 7.** Information needed for 7a through 7o corresponds to the items in section 6and the diagram in item 9. Provide the distance, to 1/100 foot, for each of the following:
  - **7a:** Provide the distance from the point on the runway centerline at landing threshold to the point on runway centerline at ground point of intercept (GPI)
  - **7b:** Provide the distance from the point on the runway centerline at landing threshold to the point on runway centerline abeam PAR antenna.
  - **7c:** Provide the distance from the point on the runway centerline at landing threshold to the point on runway centerline at departure end of runway.
  - **7d:** Provide the distance from the point on the runway centerline abeam PAR antenna to point on runway centerline at GPI.
  - **7e:** Provide the distance from the point on runway centerline abeam PAR antenna to the PAR antenna.
  - **7f:** Provide the distance from the PAR antenna to the point on the runway centerline at GPI.
  - **7g and 7h:** Provide the distance from the runway centerline at landing threshold to the touchdown reflector.
  - **7i:** If applicable, provide the distance from the point on runway centerline at landing threshold to the point on runway centerline for a displaced threshold.
  - **7j:** if applicable, provide the distance from the point on runway centerline at GPI to the point on runway centerline at displaced threshold..
  - **7k:** Provide runway heading (magnetic).
  - **7l:** Provide magnetic variation of the airfield.
  - **7m:** Provide the glide path angle.

- ■ **7n:** Provide the touchdown crossing height.
- ■ **7o:** Provide the decision altitude.
- **Item 8.** Provide the missed approach procedure.
- **Item 9.** The diagram is provided for reference and requires no input from the controller.
- **Items 10 and 11.** Self-explanatory.

PRECISION APPROACH RADAR (GCA) DATA
For use of this form see TC 3-04.81; the proponent agency is TRADOC.

1. AIRPORT NAME			2. CITY	
Ut Nebit Dag			Balkanabat	

3. STATE/PROVINCE		4. COUNTRY	5. DATE	
Balkan Province		Turkmenistan	23 May 2008	

6a. PAR COMPONENTS AND PERTINENT RUNWAY DATA (Numbered items correspond to the diagram in item 9)	6b. LATITUDE	6c. LONGITUDE	6d. ELEVATION
	(1/100 Second)		(1/100th Feet)
(1) Runway / Landing Threshold on centerline.	39 28 36.450N	54 22 45.740E	5.20
(2) Ground Point of Intercept (GPI) on centerline.	39 28 39.845N	54 22 33.094E	5.20
(3) Point on runway centerline closest to PAR antenna.	39 28 51.007N	54 21 51.512E	5.31
(4) Departure End of Runway on centerline.	39 29 02.975N	54 21 06.900E	5.40
(5a/5b) PAR Antenna Right/Left of Runway.	39 28 47.113N	54 21 49.771E	5.53
(6a) Reflector Right of Runway.	39 28 39.345N	54 22 47.034E	5.26
(6b) Reflector Left of Runway.	39 28 33.555N	54 22 44.446E	5.47
(7) Displaced Threshold on centerline.	NA	NA	NA

7. ADDITIONAL SITE INFORMATION (1/100 feet or 1/100 degrees)

a. 1 to 3	b. 1 to 3	c. 1 to 4	d. 3 to 2	e. 3 to 5a or 5b
1049.46	4500	8201.58	3450.54	417
f. 5a or 5b to 2	g. 1 to 6a	h. 1 to 6b	i. 1 to 7	j. 2 to 7
3475.65	310	310	NA	NA
k. RWY HDG (Magnetic)	l. MAGVAR (from TRUE)	m. GPA	n. TCH	o. DA
294.31	5.2 E	3.0	55.0	206

8. MISSED APPROACH

Climb to 3500 then climbing left turn to 3800 direct GLOVE and hold.

9. DIAGRAM

10. FACILITY CHIEF'S NAME, RANK, AND PHONE NUMBER

John J. Doe, SFC, DSN 312-9999

11. FACILITY CHIEF'S SIGNATURE

DA FORM 3501-1, OCT 2010   PREVIOUS EDITIONS ARE OBSOLETE.   APD PE v1.00ES

Figure D-1. DA Form 3501-1, PAR (GCA) data

RADAR (AREA SURVEILLANCE RADAR/PRECISION APPROACH RADAR) SAFETY LIMITS

D-14. These safety limits serve as a minimum standard for controllers to determine if an aircraft can execute a safe approach using the smallest aircraft target. They are established in relation to the azimuth and elevation cursors. The limits begin at the point the aircraft reaches the FAF or intercepts the glide path and ends at the missed approach point (MAP)/DH.

D-15. The following standards will be used when applying the elevation failure procedures of FAA JO 7110.65T, if authorized, on the digital radars currently being fielded such as the ATNAVICS AN/TPN-31 and fixed base precision approach radar (FBPAR) AN/FPN-67 (figure D-2). Once the aircraft begins descent and progresses along the final approach ensure ASR from—

- Five to three miles, the target does not exceed one inch left or right of azimuth cursor.
- Three miles to one mile, the target does not exceed one-half inch left or right of azimuth cursor.
- One mile to the MAP, the target must be touching the azimuth cursor.

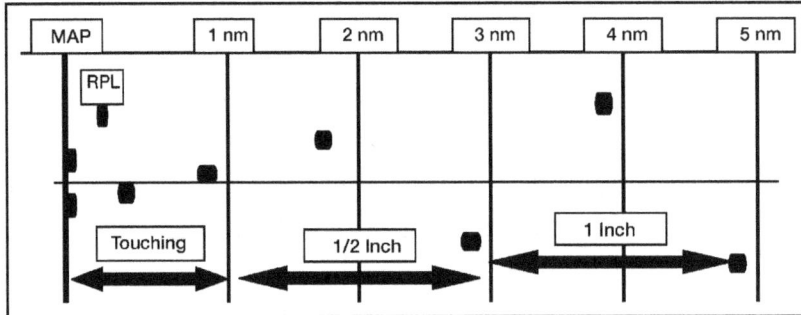

Figure D-2. Radar safety limits (ASR with digital video)

D-16. The following standards will be used during ASR approaches on the older analog radar systems currently in use worldwide such as the TPN 18A, and FPN-40 (authorized when using PAR azimuth to apply the elevation failure procedures of FAA JO 7110.65T) (figure D-3). Once the aircraft begins descent and progresses along the final approach ensure ASR from—

- Five to three miles, the target does not exceed more than two target widths left or right of azimuth cursor.
- Three miles to one mile, the target does not exceed one target width left or right of azimuth cursor.
- One mile to the MAP, the target must be touching the azimuth cursor.

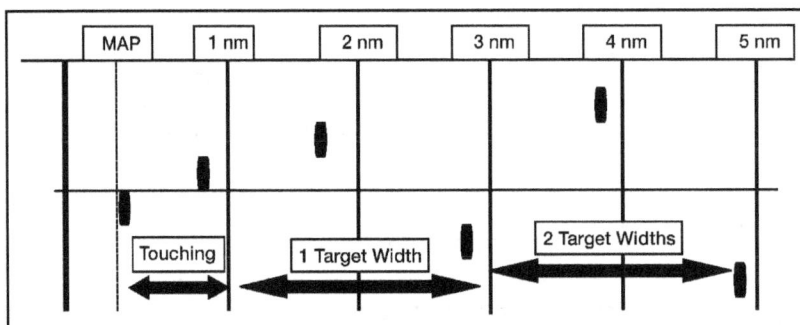

Figure D-3. Radar safety limits (ASR with analog video)

D-17. If the pilot deviates from the final approach course beyond the limits in the previous paragraph, or the pilot does not respond to trend information, apply the procedures outlined in FAA JO 7110.65T.

FLIGHT INSPECTION APPROACHES

D-18. When conducting radar approaches for FI, the pilot will perform a minimum of two approaches to check facility alignment.

D-19. One approach will be conducted under normal conditions requiring numerous glide-path information calls. This approach establishes the facility angle and course alignment. The FI pilot commonly refers to the elevation cursor as the "A" cursor (figure D-4).

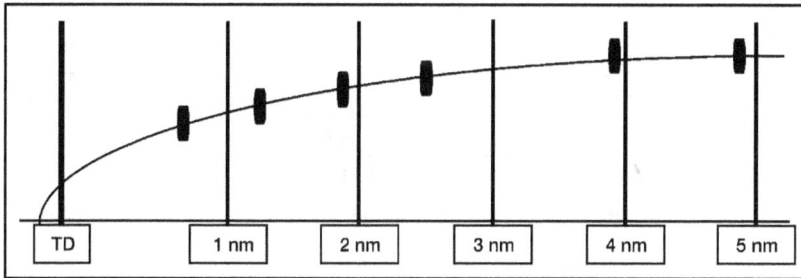

Figure D-4. PAR "A" cursor (on glide path)

D-20. The second approach will be to check the glide-path angle lower safe limits (figures D-6 and D-7, page D-10). The FI pilot will request that the controller use the "B" cursor for the approach (figure D-7). Older analog radar systems such as the FPN 40, TPN-18A do not display a "B" cursor. To execute the lower safe limit approach, use the "A" cursor to apply the following procedures using standard phraseology (figure D-6).

D-21. Descent notification will be issued 10 to 30 seconds prior to the top of the aircraft target touching or an eighth of the target width intercepting the elevation cursor. The aircraft's FAF or descent point will have to be adjusted to compensate for this type of approach.

D-22. When the top of the aircraft target touches the elevation cursor, the aircraft will be considered on-path for the lower safe limits approach using the "A" cursor (figure D-5). Approaches using the "B" cursor are identical to normal PAR glidepath except for the use of the "B" cursor and the phraseology "on-path" (figure D-6, page D-10).

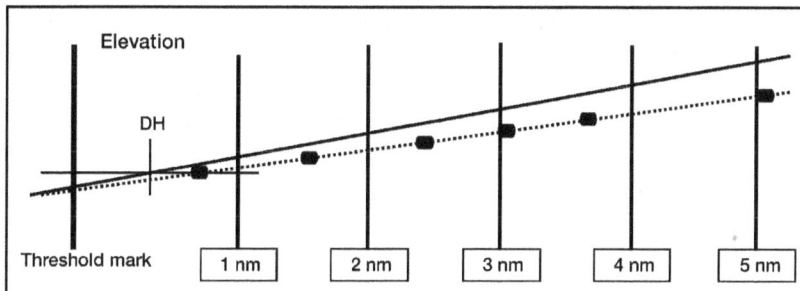

Figure D-5. "A" Cursor lower safe limits (on path)

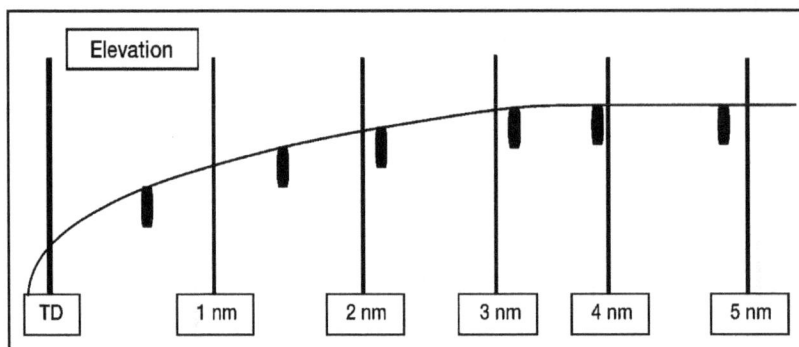

Figure D-6. "B" Cursor lower safe limits (on path)

D-23. Standard course and trend information is issued throughout the approach to maintain the aircraft on glide path.

D-24. FI approaches are normally conducted by the most experienced controller in a facility. This does not preclude familiarizing all controllers with FI procedures, terminology, and maneuvers. These procedures are further outlined in FAAO 8200.1 and will be incorporated in the FTP.

Note. IAW FAAO 8200.1, surveillance approaches will be evaluated using surveillance type radarscopes. Conducting an ASR approach on a PAR display is not acceptable for flight inspection purposes. This does not preclude controllers from exercising the elevation failure procedures of FAA JO 7110.65T

D-25. All radar facility controllers will receive this training, and it will be annotated in the individual training records as "radar safety limits."

D-26. Flight inspection of deployed radar facilities is determined by the mission requirements. See appendix E for installation and NAVAID certification requirements/guidance.

Note. The flight inspector should request operation of the PAR in circular and linear polarization modes. This feature is controllable by the operator of the AN/FPN-40 and the AN/TPN-18A radars. The AN/TPN-31 and AN/FPN-67 radars operate in circular polarization mode only and are not controllable by operators and maintenance personnel.

MINIMUM VECTORING ALTITUDE CHARTS

D-27. To provide controllers with minimum IFR altitudes for radar vectoring, facilities will prepare MVA charts for all ASR systems. Table D-2, page D-11, provides step-by-step instructions for the development of an MVA chart.

Table D-2. Instructions for the development of an MVAC

Step	Requirement	Reference
1	Identify MVA coverage area and buffer.	FAA JO 7210.3, Para 3-9-1, a. FAAO 8260.19, Para 361. TC 3-04.81, App D.
2	Gather charts/maps for coverage area in hard copy or digital form.	TC 3-04.81, App D.
3	Identify required accuracy of charts/maps.	FAAO 8260.19, App 3, Para 101.
4	Compare AC of charts/maps to required accuracy standard for MVACs.	FAAO 8260.19, Para 272, b, (4) and (5).
5	Plot NAVAID location.	FM 3-25.26, Local SOP.
6	Divide MVA Area for scanning and label.	TC 3-04.81, App D.
7	Sub-divide scanning areas by range and label.	TC 3-04.81, App D.
8	Plot adverse assumption obstacle exempt area based on landing surfaces.	FAAO 8260.19, Para 274, a, (2).
9	Scan for controlling obstructions and document on working copy of FAA Form 7210-9.	FAA JO 7210.3, Para 3-9-2, g.
10	Consult digital obstacle databases or applicable chart updating manual (CHUM/electronic chart updating manual [ECHUM]) for a source with a higher level of obstacle data accuracy.	FAAO 8260.19, Para 273.
11	Determine distance and bearing to each obstruction and document on working copy of FAA Form 7210-9.	FAA JO 7210.3, Para 3-9-2, b, 1. FAA Form 7210-9, Instructions.
12	Enclose obstructions in applicable buffer (3 NM/5 NM).	FAAO 8260.3, Para 1041 and 1045. TC 3-04.81, Appendix D.
Step	Requirement	Reference
13	Identify areas of controlled airspace and document on working copy of FAA Form 7210-9.	FAAO 8260.19, Para 362, c.
14	Determine the MVA applicable to each obstruction or airspace area and document on working copy of FAA Form 7210-9 applying— Accuracy correction. Adverse terrain assumption. Adverse assumption obstacle. Required obstacle clearance (ROC). Vegetation allowance. Allowance for controlled airspace. Round MVA altitudes up to the next 100 ft.	FAA JO 7210.3, Para 3-9-2, c. FAAO 8260.19, Para 272, b, (6). FAAO 8260.19, Para 274, b. FAAO 8260.3, Para 1041 and CFR 95. FAAO 8260.19, Para 362, a. FAAO 8260.19, Para 362, c. FAAO 8260.19, Para 362, d.
15	Identify a separate obstruction clearance altitude when MVA must be established in uncontrolled airspace.	FAA JO 7210.3, Para 3-9-2, d. FAAO 8260.19, Para 362, c.
16	Apply reductions for precipitous terrain if necessary.	FAAO 8260.19, Para 363.
17	Group or isolate obstructions into sectors to obtain an operational advantage and update the working copy of FAA Form 7210-9.	FAA JO 7210.3, Para 3-9-2, b, 3. TC 3-04.81, Appendix D.
18	Label final MVA sectors and update working copy of FAA Form 7210-9.	FAA JO 7210.3, Para 3-9-2, g. FAA Form 7210-9, instructions, local SOP.
19	Prepare 2 copies of the final MVA chart and final FAA Form 7210-9 and forward for approval.	FAA JO 7210.3, Para 3-9-2, h. FAAO 8260.15, Para 13, TC 3-04.81, Appendix D.

D-28. The MVA chart may be drawn on two current 1:100,000 joint operational graphic (JOG) or FAA sectional aeronautical charts. The most current obstruction data for updating an aeronautical chart prior to use is available at the National Geospatial-Intelligence Agency (NGA) ECHUM site (http://164.214.2.62/products/webchum/index.cfm). The chart will be centered on the location of the radar antenna site and segmented into areas as required by the different MVAs. Configuration of the areas and features shown on the chart will vary with local terrain and operational considerations. Figure D-7 is a depiction of an MVA chart.

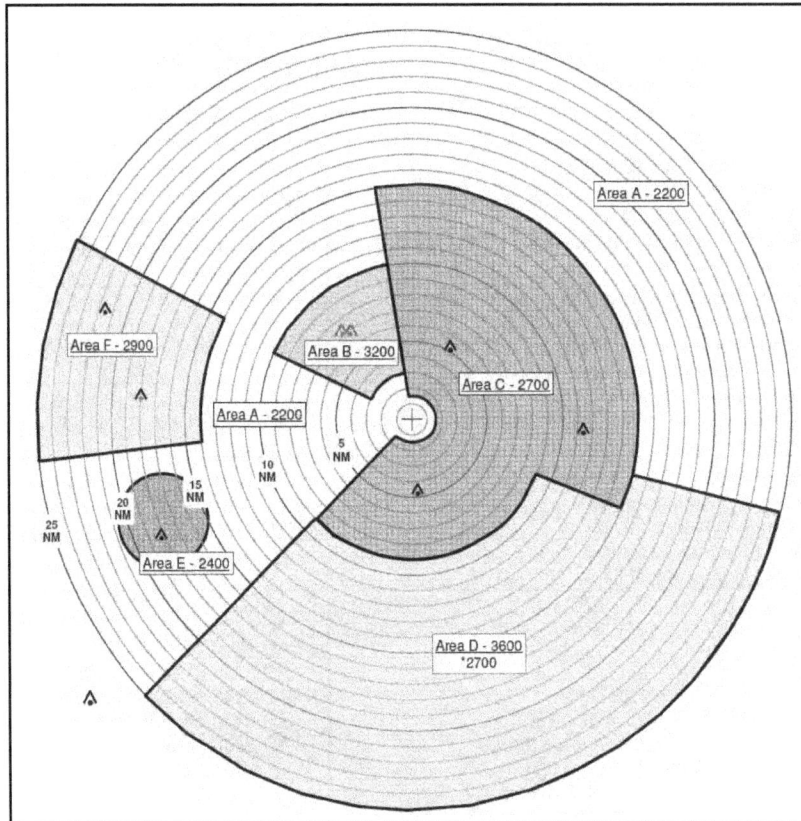

Figure D-7. Sample MVAC

D-29. The MVA on MVACs must be compatible with vectoring altitudes established for associated radar instrument approach procedures. The MVA in each area will be shown, and the controlling obstructions will be documented.

D-30. The name of the facility will be affixed to both charts, and the edition and date will be printed on the obstruction documentation of each MVAC. MVACs will be forwarded for approval. MVA documentation will be submitted using FAA Form 7210-9 as follows:

- FAA Form 7210-9 signed by the facility chief.
- Two copies of the current FAA Form 7210-9 and maps.
- Do not use large pens to mark on the charts or taped/glued labels; this can cover up obstacles.

IDENTIFYING OBSTACLES

D-31. Obstacles (manmade or natural) within 25 nautical miles (at a minimum) of a tactical NAVAID will be identified and annotated on FAA Form 7210-9. This example is completed using non-mountainous terrain ROC of 1000 feet in lieu of mountainous terrain (ROC 2000). The example also shows how the horizon may be broken down into four equal areas of ninety degrees each and ranges in increments of 5 to 10 miles. This makes it easier to scan for obstacles. When obstacles are identified, they will be used to determine the procedure altitudes for the NDB, the MVA, MSA, lowest usable glidepath, and any required adjustments to the MAP. U.S. Army ATS facilities will forward two copies of new or revised MVAC and FAA Form 7210-9 to the appropriate DAR annually for review. For U.S. Army installations outside U.S. territory and not under an FAA regional office, MVAC will be forwarded annually to Commander, USAASA or USAASD-E respective of the area of responsibility.

D-32. Use FAAO 7210.3, chapter three and FAAO 8260.19, chapter three, section seven to prepare the form and document information on charts. Also, see the back of FAA Form 7210-9 for additional instructions.

D-33. Figure D-8 depicts a completed FAA Form 7210-9.

MINIMUM ALTITUDE/MINIMUM VECTORING ALTITUDE OBSTRUCTION DOCUMENTATION

1 Area	2 Controlling Obstruction	3 Location	4 Elevation MSL	5 ROC	6 Roundoff	7 Mt. Terrain Reduction	8 Increase For Airspace	9 Other	10 MVA MIA	11 Remarks
A	Airfield	0/0.0 NM	734	1000	+16	0	0	450	2200	+250 AC +200 AAO
B	Antenna	321/6.80 NM	1915	1000	+35	0	0	250	3200	+250 AC
C	Terrain	95.00/11.40 NM	1044	1000	+6	0	0	450	2700	ATA +250 AC, +200 AAO
D	Airspace	155/10.10 NM	1205	0	+95	0	300	2350	3900	+250 AC Class E at 2100' AGL
	Terrain	155/10.10 NM	1205	1000	+45	0	0	450	*2700	+250 AC +200 AAO
E	Smokestack	244/18.30 NM	1065	1000	+85	0	0	250	2400	+250 AC
F	P-17 Terrain	288/21.50 NM	1390	1000	+60	0	0	450	2900	+250 AC +200 AAO

12. Name of Facility (The following charts are used in this review:) Carl Folsom Radar

Name of Chart	Edition	Date	Name of Chart	Edition	Date
New Orleans Sectional	83	09/2008			
			Approved By		
			Air Traffic Manager Date	FIFO Manager	Date

FAA Form 7210-9 (10-91) (computer generated) (Supersedes FAA Forms 7210-7 and 7210-9) Page 1 of 1

Figure D-8. Completed FAA Form 7210-9

This page intentionally left blank.

Appendix E

Facility and Navigational Aids Equipment Standards

This appendix provides guidance for the standardization of Army ATC and NAVAID facilities at AAFs and AHPs. Tactical facilities will refer to applicable 10/20/30 TMs for installation and operational characteristics of ATS equipment. This appendix is intended to provide the user with information on current, standard ATC/NAVAID structures and equipment. This appendix includes sections on visual air navigation facilities, installation flight-following facilities, physical security, and environmental control of ATC/NAVAID facilities. The major consideration in achieving this purpose is the installation of standard equipment at all ATC and NAVAID facilities in preplanned configurations.

GENERAL

E-1. This section provides the standards for planning new facilities or improving existing ones and applies to all active ACOMs, ARNG, and USAR units having requirements for installation ATC/NAVAID facilities. AR 95-2 sets guidance for establishing, relocating, altering, and terminating these facilities. UFC 3-260-01 provides guidance to assure AAF/AHP facilities are properly planned and constructed. FAAO 8260 series sets terminal instrument approach procedures to be used with all NAVAID planning. UFC 3-535-01 provides guidance and criteria for planning and building Army aviation lighting facilities. This UFC specifies operational procedures for ATC/NAVAID facilities.

ENGINEERING STANDARDS

E-2. Equipment configuration and standards for ATC/NAVAID facilities are contained in appropriate UFC's and engineer change package (ECP). ECPs contain standard design criteria, technical data, and guidance for planning and engineering installation and preparing final detailed engineering installation packages (EIPs). When ECPs apply, they will be used for installation of ATC/NAVAID facilities.

E-3. Equipment configuration and standards are contained in appropriate United States Army information systems command (USAISC) ECP for ATC/NAVAID facilities. EIPs are technical documents that translate validated ATC/NAVAID requirements into final engineering packages and are tailored to the individual sites.

E-4. The ATSCOM will review all ATC/NAVAID ECP or EIPs and changes to assure adherence to findings of ATC requirement surveys, established ATC operational requirements, and equipment configurations. The Department of Army, G-3/5/7, has final authority on matters affecting ATC operations and configuration.

E-5. Integrity of ATC/NAVAID facility layout and equipment configuration of AAF or AHP is maintained through a configuration management (CM) program. Commander, ATSCOM will publish CM policies and procedures to be applied to ATC/NAVAID systems.

E-6. The human engineering factors of military standard (MIL-STD) 1427B, including voice levels and environmental control of air, will be applied to the facilities described in this chapter. Additional criteria are also included in this chapter pertaining to environmental factors/controls to be applied to ATC/NAVAID facilities.

E-7. All ATC/NAVAID facilities on or near an Army installation are required to implement the physical security provisions of AR 190-51 to prevent or reduce loss or damage from theft, espionage, sabotage, and other criminal or disruptive activities.

APPLICATION

E-8. ATC/NAVAID facilities must be upgraded and modernized per AR 95-2. An ATC/NAVAID requirements survey is conducted to analyze and evaluate operational requirements; decide configuration of equipment; and recommend installation termination, alteration, or relocation of ATC/NAVAID facilities required to best support local aviation missions. The engineering site survey will confirm or determine new site location.

E-9. Existing structures are exempt from these standards if they meet the ATC operational needs and Office of the Chief Engineer (OCE) requirement for safety, and conform to the minimum environmental control system criteria specified in appropriate sections of this chapter. When practical and cost effective, existing structures will comply with the provisions of this chapter. Those structures that must be replaced (cannot be economically rehabilitated) will have operational requirements validated under AR 95-2.

E-10. Continued use of existing structures or equipment is determined on a case-by-case basis with consideration for the following:

- Age and condition of the existing equipment and materials.
- Suitability, maintainability, supportability, and reliability (safety) for continued use.
- Cost of replacement and funding.
- Operational requirements for the AAF or AHP in connection with functional requirements of the equipment.
- Availability of new equipment and materials.
- Backup power system requirements.

E-11. Backup power systems in support of ATC facilities are a critical requirement for assuring continuous, reliable operation of these facilities. To prevent serious ATC facility outages (because of primary power interruptions), all ATC facilities (such as ARAC, ATC TWRs, GCA, and those NAVAID facilities) that are published for IFR use will require backup power. Those facilities not published for IFR use may qualify if located in a geographical area considered sensitive to national security or having a history of poor climatic conditions and/or excessive power outages. Training and advisory facilities under certain conditions may also qualify. The use of uninterrupted power supplies (UPS) is required to provide uninterrupted power to equipment during the transfer from primary to back-up power sources. Additionally, UPS has filtering networks that reduce the risk for equipment damage as the result of lightning strikes or power surges. The decision to provide backup power for facilities not published for IFR use will be made on a case-by-case basis and determined during the ATSCOM requirements survey.

E-12. Backup engine generator facilities requires a fuel storage tank with adequate capacity for sustained backup power operation depending on mission requirements and/or availability and dependability of primary power. The average diesel generator consumes fuel at the approximate rate of one gallon per hour for each 10 kilowatt (kw) of generated power. The maximum time required for the generator to assume full load when primary power fails is 15 seconds. The minimum shutdown time for the generator when primary power is restored is 30 minutes.

E-13. Reliable operation of ATC facilities depends on the communications equipment room environmental design. Additional requirements, including backup exhaust systems and environmental control guidance are specified later in this chapter.

E-14. Commissioned NAVAID facilities (NDB), ILS, and terminal (very high) frequency omnidirectional range [TVOR]) will be monitored using equipment specified. NAVAID facilities will be monitored IAW this TC.

E-15. Voice recording of ATC facilities is specified in appropriate sections of this TC. The order of recording priority will be IAW this TC.

E-16. Grounding, bonding, and shielding techniques, including lightning protection of ATC/NAVAID facilities, will be done IAW FAA-STD-019.

E-17. Obstruction lighting for ATC/NAVAID facilities will be designed IAW UFC 3-535-01 and current edition of FAA advisory circular 70/7460-1.

E-18. Proposed new facilities that violate UFC 3-260-01 require a waiver IAW AR 95-2 before the project is approved.

ARMY RADAR APPROACH CONTROL

E-19. An ARAC is an ATC facility, located at a U.S. Army installation that uses surveillance radar (normally collocated with PAR) and air/ground communications equipment. ARAC facilities offer approach control services to aircraft arriving, departing, or transiting the airspace controlled by the facility. Service is available to both civil and military airports located within approach control airspace.

EQUIPMENT GUIDANCE

E-20. The order of priority of channels for voice recording is contained in this TC. In addition to position recording channels, enough channels should be available for discrete frequency recording of emergency and primary frequencies. ARAC facilities require, as a minimum, a 48-channel recorder.

E-21. The ARAC facility is the primary monitor location for NAVAID facilities.

Structural Standard

E-22. Standard drawings have not been made by the OCE because of differences in structural layout at many ARAC facilities. As a minimum, the following should be included when considering design of an ARAC facility:

- Operations (IFR) room.
- Equipment room.
- Ready room.
- Maintenance shop and supply room.
- Offices for chief of maintenance and chief of operations.
- Training room.
- Locker room.
- Latrine.

E-23. Design and layout of an ARAC structure should also include a maximum human engineering effort. ARAC facilities planned for future installations will make the greatest use of the structure drawings of present ARAC facilities. Table E-1, page E-4, lists standard equipment and systems used in ARAC facilities.

Table E-1. Major equipment (ARAC)

Function	Type
Airport surveillance radar	ASR
ATC beacon interrogator	Secondary radar
Automatic radar terminal system	Standard Terminal Automation Replacement System (STARS)
Video mapper	
Flight data entry and printout equipment	FDIO
*Precision approach radar	Installation PAR (AN/FPN-67)
Communications control system	enhanced tower voice switch (ETVS)
Console, ARAC modular	FAA type
Recorder reproducer	DALR as directed by site survey, DVRS, 48 channel
Wind speed and direction indicator	AN/FMQ-13
Receiver-transmitter radio	Single-Channel Ground and Airborne Radio System (SINCGARS)
UHF/VHF/AM transceiver B/U	AN/GRC-171/211
VHF/AM transmitter set	GRT/or CM200

Table E-1. Major equipment (ARAC)

Function	Type
UHF/AM transmitter set	GRT/or CM200
VHF/AM receiver	GRR/or CM200
UHF/AM receiver	GRR/or CM200
Modems	Interfacility data
Digital altimeter indicator system	As directed by site survey
Weather information display system	As directed by site survey
Note. When located on the same airfield, PAR scopes are collocated with the ARAC scopes.	

E-24. The communications equipment room environmental conditions will be 73 ± 2 degrees Fahrenheit dry bulb for summer and winter with relative humidity (RH) 450 ± 5 percent. Thermostats will be set to 730, humidistat to 45 percent.

E-25. Positive space pressure is required to reduce air infiltration.

E-26. Operational areas will be designed to make sure sound levels will not exceed MIL STD-1472D.

Electrical Power Standards

E-27. Minimum needs for full load operation are as follows:

- Power: 60 kw (does not include power for environmental control).
- Voltage: 120/208, ±10 percent, 3 phase, 5 wire.
- Frequency: 60 hertz (Hz) ±5 percent.

E-28. The ARAC facility, including the ARAC operations and communications equipment, lights and their independent environmental control systems, must have backup power with automatic start and load transfer capability if the primary source fails.

ARMY AIR TRAFFIC CONTROL TOWERS

E-29. ATC TWRs are terminal facilities that use air and ground communications, visual signaling, and other devices, and give ATC service to airborne and surface aircraft operating on or near an AAF or AHP.

E-30. TWRs normally have three functional positions: GC, LC, and FD. In some cases, a supervisory position may be necessary.

E-31. When space permits and where applicable, TWRs may also have the GCA and AIC facility located within the TWR structure.

E-32. To accommodate the various ATC functions described above and maintain reasonable flexibility to meet mission needs efficiently and economically, two types of ATC TWR structures have been accepted as standard by the ATSCOM:

- **Type A (high density).** TWR is a permanent structure used primarily at those locations where the mission needs all the functional positions listed above, including GCA and AIC.
- **Type B (low density).** TWR is a permanent structure primarily used at those locations where the mission is less than type A (for example no GCA).

E-33. A type A TWR will have a 24 X 24 cab and a type B TWR will have 20-foot-by-20-foot cab minimum and finished floors for a latrine/break area and a mechanical room. The equipment room, AIC, and GCA, if required, may be in a separate collocated building. This and the height of the TWR will be determined by a requirement survey.

EQUIPMENT GUIDANCE/FACILITY SPECIFICATION

E-34. The order of priority of channels for voice recording is contained in this TC. Besides position recording channels, there should be enough channels for discrete frequency recording of emergency and primary frequencies.

E-35. Table E-2 is a list of the standard equipment used in type A and type B towers.

Table E-2. Major equipment (Type A and Type B TWRs)

Function	Type
Receiver-transmitter radio	SINCGARS
UHF/VHF/AM transceiver B/U	AN/GRC-171/211 or equivalent
VHF/AM transmitter set	GRT/or CM200
UHF/AM transmitter set	GRT/or CM200
VHF/AM receiver	GRR/or CM200
UHF/AM receiver	GRR/or CM200
Communications control system	ETVS or small tower voice switch (STVS).
Recorder/reproducer	DALR; directed by site survey, DVRS, 16 or 48 channel
Wind speed and direction indicator	As directed by site survey
Digital altimeter indicator system	As directed by site survey
Weather information display system	As directed by site survey

E-36. The weather information equipment is operated by the U.S. Air Force weather station. The recommended equipment is a computer display of the airfield observing system from the New Tactical Forecast System (NTFS) or as NTFS is replaced, the ATC portlet available from the joint environmental toolkit.

E-37. In the absence of an ARAC facility, NAVAID facilities will be monitored in the control TWR cab.

E-38. The radio communications equipment for the crash rescue net will be interfaced with the ATC communication system. Purchase, equipment type, and maintenance of crash net equipment are a post responsibility.

E-39. A standard key system will be part of the new ATC communication system (STVS/ETVS) when it is installed.

STRUCTURAL STANDARDS

E-40. The communications equipment room (including GCA room) design environmental conditions for type A and type B TWRs will be 75 ±30 degrees Fahrenheit dry bulb for summer and winter with RH less than 50 percent. Thermostats will be set to the dry-bulb temperature that is currently recommended based on considerations involving energy conservation and economics. Thermostats setting for summer cooling will be 78 to 80 degrees Fahrenheit; winter heating, 65 to 68 degrees Fahrenheit. Positive space pressure is necessary to decrease air infiltration.

E-41. Operational areas (including the GCA/AIC room) will be designed to make sure sound levels will not exceed provisions of MIL-STD-1472F. To enhance safety of flight, TWR cabs must be designed to decrease the high ambient noise generated on AAFs and AHPs, to achieve 98 percent sentence intelligibility with normal noise communication. Maximum ambient cab voice level should be approximate 55 decibel (dB), but it should not exceed 60 dB.

ELECTRICAL POWER STANDARDS

E-42. Minimum needs for full-load operations (power for environmental control not included) are contained in table E-3.

Table E-3. Power standards

Type Tower	Power	Voltage	Frequency
A & B	15 kw	120/208, ±10%, 3 phase, 5 wire or 120/240, ±10%, 1 phase, 4 wire	50 or 60 Hz ±5%

E-43. The control TWR facilities, including the operations and communications equipment, GCA/AIC room, lights, and environmental control systems require backup power with automatic start and load transfer capability.

REMOTE COMMUNICATIONS FACILITY

E-44. A remote communications facility includes an equipment building with associated antenna platform(s). The ground radio equipment used for communications between air traffic controller and aircraft is installed in the building. The remote communications facility can be either a separate transmitter site, receiver site, or both. Transmitter and receiver sites are located a minimum of 1/4 mile to 1 mile apart to reduce or eliminate mutual interference. UHF and VHF multi-couplers and vertically stacked antennas are used to enhance frequency isolation and reduce total number of antennas needed.

Special Provisions

E-45. USAISC (or an appropriate engineering agency) will conduct a study of the electromagnetic current (EMC) to decide adequate separation of transmitting antennas, from each other and from receiving antennas. Location and height of antenna masts should not violate airfield obstruction clearance criteria of UFC 3-260-01.

E-46. Table E-4 lists standard equipment used in remote communications facilities.

Table E-4. Standard equipment

Function	Type
VHF/AM transmitter set*	Ground radio transmitter (GRT)/or CM200
UHF/AM transmitter set*	GRT/or CM200
UHF transmitter**	GRT/or CM200
VHF transmitter**	GRT/or CM200
VHF/AM receiver	GRR/or CM200
UHF/AM receiver	GRR/or CM200
*These items include 50-watt amplifiers and require special justification. **These items require detailed justification for power output of greater than 10 watts.	

STRUCTURAL STANDARDS

E-47. OCE made standard design drawing 38-04-34, including specifications. These plans generally require the local district or facility engineer office to adjust the site before it is constructed, at an approved site.

E-48. The communications equipment room design environmental conditions will be 75 ±3 degrees Fahrenheit dry bulb for summer and winter with RH less than 50 percent. Thermostats will be set to the dry-bulb temperature that is currently recommended based on considerations involving energy conservation and economics. Thermostat setting for summer cooling will be 78 to 80 degrees Fahrenheit; winter heating, 65 to 68 degrees Fahrenheit. Positive space pressure is necessary to decrease air infiltration.

E-49. As a backup to the environmental control system, a thermostatically controlled roof-mounted exhaust unit must be supplied. A motorized damper will be slaved to the exhaust unit control, to control airflow through a filtered, sidewall return-air inlet.

INSTRUMENT LANDING SYSTEM

E-50. The ILS facility consists of a precision, three-element system designed to supply aircraft with alignment, descent, and range data during approach to the runway under adverse weather conditions and poor visibility. The ILS uses solid-state transmitters that send signals through a directional localizer (course), glideslope (rate of descent), marker beacons (approach fix and range) system, and associated monitor equipment.

EQUIPMENT GUIDANCE

E-51. Table E-5 lists the Mark 20 ILS system and its subsystems.

Table E-5. Major equipment – ILS

Function	Type
Instrument Landing System	Mark 20
The FAA/Army standard Mark 20 ILS series equipment is recommended for use at AAFs.	

Structural Standards

E-52. The ILS shelters are environmentally controlled and form an integral part of the ILS facility.

Electrical Power Standards

E-53. The localizer and glideslope facility, including the environmental control system, needs backup power with automatic start and load transfer capability in the event the primary power source fails.

E-54. Backup power for the marker beacons is part of the system and will be supplied by a 24-volt battery capable of 165 ampere-hours, sufficient for continuous operation for one week with transmitter output of 2.5 watts. This does not include exhaust blower or heater.

GROUND-CONTROLLED APPROACH

E-55. The GCA is a radar approach system operated from the ground by ATC personnel transmitting instructions to the pilot by radio. The approach may be conducted with ASR, PAR, or a combination of both.

EQUIPMENT GUIDANCE

E-56. Table E-6 lists standard equipment and (or) systems used in a GCA facility.

Table E-6. Major equipment – GCA

Function	Type
Radar system	AN/FPN-67
Note. The AN/FPN-67 comes with a built in simulator. Communication console (ETVS) and meteorological display console are also included. UHF, VHF, and VHF/FM radios are collocated with the control TWR radios and are the same as those listed in table E-2.	

Structural Standards

E-57. The radar receiver/transmitter group (R/T) is weatherproof and does not need a dome. Layout of a concrete pad will be as per system design. GCA indicators are installed in the radar room.

E-58. The shelter is environmentally equipped.

Electrical Power Standards

E-59. Minimum requirements for full-load operation are contained in tables E-7 and E-8.

Table E-7. Electrical power standards (GCA)

Facility	Power	Voltage	Frequency
Indicator site	2 kiwi*	120/240, ±10%, 1 phase, 4 wire	50 or 60 Hz ± 5%
Receiver-transmitter site	9 kiwi**	120/240, ±10%, 1 phase, 4 wire	50 or 60 Hz ± 5%
Notes. *Does not include power requirements for environmental control. **Includes 4 kiwi for S-70/G shelter environmental equipment and interrogator group.			

E-60. The input power requires the following regulation, which generally needs an external voltage regulator and separate low-pass filter for effective suppression of ripple voltage.

Table E-8. Power conditioning requirements

Voltage Regulation	Ripple Voltage	Harmonics
±3 volts	Maximum response time, 100 milliseconds	Maximum 3%

E-61. If separate power sources are used to supply the system indicator site and receiver-transmitter site, the power sources need not be synchronized.

E-62. The GCA facility, including the radar room, lights, and environmental control systems must have backup power with automatic start and load transfer capability if primary power fails.

TERMINAL (VERY HIGH) FREQUENCY OMNIDIRECTIONAL-RANGE

E-63. A TVOR facility is a ground-based electronic NAVAID transmitting VHF navigation signals, 360 degrees in azimuth, oriented from magnetic north. The facility is used for air navigation. The TVOR periodically identifies itself by mores code and may have an additional voice identification feature. Voice feature may be used by ATC for transmitting routine information to pilots by way of an ATIS recorder.

E-64. The ATIS system (not part of the TVOR facility) is physically located in the control TWR equipment room with a remote control unit in the control TWR cab. Connection to the TVOR or a discrete transmitter is by telephone lines.

EQUIPMENT GUIDANCE

E-65. Table E-9 lists standard equipment and (or) system.

Table E-9. Major equipment – TVOR

Function	Type
TVOR	AN/FRN-41(V)1, AN/FRN-41(V)2, AN/FRN-41(V)T1
ATIS	AN/GSH-45
Notes. The (V) 1 configuration is complete with 21-foot shelter (S 597/FRN-41). The (V) 2 configuration is the same as (V) 1, less the shelter. The AN/FRN-41(V) T1 is a trainer configuration, which uses all of the radio transmitting set AN/FRN-41(V) except for antenna AN 3323/FRN-41 and RF detector DT-603/FRN-41. The ATIS is located at designated control TWRs with voice transmission by way of the TVOR facility. A TVOR is not required for an ATIS; it can have a stand-alone transmitter.	

Structural Standards

E-66. The TVOR transmitter group is supplied with a shelter. Support construction consists mainly of a concrete base to support the shelter. The local district or facility engineers will help in design and construction of the TVOR support base.

E-67. Each sheltered TVOR comes complete with an environmental control unit. A backup environmental system is not supplied.

E-68. The TVOR shelter design environmental conditions for existing buildings will be 75 ± 3 degrees Fahrenheit dry bulb for summer and winter with RH less the 50 percent. Thermostats will be set to the dry-bulb temperature that is currently recommended based on considerations involving energy conservation and economics. Summer cooling will be 78 to 80 degrees Fahrenheit; winter heating, 65 to 68 degrees Fahrenheit.

Electrical Power Standards

E-69. Table E-10 outlines the minimum requirements for full-load operation.

Table E-10. Electrical power standards

Facility	Power	Voltage	Frequency
TVOR	10 kw	120/240, ±10%, 1 phase, 4 wire	50 or 60 Hz ±5%

E-70. The TVOR facility, including lights and the environmental control, needs backup power with automatic start and load transfer capability if the primary power source fails.

NON-DIRECTIONAL BEACON

E-71. The NDB facility transmits a non-directional signal whereby the pilot of a suitably equipped aircraft can determine the bearing to or from the facility. The facility operates in the frequency range of 200 to 535.5 kHz and transmits a continuous carrier with 1020 Hz modulation keyed to give identification.

EQUIPMENT GUIDANCE

E-72. Table E-11 is a list of standard equipment used at NDB facilities.

Table E-11. Major equipment – NDB

Function	Type
Non-directional beacon	FA-9782
Antenna tuning unit	FA-9782
Monitor receiver	R-2176/FRN
Shelter	FAA Mark 1D or Federal Aviation Administration-equipment (FAA-E)-2221B equal

Structural Standards

E-73. FAA design shelter, type Mark 1D marker beacon transportable shelter or equal will be used as the NDB shelter. Shelter specifications are in FAA-E-221B.

E-74. The environmental control system will consist of a filtered power ventilation system with thermostatic control.

Electrical Power Standards

E-75. Minimum requirements for full-load operation are listed in table E-12.

Table E-12. Electrical power standards

Facility	Power	Voltage	Frequency
NDB	1 kw*	120/240, ±10%, 1 phase, 4 wire	50 or 60 Hz ±5%

*Power for environmental control is not included.

E-76. The NDB transmitter will need battery backup power with automatic load transfer capability if the primary power source fails. Storage batteries capable of operating the transmitter for a minimum of 12 continuous hours are essential.

AIRFIELD ADVISORY OR OPERATIONS FACILITY

GENERAL PROVISIONS

E-77. Airfield or heliport advisory service consists of giving information to arriving and departing aircraft concerning wind direction and speed, preferred runway, altimeter setting, pertinent known traffic and field conditions, airfield taxi routes and traffic patterns, and authorized instrument approach procedures. Airfield or heliport advisory service is at an AAF or AHP not served by a control TWR or during hours the control TWR is not operational. When the TWR is not operational, control of the communications radios is transferred to remote control console located in the airfield or heliport operations room. Advisory facilities at locations not served by a control TWR will have a small multi-channel communication switch.

Special Provisions

E-78. If the control TWR is the NAVAID monitoring facility, the advisory facility will become the alternate NAVAID monitoring facility during hours the control TWR is not in operation.

Equipment Guidance

E-79. Table E-13 is a list of standard equipment used in advisory facilities.

Table E-13. Major equipment

Function	Type
Remote control communication console	STVS, ETVS
Wind speed and direction indicator	AN/FMQ-13
*VHF/FM receiver-transmitter radio	SINCGARS
*UHF transmitter	GRT/or CM200
*VHF transmitter	GRT/or CM200
*VHF receiver	GRR/or CM200
*UHF receiver	GRR/or CM200
* Normally, a part of the control TWR equipment.	

Structural Standards

E-80. Standard structures do not exist for ATC advisory facilities. Adequate space for the electronic equipment with consideration toward maximizing human engineering is necessary.

E-81. Degree of environmental control necessary for a particular site is decided at the time of the site survey and is based on local conditions and technical characteristics of equipment involved.

Electrical Power Standards

E-82. Minimum requirements for full-load operation are listed in table E-14. Backup power is not required for an advisory service.

Table E-14. Electrical power standards for full-load operation

Facility	Power	Voltage	Frequency
Airfield advisory/operations facility	1 kw*	120/240, ±10%, 1 phase, 4 wire	50 or 60 Hz ±5%
*Power for environmental control is not included. This power requirement provides for consoles only. Power requirements for remote communications sites are contained in Section IV of this chapter.			

WIND-MEASURING EQUIPMENT

GENERAL PROVISIONS

E-83. Wind measuring set, AN/FMQ-13 or equivalent, determines runway wind velocity in the area where aircraft will be landing or taking off. The wind sensor is located in an area that allows unobstructed wind flow from all directions. The site must not be exposed to wind eddies caused by aircraft (rotor wash, prop wash, or jet blast) and must be accessible for inspection and servicing of the transmitter. Readouts are in the ARAC facility, control TWR cab, GCA room, advisory or operations, and weather facilities. All readouts must be paralleled to the individual runway sensor they are serving. Some airfields and/or heliports may require more than one wind speed, direction sensor, and readout indicator because of the simultaneous use of runways or helipads or peculiar terrain and distance characteristics.

Equipment Guidance

E-84. Table E-15 lists the major standard equipment used at wind measuring facilities.

Table E-15. Major equipment

Function	Type
Wind measuring set	AN/FMQ-13
Note. This item is normally supported and maintained by the U.S. Air Force.	

Structural Standards

E-85. The wind transmitter is self-contained and needs no external structure.

Electrical Power Standards

E-86. Minimum requirements for full-load operation are listed in table E-16.

Table E-16. Electrical power standards

Facility	Power	Voltage	Frequency
Wind measuring set	1 kw	115/230, ±10%, 1 phase, 4 wire	47-63 Hz

E-87. This set will be in the backup power circuitry when such power is otherwise supplied at the airfield.

AIRSPACE INFORMATION CENTER FACILITIES

GENERAL PROVISIONS

E-88. In flight following, the en route progress and/or flight terminations of an aircraft are determined by aircraft position reporting procedures. This includes relaying to aircraft data on known factors affecting a flight such as weather conditions and planned artillery fires and air strikes.

Special Provisions

E-89. A remote communications facility may be provided to minimize radio interference.

Equipment Guidance

E-90. Table E-17 lists the major standard equipment used in flight-following facilities.

Table E-17. Major equipment – installation AIC

Function	Type
VHF/FM receiver-transmitter	SINCGARS
UHF/VHF/AM transceiver B/U	AN/GRC-171/211
VHF transmitter set	GRT/or CM200
UHF transmitter set	GRT/or CM200
VHF receiver	GRR/or CM200
UHF receiver	GRR/or CM200
Recorder/reproducer	DALR as directed by site survey
Communications console	ETVS
Speech security	SINCGARS with integrated communications security (ICOM)
Note. 50-watt amplifiers for transmitters will require special justification.	

Structural Standards

E-91. OCE has not established standard drawing requirements for flight-following facilities. As a minimum, the following floor space requirements (table E-18) should be included when considering design of a facility.

Table E-18. Space and amenity requirements

Function	Operations Room	Maintenance/Equipment Room
AIC	13' by 15' minimum	13' by 15' minimum
Notes. 1. Each facility will have a latrine and comfort station. 2. A remote communication site is essential.		

E-92. The communications equipment room environmental conditions will be 75 ± 3 degrees Fahrenheit dry bulb for summer and winter with RH less than 50 percent. Thermostats will be set to the dry-bulb temperature that is currently recommended, based on considerations involving energy conservation and economics. Thermostat setting for summer cooling will be 78 to 80 degrees Fahrenheit; winter heating, 65 to 68 degrees Fahrenheit.

E-93. Positive space pressure is necessary to reduce air infiltration.

E-94. As a backup to the environmental control system, a thermostatically controlled, roof-mounted exhaust unit must be supplied. A motorized damper will be slaved to the exhaust unit control, to control airflow through a filtered, sidewall exhaust-air inlet.

E-95. Operational areas will be designed to make sure sound levels will not exceed MIL STD-1472F.

Electrical Power Standards

E-96. Minimum requirements for full-load operation are listed in table E-19, page E-13.

Table E-19. Electrical power standards

Facility	Power	Voltage	Frequency
AIC	10 kw	120/240, ±10%, 1 phase, 4 wire	50 or 60 Hz ±5%
Note. Power for environmental control is not included in above requirements.			

E-97. The flight-following facility, including the operations and communications equipment, lights, and environmental control system, must have backup power with automatic start and load transfer capability in the event of a primary power failure.

AIRPORT/AIRFIELD LIGHTING SYSTEMS

GENERAL PROVISIONS

E-98. Lighting systems include all the lights, signs, symbols, markings, and other devices located on or near an airfield to give pilots visual reference to guide aircraft on the ground or in the air. Standard types of runway lighting systems used by the Army include the following.

E-99. At non-precision approach installations, a medium intensity runway lighting system (MIRLS) without approach lights is essential. If more flight guidance is necessary because of operational criteria (such as poor weather conditions) medium intensity approach lighting systems (MALS) may be authorized. Omnidirectional Approach Light Systems (ODALS) is authorized and recommended at AAFs and AHPs servicing predominantly category A or B fixed-wing and/or rotary-wing aircraft, if other approach light systems offer no significant or essential operational advantages.

Note. No approach lights are required.

E-100. Where precision approach light systems are authorized, a High Intensity Runway Lighting System (HIRLS) is used with 1,500-foot Short Approach Lighting System (SALS).

E-101. When longer approach light systems are required to permit significant and required operational advantage, the high intensity approach lighting system F-1 or simplified short approach lighting system (SSALS) with runway alignment indicator lights (RAIL) is used. The latter combination is designated SSALR. Both systems include condenser discharged flashing lights (flasher or RAIL). Flashers or RAIL are physically identical, flashing a brilliant blue-white light in sequence toward the runway. When installed on centerline along the approach light system, the condenser discharged flashing lights are sequence flashers.

E-102. Control systems for runway and approach lighting facilities are an integral part of the control system for all airfield and heliport lighting facilities. This remotely energizes and de-energizes the selected runway and approach lighting systems and remotely controls the brightness of these systems, as needed by the operation of the airfield or heliport. The runway and approach lighting system controls (including rotating beacon, windsock, and wind tee) will be located in, and controlled from, the control TWR cab. Separate intensity controls for runway and approach lighting systems are necessary. Several lighting control options are available depending on the operational requirements.

Manual Remote Control

E-103. The airfield lighting system is manually remote controlled from the control TWR cab; the control TWR can control transfer to operations when the control TWR is not manned.

Pilot Control of Airport Lighting

E-104. Table E-20, page E-14, describes pilot controlled airport lighting.

Table E-20. Pilot controlled airport lighting

Type	Activation	Duration of Lighting
Three-step system	Pilot keys microphone 5 times within 5 seconds Activates lighting at medium intensity Can be adjusted to high or low intensities	15 minutes
Two-step system	Pilot keys microphone 5 times within 5 seconds Can only adjust to medium intensity	15 minutes
One-step system	Pilot keys microphone 5 times within 5 seconds, activating runway lighting.	15 minutes

Table E-20. Pilot controlled airport lighting

	Intensity is not adjustable by pilot; it will be the intensity selected by the controller at the end of the duty day	
Type	*Activation*	*Duration of Lighting*
Photoelectric system	Activated (on/off) by a photoelectric cell; Intensity is determined by controller at the end of each duty day	During the hours of darkness
The lighting system can also be controlled locally at the lighting vault, which is usually located near the runway.		

Photo Electrically Controlled

E-105. Light systems are set at a certain level of brightness by the air traffic controller at the close of business each day. The system is activated (on/off) by a photoelectric cell.

Note. The lighting system can also be controlled locally at the lighting vault, which is usually located near the runway.

EQUIPMENT GUIDANCE

E-106. Table E-21 lists standard visual aids that may be used at AAFs and AHPs.

Table E-21. Major equipment

Function	Type
Rotating beacon (light 24")	UFC 3-535-01
Lighted wind cone (18" D X 8' L)	UFC 3-260-1
Lighted wind tee	UFC 5-535-01/AC 150/5340-21
Visual approach slope indicator (VASI)/precision approach path indicator (PAPI)	*FAA-AC 150/5340-14 *FAA-AC 150/5345-28
Signal light	PTS 44859B
*FAA Advisory Circular	

Structural Standards

E-107. See UFC 3-535-01 for information on supporting structures for visual aids.

Electrical Power Standards

E-108. See UFC 3-535-01 for power requirements.

Engineering Installation Standards

E-109. The installation of visual aids and associated electrical power supplies, control wiring, and construction of mountings will conform to applicable criteria in UFC 3-535-01.

AIR TRAFFIC CONTROL MISSION ESSENTIAL PECULIAR ITEMS

E-110. This section describes items difficult to identify but essential for U.S. Army ATC facilities.

ACOUSTICAL FLOOR COVERING (CARPETING)

E-111. Electro static discharge carpeting is required in operational areas of control TWR, ARAC, GCA, and AIC facilities IAW FAA-STD-019.

BOOKCASE, DESK, FILE CABINET, AND CHALKBOARD

E-112. Table E-22 describes items of furniture included on facility CTA 50-909.

Table E-22. Furniture specifications

Furniture	Location
Bookcase	ATC facilities
Desk	ATC facilities
File cabinet	ATC facilities
Chalkboard	ATC facilities
*High back chairs (2)	ATC TWR
*Note. Approved by DA for inclusion in CTA 50-909.	

FLIGHT PROGRESS STRIPS/STRIP HOLDER

E-113.   Table E-23 describes flight strip holders required at all ATC facilities.

Table E-23. Progress strips/strip holders

ARAC	FAA Form 7230-7.2, NSN 7530-01-449-4250.	Perforated strips, no holder necessary.
Tower	FAA Form 7230-8, NSN 7530-01-449-4239 Strip holder, type 4 NSN 6605-00-485-2879.	
Flight following	FAA Form 7230-21, NSN 7530-01-449-4244 Strip holder, type 5 NSN 6605-00-485-6649.	

HEADSET/MICROPHONE

E-114.   One per controller is essential in all ATC TWRs, GCAs, AICs, and ARACs for the control of air traffic. Reciprocating Counter

E-115.   Hand-hold tally registers are required in all control TWRs. These four-wheeled, registers to 9,999 and comes with reset knob, NSN 6680-00-641-3206.

PORTABLE SIGNAL-LIGHT GUN SUPPORT EQUIPMENT

E-116.   Two signal light guns are required in each control TWR. Battery powered signal light guns that meet FAA specifications FAA-E-2214a are acceptable.

VACUUM CLEANER

E-117.   Authorized by CTA 50-909 for those ATC facilities authorized carpeting.

WINDOW SHADES

E-118.   Window shades are required at all ATC TWRs for use in bright sunlight and snow conditions. Shades must meet FAA specification E-2470b/12520-5 Suggested type is manufactured by Plastic-View ATC, 4584 Runway, Suite B, Simi Valley, California 93063. The number of shades will be determined locally and will be on all sides to reduce rear and side reflections.

BINOCULARS

E-119.   Each TWR is authorized two sets of binoculars.

PHYSICAL SECURITY REQUIREMENTS

E-120.   AR 190-13 requires that a physical security plan be written by the installation commander. As an annex to this security plan, a physical security plan for aviation facilities located on, or close to, an Army installation is essential (AR 190-51).

E-121. Security of aviation facilities includes ATC TWRs, ARACs, flight-following facilities, advisory/operations, remote communications facilities, wind measuring equipment, ILS (excluding marker beacons), and GCA facilities.

STANDARDS FOR AIR TRAFFIC CONTROL AND NAVIGATIONAL AID FACILITIES

E-122. In addition to the provisions of AR 190-51 governing physical security of Army property at unit and installation level, the following requirements apply to ATC and NAVAID facilities:

E-123. Control TWRs and ARAC facilities will have a remotely controlled release lock for the main entrance door with intercom between entrance and supervisor position.

E-124. TVOR facilities located off the confines of the AAF or AHP will be provided a security fence constructed of wood or other non-metallic material. The fence will be a minimum of 150 square feet, 6 feet high, and include vehicle entrance gate and padlock.

E-125. NDB and ILS marker beacon facilities located off the confines of the AAF or AHP will require a chain link fence under AR 190-51, appendix E. The fence will surround the plot to include vertical antenna or lean-ins to flat top antennas.

E-126. Windows and doors of ATC and NAVAID facilities will be secured as defined in AR 190-51, appendix C.

ENVIRONMENTAL CONTROL STANDARDS FOR AIR TRAFFIC CONTROL AND NAVIGATIONAL AID FACILITIES

ENVIRONMENTAL GUIDANCE

E-127. This section provides environmental guidance for planning and designing ATC and NAVAID environmental control systems. Environmental control (conditioned air) is defined as the process of treating air to control, simultaneously, its temperature, humidity, cleanliness, and distribution to meet the requirements of the communications equipment space.

Critical/Noncritical Applicability

E-128. Critical standards are applicable to—
- Communications equipment spaces having equipment or supplies that need close control of space environment to reduce operational and maintenance problems and comply with equipment manufacturer recommendations.
- ARAC facilities.
- Areas that include a combination of critical and noncritical space/equipment.
- Noncritical standards apply to—
  - All other ATC facilities.
  - NAVAID equipment spaces.

Critical/Noncritical Standards

E-129. Standards for critical and noncritical space/equipment are shown in table E-24.

Table E-24. Critical/noncritical environmental control standards

Standard	Critical	Noncritical
1. Air conditioning, heating, ventilation, humidification, dehumidification, vapor barrier, and space ventilation.	Required	
2. Heating, ventilation, and space pressurization.		Required
3. Air conditioning, if within permissive weather zone, as indicated in AR 420-1, chapter five, or MIL-STD-3007.		Required
4. Humidification during heating system season, if within a low humidity area.		Permitted
5. Temperature and humidity design requirements.		
(a.) Outdoor.		
(1) Summer:		
(a) 1 % direct current, 1% FWB*.	Required	
(b) 2 ½ % FDB*, 5% FWB.		Required
(2) Winter: 97 ½ %.	Required	Required
(b.) Interior.		
(1) Summer:		
(a) 73 FDB ± 2 FDB. 45% ± 5% RH*.	Required	
(b) 78 – 80 FDB, 50% ± 5% RH.		
(2) Winter:		
(a) 73 FDB ± 2 FDB. 45% ± 5% RH.	Required	
(b) 65 – 68 FDB when occupied.	Required	
(c) 55 FDB when not occupied.		Required
6. Portable, clock wound, 24-hour chart, temperature/RH recorder.	Required	
7. Ventilation and space pressurization.		
(a.) Equipment-space positive-pressure relative to exterior and adjacent non-equipment spaces.	Required	Required
(b.) Ten CFM* minimum ventilation air per equipment-space occupant.	Required	Required
8. Air filters.		
(a.) Replaceable type with filter air seals and filter gauge.	Required	Required
(b.) Filter efficiency (ASHRAE* STD 52-68).		
(1) Direct outdoor air.		
(a) 5% – 15% pre-filter.	Required	Permitted
(b) Good quality air; 30% – 60% filter.	Required	Required
(c) Poor quality air due to excess dust; 85% – 95% filter.	Required	
(d) Ultra-high or carbon filter.	Required	
(2) Indirect outdoor air (as indicated in paragraph 7c) 30% – 60% filter.	Required	Required
9. Effective vapor barrier on equipment-space walls, floor, subfloor, ceiling, or roof.	Required	
10. Equipment-space sidewall, ceiling, floor, subfloor coating to reduce surface erosion, which contributes to space-dust level.	Required	
11. Weather stripping at doors opening to exterior and adjacent non-equipment spaces.	Required	Required

Table E-24. Critical/noncritical environmental control standards

Standard	Critical	Noncritical
12. Automatic door closures on primary traffic doors opening to exterior and non-equipment spaces.	Required	Required
13. Air locks at primary exterior entrance doors wherever poor quality outdoor air, extreme low/high outdoor temperature, and high humidity are prevalent.	Required	Required
14. Air seals.		
(a.) At equipment-space conduit pipe, air duct, cable, tray, and side wall penetrations.	Required	Required
(b.) Around raised floor penetrations, raised floor perimeter, and interface of raised floor and supporting stringers and pedestal heads.	Required	
(c.) At interface of raised floor and air condition support stand.	Required	
(d.) Required on all modulating air campers to reduce damper air leakage when closed.	Required	Required
15. Raised floor conditioned air supply plenum.		
(a.) RH less than 80%.	Required	
(b.) Plenum air pressure greater than 0.3 inches water gauge to serve communications equipment having floor cutout air inlets at floor and equipment interface.	Required	
(c.) Subfloor drains with cleanout.	Required	
(d.)16 – 18 inch minimum elevation between concrete subfloor and bottom of raised floor support stringers.	Required	
(e.) Insulate air plenum water, drain, and refrigerant lines.	Required	
16. Raised floor, mounted air registers or perforated panel air outlets.	Required	
(a.) Readily relocatable.	Required	
(b.) Volume control damper.	Required	
(c.) Load-bearing strength equal to that of floor panel.	Required	
(d.) Compute quantity (N) of air outlets $N= \dfrac{TR-TE-TC}{Q} + 10\%$ Where: TR = Space-total computed air quantity, CFM. TE = Air quantity required by communication equipment having direct cooling air, supplied through raised floor cutouts within equipment base area. TC = Estimated raised-floor air leakage by way of cable cutouts, and CFM. Q = Recommended air outlet airflow rate, CFM.		Required
17. Equipment-space air-distribution system requires built-in flexibility, which will permit ready air redistribution to satisfy needs of new or relocated equipment.	Required	Required
18. Conditioned air distribution will assure equipment space:		
(a.) "Hot spots" do not occur.	Required	Required
(b.) Space temperature, at elevation, is uniform throughout equipment space.	Required	Required
(c.) Air supply does not short-circuit back to return inlets.	Required	Required
(d.) Return-air path to return-air inlets is minimal.	Required	Required

Table E-24. Critical/noncritical environmental control standards

Standard	Critical	Noncritical
(e.) Equipment enclosure, temperature rise does not exceed 16°F*, or reach equipment temperature cutoff set point.	Required	Required
19. Rate of heat gain per equipment-space occupant.		
(a.) 250 BTU*/hour sensible.	Required	Required
(b.) 200 BTU/hour latent.	Required	Required
20. Rest room, if within equipment-environmental zone, exhaust rate should not exceed 20 CFM per rest room occupant.	Required	Required
21. Vibration noise isolators required between air conditioners/pumps and supports, and at interconnection with piping, conduit, and ductwork.	Required	Required
22. Outside ventilation air damper will close when equipment-space is not occupied.	Required	Required
23. Utilized, computer-room-type air conditioning units with redundancy.	Required	
24. Life-cycle-cost-economic analysis will be used to determine the most effective air conditioning system.	Required	Required
25. Occupied communications equipment-installed-space air conditioners, air-supply outlets, return-air-grille, ductwork sound level will not exceed noise criteria NC-45, MIL-STD 1472F.	Required	Required
26. Inclined, water-gauge manometer is required to indicate raised-floor plenum/equipment-space differential pressure.	Required	
27. Outdoor air cooling (economizer cycle). (a.) Comply with paragraph 8-5.16A and 8-5.16B of MIL-STD-3007. Note. Exceptions to requirements as indicated within paragraph 5.6 of ASHRAE Standard 90-75.		Required
(b.) Economizer activation. • Enthalpy controller whenever humidity is excessive. • Outdoor-air, dry-bulb controller otherwise.		Required
28. Consideration must be given to the use of energy recovery systems to reduce energy requirements.	Required	Required
29. Battery ventilation. Provisions will be made for sufficient diversion and ventilation of gases from battery to prevent accumulation of an explosive mixture. (National electrical code) accumulation of hydrogen gas will not exceed a level of 3% by volume in the room air at anytime. For a maximum of 3% concentration of hydrogen, the minimum amount of exhaust ventilation needed is given by the equation Q = 0.009IN (2). Where -- Q = air (CFM). I = charging current. N = Number of battery cells. (2) = Factor to compensate for inefficiencies in ventilation system. If battery room is air conditioned as part of a general building-wide air conditioning system, the exhaust air from the battery room should not be returned to the air distribution system. The room should have its own exhaust system direct to the outdoors.		

*Notes.
ASHRAE - American Society of Heating, Refrigeration, and Air Conditioning Engineers
BTU - British thermal unit
CFM - Cubic feet per minute
F – Fahrenheit
FDB - Fahrenheit dry bulb
FWB - Fahrenheit wet bulb
RH - Relative humidity

This page intentionally left blank.

Appendix F
Evaluations and Training Records

Evaluations and training records will be managed according to the procedures in this appendix. They are a part of the facility's permanent records and subject to review by authorized personnel or agencies. Entries on all evaluations and training records will be neat and accurate. When practical, entries should be typewritten (computer generated forms may be used); however, entries may be printed in ink. Incorrect entries will not be erased or struck over. When an entry must be corrected, a line will be typed or drawn through the incorrect portion and the correct entry made. The controller correcting the error will initial the correction.

TRAINEE/CONTROLLER EVALUATION

F-1. The DA Form 3479-1, Trainee/Controller Evaluation provides a written evaluation of an individual's training progress or job performance for a specific time while signed on one or more operating positions within a facility. It also provides a means for documenting areas of weakness that need training attention. This form is also used to document observed trends in the controller performance since the last evaluation. Instructions for completing DA Form 3479-1 are outlined in table F-1.

Table F-1. Instructions for completing DA Form 3479-1

Block 1: Facility.	Enter the facility for which the evaluation is being conducted.
Block 2: Positions.	Lines one and two will be used to show the positions evaluated. Separate multiple positions with a comma (LC, GC, and FD). Indicate combined positions with diagonal slash (/) (FD, LC/GC) Identify similar positions with an additional alphanumeric character (FD, GC, LCN, and LCS).
Block 3: Traffic density and conditions.	From the presented choices, select the options, which most correctly indicate the density and condition of traffic compared to the facilities normal load.
Block 4: Demonstrated performance.	Select or manually enter the evaluation results, which most accurately indicate the demonstrated performance and training progress of the trainee/controller when compared against the standard of a rated/full performance level controller using the following standards listed below.
Satisfactory (S).	A selection of "Satisfactory" indicates the trainee/controller is performing at a level that is satisfactory for position qualification or the rating held.
Unsatisfactory (U).	A selection of "Unsatisfactory" indicates that the trainee/controller is not performing at an acceptable level. Examples would be continued errors in the subject area with little or no improvement shown and failure to complete study assignments. Selections of this performance level should not be taken lightly nor considered normal. The evaluator and the trainee should place additional emphasis on training in these areas.
Needs Improvement (NI).	A selection of "Needs Improvement" indicates the trainee/controller is performing at a level less than satisfactory for position qualification or the rating held. As applied to trainees, it should be considered an

Table F-1. Instructions for completing DA Form 3479-1

	extension of a "SATISFACTORY" selection and indicates the trainee is at a level expected at this point in the training program, but still exhibits deficiencies that must be corrected prior to position qualification. A selection of "Needs Improvement" in blocks a-z indicates satisfactory training progress. As applied to rated controllers, it should be considered an extension of an "UNSATISFACTORY" selection and indicates the controller exhibits deficiencies that are unacceptable from a rated/full performance level controller and must be corrected prior to restoring full duties.
Not Applicable (NA).	A selection of "Not Applicable" indicates the evaluation area does not apply to the position evaluated. Areas marked "NA" should be standardized for each position within the facility by the facility chief.
Block 4: Task Evaluated.	Select or manually entered whether the task was evaluated under live traffic conditions or during simulator training.
Block 4a. Separation is ensured.	Provides control instructions or restrictions to ensure separation standards are maintained at all times. Satisfactory if— • Issues appropriate control instructions or restrictions, including speed control, vectoring techniques, and visual separation. • Ensures traffic entering/departing his airspace is not in conflict or about to lose separation. • Obtains specific approval prior to entering another position/facility's area of jurisdiction. • Ensures traffic is not in conflict with other aircraft or vehicular traffic on runway(s) and/or any movement area.
Block 4b. Safety alerts are provided.	Recognizes safety alerts are a first-priority duty along with separation of aircraft, and remains constantly alert for unsafe proximity situations. Satisfactory if— • Informs pilot or appropriate controller when unsafe situation has been observed. • Issues alternate course of action when feasible.
Block 4c. Performs handoffs/pointouts.	Performs handoffs/pointouts correct, and at the appropriate time/position.
Block 4d. Required coordination is performed.	Coordinates all information pertinent to the situation. Ensures personnel receiving the information have all necessary information. Acknowledges all information received on position. Satisfactory if— • Coordinates restrictions or SPINS. • Verifies aircraft/vehicle position and/or altitude at the time of coordination. • Verifies and acknowledges all information exchanges.
Block 4e. Good control judgment is applied.	Issues control instructions or restrictions that are correct. Carefully plans procedures prior to issuing instructions to provide a safe, expeditious traffic flow. Satisfactory if— • Uses correct speed control procedures/techniques. • Applies effective vectoring techniques. • Considers aircraft performance capabilities in control decisions, and demonstrates awareness of aircraft equipment capabilities and limitations that affect ATC instructions.

Table F-1. Instructions for completing DA Form 3479-1

	• Uses control procedures that do not place workload or stress on other controllers/facilities. • Considers subsequent controller requirements. • Does not terminate or activate radar control prematurely. • Informs aircraft and appropriate personnel of significant situations. • Applies effective techniques for taxiing to, from, and crossing runways.
Block 4f. Priority of duties is understood.	Properly prioritizes actions according to their significance in the overall traffic situation. Satisfactory if— • Maintains situational awareness. • Performs duties in the order of their importance. • Applies effective prioritization during operations where anticipated separation is utilized.
Block 4g. Positive control is provided.	Takes command of control situations and does not act in a hesitant or unsure manner. Observes present and considers forecasted traffic to predict if an overload may occur, and takes appropriate action to prevent or lessen the situation. Satisfactory if— • Demonstrates confidence and takes command of control situations. • Maintains positive control during stressful situations. • Recognizes potential overload situations.
Block 4h. Effective traffic flow is maintained.	Takes into account aircraft characteristics and their effect on traffic control. Uses runways and taxiways effectively. Satisfactory if— • Makes effective use of runways and taxiways. • Provides orderly traffic flow with proper aircraft spacing, and avoids use of excessive separation/restrictions. • Considers aircraft characteristics and their effect on traffic flow and properly sequences traffic. • Manages ground traffic effectively and efficiently. • Implements and recovers from holding procedures efficiently. • Adheres to flow control procedures.
Block 4i. Aircraft identity is maintained.	Maintains positive identification during the entire time the aircraft are within the area of responsibility. Satisfactory if— • Uses radar displays to assist in maintaining identity. • Re-identifies aircraft when doubt exists. • Detects errors in aircraft identity. • Employs correct beacon and radar procedures in identifying aircraft. • Maintains awareness of non-radar, untracked, unassociated, or primary targets within delegated airspace. • Remains aware of previously coordinated traffic.
Block 4j. Strip posting is complete/correct.	Posts all required information on strips, and updates as required. Satisfactory if— • Receives flight plans and distributes strips to correct operational positions in a timely manner.

Table F-1. Instructions for completing DA Form 3479-1

	• Posts all required information on strips, and reviews and updates as required. • Posts data in correct area on strips. • Ensures postings are legible. • Detects and corrects strip errors, ensuring actual altitude and route agree with strip information. • Selects appropriate sorting and posting options so the aircraft list is easily referenced for necessary flight information. • Enters all required information into the automated systems and updates as required.
Block 4k. Clearance delivery is complete, correct, and timely.	Transmits/issues clearances in correct format, is specific, and uses correct phraseology. Satisfactory if— • Uses specific terms to describe a fix. • Adheres to read-back procedures. • Adheres to pre-departure clearance (PDC) procedures.
Block 4l. LOAs/directives are adhered to.	Ensures performance of control instructions/duties is incompliance with handbooks, facility procedures, and directives. Satisfactory if— • Adheres to LOA requirements. • Adheres to facility directives and local routing instructions.
Block 4m. Additional services are provided.	Follows the required format for providing navigational assistance, weather information, and traffic advisories. Satisfactory if— • Provides navigational assistance when operational advantage would be gained by pilot or controller. • Provides significant weather information in a timely manner to aircraft and controllers/facilities. • Solicits PIREPs as required. • Adheres to NOTAM, significant meteorological information (SIGMET), and center weather advisory procedures. • Issues complete traffic information in required format for both radar-identified and non radar-identified aircraft as required. • Provides chaff services and bird activity information when necessary.
Block 4n. Rapidly recovers from equipment failures and emergencies.	Handles equipment failures, unusual or nonstandard situations, and emergencies correctly. Satisfactory if— • Handles aircraft emergencies effectively, including radio failures, hijacks, and bomb threats. • Appropriately handles special flight operations, and unusual or nonstandard situations. • Is knowledgeable of available backup equipment and properly transitions to its use.
Block 4o. Scans entire control environment.	Checks assigned control environment and equipment for changes in data or presentation. Satisfactory if— • Monitors equipment, equipment alarms, displays, and status information area for changes in data or presentation. • Scans assigned control environment for potential errors or conflicts and weather-related problems.

Table F-1. Instructions for completing DA Form 3479-1

	• Scans runways for landing, departing, and crossing situations. • Acts rapidly to correct errors. • Recognizes when incorrect information has been passed to aircraft or other positions. • Remains alert for possible problem situations from other controllers/facilities.
Block 4p. Effective working speed is maintained.	Paces control actions and associated tasks at an acceptable rate. Satisfactory if— • During periods of inactivity, reviews and updates pending/current information for familiarity and plans actions to be taken. • Records information at the same time it is received from pilots/controllers/facilities. • Records information at the same time it is issued to pilots/controllers/facilities.
Block 4q. Equipment status information is maintained.	Maintains knowledge of equipment operating status. Satisfactory if— • Determines status of equipment performance. • Reports malfunctions.
Block 4r. Equipment capabilities are utilized/understood.	Uses available equipment to the fullest extent possible. Knowledgeable on capabilities and limitations of equipment. Satisfactory if— • Enters all required data into computer for required area display. • Displays appropriate area of jurisdiction. • Adjusts radar presentation to present best display possible. • Displays appropriate filter limits. • Demonstrates knowledge of required computer entries and ensures entries are complete and correct. • Enters necessary corrections/updates in a timely manner. • Demonstrates knowledge of procedures for operating all equipment. • Is aware of equipment peculiarities.
Block 4s. Functions effectively as a facility team member.	Accepts equal responsibility for the safe and efficient operation of the position. Satisfactory if— • Maintains a spirit of cooperation. • Maintains professional manner. • Is receptive to instructor's/supervisor's/team members' suggestions for improvement of job performance. • Remains calm under stress. • Conveys pertinent information to other team members in a timely manner.
Block 4t. Communication is clear and concise.	Ensures all data passed or received is understood. Satisfactory if— • Demonstrates professional, positive voice. • Demonstrates moderate, rather than too fast or too slow, speech rate.

Table F-1. Instructions for completing DA Form 3479-1

	• Listens carefully and verifies correct information is transmitted and received. • Demonstrates clear pronunciation. • Does not transpose words, numbers, or symbols.
Block 4u. Uses prescribed phraseology.	Uses words and phrases IAW the requirements of the duty being performed. Satisfactory if— • Uses approved procedures, words, phrases, and formats. • Issues specific instructions.
Block 4v. Makes only necessary transmissions.	Transmits required information only by radio or interphone. Satisfactory if— • Uses radio/interphone only when necessary. • Transmits only required information/instructions. • Does not use abusive or profane language. • Does not transmit separate message when it would be more effective to combine information.
Block 4w. Uses appropriate communications method.	Transmits information using the appropriate communications method. Satisfactory if— • Formulates message before transmitter is keyed. • Uses radio/interphone when required.
Block 4x. Relief briefings are complete and accurate.	Ensures duty familiarization and transfer of position responsibility are complete and accurate. Follows approved checklist when exchanging information, and both individuals acknowledge the positive transfer of responsibility. Satisfactory if— • Communicates pertinent status information. • Communicates weather information to relieving specialist as necessary. • Communicates overall traffic situation. • Ensures unresolved questions about the operation of the position are resolved before transfer of responsibility. • When assuming a position, completes the appropriate position log to indicate responsibility for a specific position or combined position.
Block 4y. Facility training program progress.	Satisfactory if -achieves FTP goals in a timely manner.
Block 4z. Blank.	For local use as needed. Use block 5 z for unique facility specific items or an area of extra emphasis.
Block 5: Evaluator Comments.	Evaluator should include comments on areas marked "Needs Improvement" or "Unsatisfactory", as well as positive comments on improved or exceptional areas of the trainee/controller: A statement indicating the time span of the evaluation will be included. The evaluator's will terminate their comments with the acronym "EOS" to indicate "End of Statement". If additional space is needed, a continuation block is provided on the reverse of the first page. Continuation page not required, if not needed.

Table F-1. Instructions for completing DA Form 3479-1

Block 5a: Evaluator's printed name, rank, and position.	Print evaluator's first name MI last name, rank/grade, and abbreviated duty position; (FACF instead of Facility Chief).
Block 5bEvaluator's signature.	Evaluator will sign the form either digitally or otherwise when their comments have been completed.
Block 6: Trainee/controller Comments.	The evaluated trainee/controller will review the form and the evaluator's comments. At a minimum, the trainee/controller will enter whether they "Agree" or "Disagree" with the evaluator's comments or the overall rating. Trainee/controller should utilize the remaining comment area to include any specific disagreements with the evaluator as well as circumstances or irregularities they feel affected the evaluation. The trainee/controller's will terminate their comments with the acronym "EOS" to indicate "End of Statement". Facility personnel may not continue to restrict or otherwise limit the trainee/controllers comments. If additional space is needed, a continuation block is provided on the reverse of the first page. **Continuation page not required if not used.**
Block 6a: Trainee/controller's printed name.	Print trainee/controller First Name MI Last Name. Rank, grade, or position is not necessary for the purpose of the evaluation.
Block 6b: Trainee/controller's signature.	The trainee/controller will sign the form either digitally or otherwise when their comments have been completed. The trainee/controller will NOT sign the form if the Evaluator has not completed all blocks, entered their comments, and signed the evaluation.
Block 7: Training Day/Hours.	Enter Training Day count for controllers in fixed site training programs. Enter Total Position Hours for Tactical Training programs. • Training days will be counted IAW AR 95-2. • Hours will reflect total position time on all positions to date. Include hours up through evaluation period.
Block 8: Type training.	Enter Q for "qualification", P for "proficiency"', or R for "remedial" to define the type of training being evaluated.
Block 9: Date.	The evaluator will enter the date the evaluation was conducted. Dates will be entered in the format DD MMM YY: (07 JAN 12).
Block 10: Overall rating/Reviewer	The overall rating is an indication of trainee/controller performance. The evaluator considers the amount of time a trainee has been on the position and where they would expect a trainee to have progressed at this point as reflected by the FTP schedule and cumulative down time. The evaluator then selects either SAT or UNSAT IAW the following guidance: • If any areas are marked UNSAT in Block 4, Items a-z the overall rating will be UNSAT. • A trainee who has some areas marked SAT and others NEEDS IMPROVEMENT, but none marked UNSAT, could receive a SAT overall rating. This would indicate the trainee/controller is progressing satisfactorily but still needs additional training and experience to reach the PQ level of competency.

Table F-1. Instructions for completing DA Form 3479-1

	As applied to rated controllers the overall rating indicates whether the controller meets the level of proficiency and ability necessary for a rated/full performance level controller at that facility. Therefore, any areas marked NEEDS IMPROVEMENT for a rated controller will result in an overall UNSAT score.
Reviewer.	The reviewer will— • Verify the administrative information on the form. • Review comments of the evaluator and trainee/controller. • Ensure the evaluation was annotated correctly, commented appropriately, and signed by the evaluator. • Ensure the form has been commented, and signed by the trainee/controller. • Initial to the right of the overall rating.

USE

F-2.   DA Form 3479-1 will be completed at the time of the evaluation with the results of the evaluation explained in detail to the trainee. A single evaluation form may be used to evaluate the performance of a trainee/controller at more than one control position.

> *Note.* Proficiency evaluations will not be used while a controller is progressing toward a rating. Evaluations of trainee performance on positions previously position qualified on will be indicated as "Q" Qualification training until the rating is completed.

F-3.   DA Form 3479-1 provides a written evaluation of a controller's ability to perform at a position. It is also used to evaluate a trainee's progress toward becoming PQ. If his proficiency or training progress is not satisfactory, the trainee/controller must be told why and what he must do to improve. This may include study assignments, oral or written tests, or extra time on a position. The facility chief should use the results of trainee/controller evaluations to determine training trends, time extensions, and FTP modifications. DA Form 3479-1 is also used to support reclassification requests.

FREQUENCY

F-4.   Supervisors determine when to conduct trainee/controller evaluations based upon demonstrated performance. Supervisors should conduct evaluations based upon observed trends during training and to emphasis and reinforce training points. As a minimum, these evaluations will be completed as Qualification, Proficiency, or Remedial type evaluations under the following circumstances —

QUALIFICATION

- To document the successful removal of a controller from remedial training.
- To document RL advancement in a tactical facility.
- To document progression in an installation (fixed-site) facility every 14 calendar days while working toward a rating.
- To document the results of live-fly and simulator training events undertaken by trainees in a tactical rating program.
- To document position qualifications and facility ratings.

PROFICIENCY

- To document the reinstatement of a controller who has failed to maintain currency.
- To document the results of annual or biennial skills evaluations.

- To document the results of live-fly and simulator training events undertaken by controllers maintaining proficiency in tactical ratings.
- To document the initial results of unsatisfactory evaluations.

REMEDIAL

- To document the progression of controllers undergoing remedial training.

Note. The 14 calendar day evaluation will include an assessment of proficiency for position(s) the controller has been qualified on as well as an assessment of performance for the position on which the controller is currently training. Separate evaluations for proficiency and qualification are not required while undergoing training. Additionally, the documentation of recommendations for position qualification are not necessary unless deemed appropriate by ATC managers.

F-5. If an evaluation is given outside of the 14 calendar day requirement, or insufficient traffic exists during a live-fly event in a tactical setting, a section III entry is required explaining the reason for the overdue evaluation.

LOSS OF CURRENCY

F-6. Evaluations given to assess proficiency after a loss of currency will be administered on all control positions with direct one-on-one supervision. The evaluation will be conducted under normal traffic conditions and last long enough to provide a reliable performance sample of all duties associated with each position and the facility rating hold. It must be completed satisfactorily before the controller assumes position responsibility without supervision. The evaluation given for a loss of currency may include classroom academics, simulation exercises, written and oral examinations in conjunction with practical evaluations conducted on all positions associated with the facility rating. The ATC/facility chief will determine training requirements necessary for the controller to achieve proficiency. All training conducted for loss of currency will be recorded in sections II and III of DA Form 3479. Evaluations given for a loss of currency will be administered by the facility chief, ATC training supervisor, or SL. The ATC chief may administer the evaluation, if he is facility-rated and current in the facility.

F-7. Remedial training will be noted in sections II and III of DA Form 3479, if additional training is needed to regain proficiency because of an unsatisfactory evaluation. The amount of training devoted to regaining proficiency is determined by the facility chief and will be outlined in section III of DA Form 3479. Individuals unable to regain proficiency will be processed IAW AR 95-2.

RETENTION

F-8. When the reviewing authority signs an evaluation, it will be placed on top of written tests and other evaluations and attached to the right inside portion of DA Form 3479. The results of all evaluations will be entered in section II of the controller's training record. Evaluations will be retained until facility rating and then returned to the controller. Evaluations for facility ratings, loss of currency, no-notice evaluations, or annual or biennial evaluations will be retained for one year or until the next annual or biennial skills evaluation. Figure F-1, page F-10, provides an example of the completed DA Form 3479-1.

TRAINING AND PROFICIENCY RECORD - AIR TRAFFIC CONTROLLER
For use of this form, see TC 3-04.81; the proponent agency is TRADOC.

1. FACILITY	2. POSITIONS
LAWSON AAF	LC

3. TRAFFIC DENSITY and CONDITIONS: ☐ None ☐ Light ☒ Moderate ☐ Heavy ☐ Stable ☐ Fluctuating

4. **DEMONSTRATED PERFORMANCE**
S = Satisfactory; U = Unsatisfactory; NI = Needs Improvement; NA = Not Applicable

TASK EVALUATED	LIVE	SIM	TASK EVALUATED	LIVE	SIM
a. Separation is ensured.	NI		n. Rapidly recovers from equipment failures and emergencies.	NA	
b. Safety Alerts are provided.	NA		o. Scans entire control environment.	U	
c. Performs handoffs/point-outs.	NA		p. Effective working speed is maintained.	S	
d. Required coordination is performed.	S		q. Equipment status information is maintained.	S	
e. Good control judgment is applied.	NI		r. Equipment capabilities are utilized/understood.	S	
f. Priority of duties is understood.	S		s. Functions effectively as a facility team member.	S	
g. Positive control is provided.	S		t. Communication is clear and concise.	S	
h. Effective traffic flow is maintained.	S		u. Uses prescribed phraseology.	S	
i. Aircraft identity is maintained.	S		v. Makes only necessary transmissions.	S	
j. Strip posting is complete/correct.	S		w. Uses appropriate communications method.	S	
k. Clearance delivery is complete/correct/timely.	NA		x. Relief briefings are complete and accurate.	S	
l. LOAs/directives are adhered to.	S		y. Facility training program progress.	NI	
m. Additional services are provided.	S		z. Airfield and airspace knowledge.	S	

5. **EVALUATOR COMMENTS**

Mr. Public was monitored on the LC position for 6 hours. Multiple times during the evaluation Mr. Public failed to scan the landing surface prior to issuing landing clearances to arriving aircraft. Good control judgment was not applied and the separation of aircraft could not be assured. Mr. Public is two weeks behind in FTP academics. One 4 hour simulator training session has been scheduled to improve his performance in these areas. EOS--------------WJ

a. EVALUATOR'S PRINTED NAME, RANK, AND POSITION: William B. Jones, GS-12, Facility Chief
b. EVALUATOR'S SIGNATURE: *William B Jones*

6. **TRAINEE/CONTROLLER COMMENTS**

Concur. I will complete required tests. JP

a. TRAINEE / CONTROLLER'S PRINTED NAME: John Q. Public
b. TRAINEE/CONTROLLER'S SIGNATURE

7. TRNG DAY/HOURS	8. TYPE TRNG	9. DATE	10. OVERALL RATING/REVIEWER
100	Q	2 Jun 1998	UnSatisfactory / WJ

DA FORM 3479-1, OCT 2010 — PREVIOUS EDITIONS ARE OBSOLETE. — Page 1 of 2
APD PE v1.00ES

Figure F-1. Sample DA Form 3479-1

TRAINING AND PROFICENCY RECORDS - AIR TRAFFIC CONTROL

F-9. DA Form 3479 is a permanent and comprehensive record of training, certification, qualification, proficiency, ratings, and ATC duty assignments.

F-10. Each organization will maintain a complete and current DA Form 3479 for all assigned or attached ATC specialists or ATS specialists. DA Form 3479 will be stored and maintained IAW the requirements for ARIMS file 95-2d.

F-11. Pages in DA Form 3479 will be numbered with the section number followed by an incremented page number starting at "0", for example, "2-__" or "2-0" would indicate the first page of section II and "2-5" would indicate the sixth page of section II.

F-12. Abbreviations or contractions used will be IAW AR 25-52, JP 1-02, FAA JO 7340.2, and this publication.

IMPLEMENTATION GUIDANCE FOR DEPARTMENT OF THE ARMY FORM 3479

F-13. DA Form 3479 (JUN 2003) is obsolete effective with the authentication of this publication. Facility chiefs and training supervisors will apply the following guidance to transition from the old forms to the updated forms. Table F-2 provides instructions for the disposition of obsolete forms.

Table F-2. Disposition guidance for obsolete records

Old DA Form 3479	Action Required	New DA Form 3479 Section
I	Transcribe and validate.	Section I
II	Return to controller.	None
III	Retained behind reviewed records on the left side of training records.	Section II
IV	Retained behind reviewed records on the left side of training records.	Section II
V	Retained behind reviewed records on the left side of training records.	Section II
VI	Retained behind reviewed records on the left side of training records.	Section III
VII	Transcribe and validate.	Section IV

F-14. Existing sections III, IV, V will be closed out per existing guidance and will remain in the records folder below the current DA Form 3479 as a historical reference to previous training with all future entries will be recorded on the revised DA Form 3479.

DEPARTMENT OF THE ARMY FORM 3479, SECTION I

F-1. DA Form 3479, section I is used to record units and locations of ATC assignments, duties performed, periods of assignment, ratings, or certifications received, and awards. Figure F-2, page F-13, is an example of a completed DA Form 3479, section I.

F-2. Additional duty position designations may be used based on civilian job descriptions or unit mission provided they do not duplicate those shown above. Standard duty position abbreviations may be used.

F-3. The following instructions aid in completion of this form:
- **Name:** Enter last name, first name, and middle initial of the individual. Use both available lines if needed.

- **ASGN INIT:** enter the assigned operating initials of the individual. This entry may be automated, written in ink, or entered in pencil.
- **Rank:** Enter the standard three-letter rank abbreviation for military personnel, "DAC" for Department of the Army civilians, "LN" for local national non-DOD civilians, and "CIV" for other civilians or contractors. This entry may be automated, written in ink, or entered in pencil.
- **CTO Number:** If applicable, enter the assigned CTO certificate number for the individual.
- **ATCS:** Enter the assigned ATCS number of the individual.
- **Facility Section, Unit of Assignment, Installation or Location:**
  - On the first line, enter the facility or section of assignment.
  - On the second line, enter the unit to which the facility or section is a part.
  - On the third line, enter the installation or location of the facility or section.
  - If the individual changes duty assignments, but the facility, location, or assignment does not change, there is no need to repeat this entry on the next line.
- **Duties Performed:** Enter the current duty assignment of the individual.
- **Date Assigned (To/From):** Using the DD MMM YY format.
- **Applicable Equipment, Certifications or Awards, and Remarks:** Self-explanatory.

TRAINING AND PROFICIENCY RECORD - AIR TRAFFIC CONTROLLER

For use of this form, see TC 3-04.81; the proponent agency is TRADOC.

GENERAL INFORMATION

This form consists of Sections I through IV. It will be used as an authoritative source of information and reference in regard to the individual's training record as an air traffic controller in the United States Army and as a comprehensive training progress report.

SECTION I - ASSIGNMENTS

NAME (Last, First, Middle initial)		ASGD INITIAL	RANK	CTO NUMBER	ATCS NUMBER
Public, John Q.		JP	SSG	123456789	1234

FACILITY or SECTION, UNIT OF ASSIGNMENT, INSTALLATION or LOCATION	DUTIES PERFORMED	DATE ASSIGNED FROM	DATE ASSIGNED TO	APPLICABLE EQUIPMENT, CERTIFICATES or AWARDS, and REMARKS
Tactical Tower Team E Co., 3/2 GSAB Republic of Korea	Trainee	15 Jul 1998	15 Jan 1998	ATCS Rated AN/TSQ-198 AN/TSW-7A
	Controller	15 Jan 1998	14 Jul 1999	
Butts Tower Butts AAF Ft. Carson, CO	Trainee	1 Sep 1999	15 Dec 1999	CTO Rated
	Controller	15 Dec 1999	1 Nov 2000	
	Shift Leader	1 Nov 2000	8 Mar 2001	
GCA Team 1/58th AOB Ft. Rucker, AL	Trainee	1 May 2001	1 Nov 2001	ATCS Rated AN/TPN-31
	Controller	1 Nov 2001	1 Dec 2001	
	Shift Leader	1 Dec 2001	1 May 2002	
	Facility Chief	1 May 2002	30 Nov 2004	
E Co, 1st Training BDE Ft. Jackson, SC	Drill Sergeant	15 Jan 2005	14 Jan 2008	
ADAM/BAE Cell 82nd ABN DIV Ft. Bragg, NC	AC2 NCO	1 Apr 2008		

DA FORM 3479, OCT 2010   PREVIOUS EDITIONS ARE OBSOLETE.   1-___

APD PE v1.00ES

Figure F-2. Sample DA Form 3479, section I

DEPARTMENT OF THE ARMY FORM 3479, SECTION II

F-4.   Section II of DA Form 3479 is used to record training received, tests and examinations, evaluations, and associated results. A blank copy is contained at the end of this publication. Figure F-3, page F-15, illustrates a completed DA Form 3479, section II.

F-5. The following instructions aid in the completion of this form:

- **Subject/Positions/Equipment:**
  - For tests and examinations enter the subject, material, or equipment tested.
  - For controller evaluations enter the facility positions which were evaluated.
  - Use a comma (,) to separate individual positions ("FD, GC").
  - Use a slash (/) to show consolidated or combined positions (for example "FD, GC/LC").
- **Type TRNG:** For controllers, enter "P" for Proficiency, "Q" for Qualification or "R" for Remedial.
- **Date:** Using the DD MMM YY format, enter the date the training, test, or evaluation was completed.
- **Results:** Enter "S" for Satisfactory/Pass/Go or "U" for Unsatisfactory/Fail/No Go.
- **Remarks:** The remarks block is used to record pertinent comments that add further detail to the entry. The following information aids in completing remarks entries:
  - Enter 1R for evaluations.
  - Written tests given.
  - Include total position hours for 1Rs. Annotate tactical position hours and all simulation hours.
  - Record RL assessments and progression.
  - Include other relevant training remarks as necessary.

SECTION II - TRAINING, TESTING, AND EVALUATIONS				
SUBJECT / POSITION / EQUIPMENT	TYPE OF TRAINING	DATE	RESULTS	REMARKS
WX Training	Q	15 Oct 1998	S	USAF
ATC Policies AR 95-2/40-8/40-501	Q	26 Oct 1998	S	Written Test
Army Driver/Operator Training	Q	28 Oct 1998	S	DA 348/OF-346 Issued
FM 3-04.120	Q	29 Oct 1998	S	Written Test
FM 3-52/3-52.1	Q	29 Oct 1998	S	Written Test
LZ/PZ Operations FM 3-21.38	Q	30 Oct 1998	S	Written Test
FAAJO 7110.65 Chpt 1-2	Q	2 Nov 1998	S	Written Test
FAAJO 7110.65 Chpt 3	Q	6 Nov 1998	S	Written Test
Unit SOPs	Q	12 Nov 1998	S	Written Test
Operate NVDs	Q	16 Nov 1998	S	
Phase I Complete	Q	16 Nov 1998	S	1-R, RL-2 Awarded
FD	Q	20 Nov 1998	S	1-R, 6+00hrs Position Training
FAAJO 7110.65 Chpt 7	Q	4 Dec 1998	S	Written Test
FAAJO 7110.65 Chpt 10	Q	6 Dec 1998	S	Written Test
FAAJO 7110.65 Appendix D	Q	7 Dec 1998	S	
FD	Q	7 Jan 1999	S	1-R, 6+00hrs Position Training, PQ FD
GC/LC	Q	7 Jan 1999	S	1-R, 2+00hrs Position Training
GC/LC	Q	11 Jan 1999	S	1-R, Tower Simulator 4+00hrs
GC/LC	Q	12 Jan 1999	S	1-R, Tower Simulator 3+00hrs
TC 3-04.81, Chpt 5-7	Q	12 Jan 1999	S	Written Test
GC/LC	Q	13 Jan 1999	S	1-R, Tower Simulator 7+00hrs
GC/LC	Q	23 Jan 1999	S	1-R, Tower Simulator 6+00hrs
GC/LC	Q	8 Feb 1999	S	1-R, 8+00hrs Position Training
GC/LC	Q	9 Feb 1999	S	1-R, 8+00hrs Position Training, PQ GC
LC	Q	10 Feb 1999	S	1-R, 9+00hrs Position Training
GC/LC	Q	21 Feb 1999	S	1-R, Tower Simulator, 4+00hrs
GC/LC	Q	23 Feb 1999	S	1-R, Tower Simulator, 3+30hrs
FAAJO 7210.3 and 8260.3	Q	25 Feb 1999	S	Written Tests
LC	Q	6 Mar 1999	S	1-R, 6+30hrs Position Training
LC	Q	13 Mar 1999	S	1-R, Tower Simulator 3+00hrs
FD/GC/LC	Q	17 Apr 1999	S	1-R, 9+00hrs Position Training, PQ LC
Pre FAA ATCS	Q	18 Apr 1999	S	Written Test
FAA ATCS	Q	19 Apr 1999	S	Written Test
ATCT Rating, Phase II Complete	Q	19 Apr 1999	S	1-R, RL-1 Awarded

DA FORM 3479, OCT 2010   PREVIOUS EDITIONS ARE OBSOLETE.   2-

APD PE v1.00ES

Figure F-3. Sample DA Form 3479, section II

DEPARTMENT OF THE ARMY FORM 3479, SECTION III

F-6.   Section III of DA Form 3479 (figure F-4, page F-16) is used to record additional information pertaining to remarks in other sections, interview data, or comments that may affect the individual's career (for example, duties not to include flying (DNIF)/FFD safe aviation via exceptional service (SAVES), TTE, reason(s) for remedial training, awards, or letters of commendation).

SECTION III - MISCELLANEOUS GENERAL COMMENTS

1
5 Oct 98-PV2 Public is assigned to the TACT and was given a briefing on the RL progression and ATCT rating program. He received initial counseling on training time limitations and his flight physical has been verified. The commander has completed his evaluation and CTL. PV2 Public is designated RL-3.

NAME, RANK, AND TITLE	SIGNATURE
John J. Doe, SFC, Facility Chief	

2
20 Nov 98-PV2 Public participated in unit team training today with 2-2 Aviation. He was observed and evaluated on multiple CTL tasks. PV2 Public has demonstrated the knowledge and skills required to install, operate, and deploy the TTCS. He has completed all components of Phase I training and is awarded RL-2. Phase II training began on this date.

NAME, RANK, AND TITLE	SIGNATURE
John J. Doe, SFC, Facility Chief	

3
7 Jan 99-PFC Public participated in unit team training today with 2-2 Aviation. He was observed on the FD position and demonstrated the knowledge and skills required to be position qualified on FD. PFC Public began training on the GC/LC positions. FD position time= 12.0hrs.

NAME, RANK, AND TITLE	SIGNATURE
John J. Doe, SFC, Facility Chief	

4
10 Feb 99-PFC Public participated in an ATS STX with 2-2 Aviation during 8-10 Feb 99. He completed training on the AN/TSW 7-A and successfully completed several CTL tasks. PFC Public was observed on the GC position and demonstrated the knowledge and skills required to be position qualified on GC. GC position time=37.5hrs.

NAME, RANK, AND TITLE	SIGNATURE
John J. Doe, SFC, Facility Chief	

5
19 Apr 99- PFC Public participated in an ATS STX with 2-1 Aviation during 17-19 Apr 99. He completed all remaining CTL tasks for a Tower Operator. PFC Public has demonstrated the necessary knowledge and skills to receive an ATCT rating. He is awarded RL-1. LC Position time=39.5hrs.

NAME, RANK, AND TITLE	SIGNATURE
John J. Doe, SFC, Facility Chief	

6

NAME, RANK, AND TITLE	SIGNATURE

DA FORM 3479, OCT 2010 PREVIOUS EDITIONS ARE OBSOLETE. 3-

APD PE v1.00ES

Figure F-4. Sample DA Form 3479, section III

F-7. Section III is completed as follows:

- Each entry will start with a date in standard DD MMM YY format.
- The body of the text area is for comments or elaboration about other entries, events, or incidents within the record.
- Each entry requires the name, rank, title, and signature of the individual making the entry.
- Mandatory entries in this section include—
  - Reason and time limits for personnel placed on remedial training.

- Failure of the pre-FAA/ATCS examination.
- Failure of the final FAA/ATCS examination.
- Gaining unit inspection of records.
- Date granted, and time limit (if applicable), for TTE.
- Position Qualification, Rating, RL Progression dates, and total position hours.
- Results of No-Notice Evaluations.
- Results of Annual Skills Evaluations.

DEPARTMENT OF THE ARMY FORM 3479, SECTION IV

F-8.   The individual radar record (figure F-5, page F-17) is a monthly count of radar approaches by type or operation conducted by the controller. This section will be closed out the last day of each calendar year by entering the yearly total—the total to date (the total of all the previous year's approaches). A controller previously rated in a radar facility, but is currently working in a tower or AIC, will enter only the date and bring forward the totals each year. Monthly entries of 0 are not necessary. If a controller has never been radar-rated, the form may be left blank. This section applies only to radar facilities; however, it must be kept for all controllers once they start radar training. S/S approaches are counted separately from live (LV) approaches.

SECTION IV - INDIVIDUAL RADAR RECORD									
* S/S = Supervised/Simulated						* LV = Live Unsupervised/Non-Simulated			
YEAR: 1998	PAR		ASR		EMERG/NO GYRO				GRAND TOTAL	REMARKS
					PAR		ASR			
	*S/S	*LV	*S/S	*LV	*S/S	*LV	*S/S	*LV		
Total Runs Brought Forward	46	76	59	72	21	18	6	12	310	

I have verified the runs brought forward are accurate.

FACILITY CHIEF'S PRINTED NAME	FACILITY CHIEF'S SIGNATURE	DATE
JOHN Q. PUBLIC	*(signature)*	6 JAN 99

YEAR	PAR *S/S	PAR *LV	ASR *S/S	ASR *LV	EMERG PAR *S/S	EMERG PAR *LV	EMERG ASR *S/S	EMERG ASR *LV	GRAND TOTAL	REMARKS
January	6	5	5	4	2			1	23	
February	12	6	2	7		1			28	
March	9	9		14		1		1	34	
April	6	14	4	9		1			34	
May	9	5	3	6	2			2	27	
June	11	3		21		3	1		39	
July	4	9	7			3			23	
october	4	13	11			2		1	31	
September	11	8	12	6	2				39	
October	9	9	4	15	1		1		39	
November	7	4	3	7	1		1		23	
December	5	4	2	9		2	1		23	
Total Runs for Year	93	89	53	98	8	13	4	5	363	
TOTAL Runs	139	165	112	170	29	31	10	17	673	

DA FORM 3479, OCT 2010   PREVIOUS EDITIONS ARE OBSOLETE.   4-___

APD PE v1.00ES

Figure F-5. Sample DA Form 3479, section IV

F-9. The facility chief will tally total runs for the year and total runs brought forward and enter results in the "Total Runs" line. Upon completion of all entries, the form will be signed, dated, and retained in the controllers file until completion of the following year. A new form will be started and placed on top of the previous year to record radar runs for the current year. All section IV radar records not indicating current year or previous year data will be returned to the controller.

Note. S/S–Supervised approaches are approaches that require direct supervision for a controller. Simulated approaches are conducted on an ATC simulator. LV approaches are those not requiring direct supervision and are not simulated.

PREPARATION AND MAINTENANCE

F-10. Each organization will maintain a complete and current training and proficiency folder for all assigned or attached ATCS or ATS specialists.

F-11. The record will be kept in a straight cut, 9 ½ inch by 11 ¾ inch, heavy-duty file folder.

F-12. Each folder will contain a file label in the upper left corner and a folder label with return mailing instructions centered on the front cover.

F-13. File label will be formatted IAW DA Pam 25-403 and the records retention standard-Army criteria for file 95-2d. Folder label will contain the text illustrated in figure F-6.

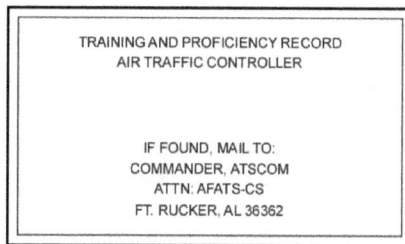

TRAINING AND PROFICIENCY RECORD
AIR TRAFFIC CONTROLLER

IF FOUND, MAIL TO:
COMMANDER, ATSCOM
ATTN: AFATS-CS
FT. RUCKER, AL 36362

Figure F-6. File folder label

F-14. The folder will be filed alphabetically by the controller's last name. A dummy folder (figure F-7) will be used and labeled IAW AR 25-400-2 and DA Pam 25-403 to reduce file labeling requirements.

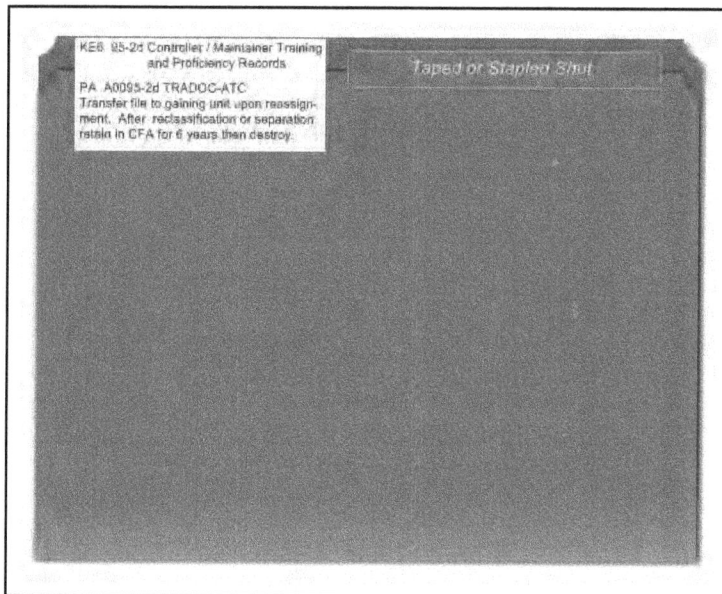

Figure F-7. Dummy folder

F-15. Each record folder will contain the following on the left side, top to bottom:
- DA Form 3479.
- FAA Form 8000-5 (Certificate of Designation) or other examiner designations per AR 95-2 retain permanently as a historical record even if expired or cancelled.
- Electronic media copy of folder contents.

F-16. Right side top to bottom contents are illustrated in figure F-8.

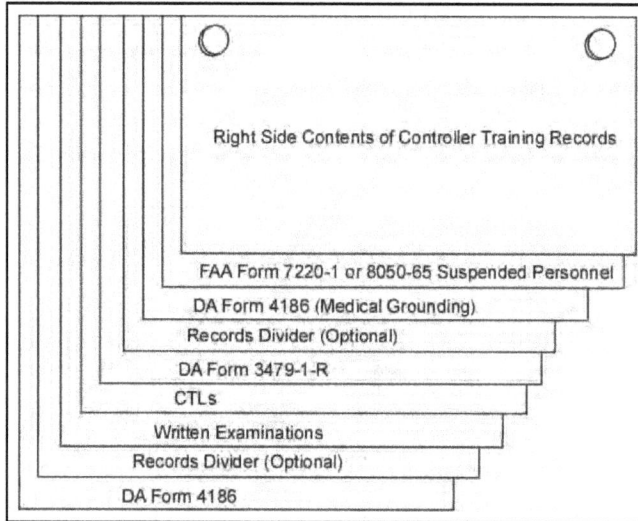

Figure F-8. Right side contents of controller training records

AVAILABILITY

F-17. File folders are available to the individual controller upon request. They will also be made available to—
- ATSCOM.
- Commanders.
- FAA authorities.
- Supervisors.
- Aircraft accident and flight violation investigators.
- ATCS or CTO examiners who facility-rate the controller for duty.

CONTESTS AND APPEALS

F-18. Individuals may contest (appeal) the entries on the DA Form 3479. Appeals will be directed through channels to the Commander, ATSCOM, AFAT-ATS-CT, 2805 Division Road, Fort Rucker, Alabama 36362-5265.

RETENTION

F-19. These records are permanent and will remain active while an individual is an ATC. The records will be returned to the individual upon completion of reclassification actions or termination of service.

MAINTENANCE CERTIFICATION RECORDS AND FORMS

F-20. This section explains the required files, forms, and records for administering the maintenance certification program. It explains the contents of the records folder, how to complete the forms, and lists the equipment requiring certification authority.

RECORDS FILE

F-21. For each technician assigned to the maintenance section who requires certification, establish and maintain an official certification and related training file. This file will be under the control of the facility maintenance chief/platoon/section. It will be kept in an area accessible only to authorized personnel who have been properly screened, cleared, and trained. Information in the file will be protected according to privacy act regulations.

F-22. Each official training file will contain documentation substantiating the technician's qualifications to possess certification authority or have responsibility on specific system/subsystems/equipment. The file will be used as a complete historical record of the technician's certification progress. It will contain such background data and supporting documents as reports, certification responsibility assignments/withdrawals, and granting/revocation of certification authority. This informational file will contain documentation to support the program responsibilities assigned to the office maintaining the file.

F-23. The pertinent records will be kept in a straight cut, 9½ inch by 11¾-inch, heavy-duty file folder. Each folder will be maintained according to AR 25-400-2. The folders will be filed alphabetically by the technician's last name. The following information will be entered on the front cover of the file folder: Air Traffic Control Maintenance Qualification and Related Training Records Folder, United States Army. If found return to: Commander, ATSCOM, AFAT-ATS-CT, 2805 Division Road, Fort Rucker, Alabama 36362-5265. The folder will contain—

- Certification and related training received.
- Performance examination sheets.
- Theory (concepts) and performance examination results.
- Grades and certifications obtained through training.
- Other correspondence related to training and certification.
- Responsibility assignment.

F-24. The left side (foldout portion) of the folder will contain DA Form 3479-9 and DA Form 3479-10 (Responsibility Assignment). No other forms, records, or papers will be on this portion of the folder. The right inside (foldout portion) of the folder will contain performance examination results as well as other correspondence related to ATC maintenance training.

F-25. Upon request, technicians may review the contents of their records folder. The folders are available for review to—

- ATSCOM representative.
- Commanders.
- FAA authorities.
- Supervisors (training or maintenance).
- Aircraft accident investigators.
- Mobile maintenance contact teams.
- Systems managers and their authorized representatives.
- Examiners who administer theory (concepts) and performance examinations.

F-26. When a technician is reassigned to another maintenance facility/shop, the losing organization will note the effective reassignment date and location (if known) on the DA Form 3479-9, section II. The ATC facility retains the active paper records until individual transfers. These paper records are transferred with the military personnel records jacket or civilian personnel folder, as appropriate. Automated management information at the primary location is retained until no longer needed for current operations. AR 5-400-2 explains record retention and disposal procedures.

F-27. When civilian and military personnel retire or separate from federal service, their records are retired. Civilian personnel records are sent to the National Personnel Records Center, 111 Winnebago Street, St. Louis, Missouri 63118; military personnel records are sent to the U.S. Army Personnel Center and U.S. Army Reserve Components Personnel and Administration Center, 9700 Page Boulevard, St. Louis, Missouri 63132.

FORMS

F-28. DA Form 3479-9 and DA Form 3479-10 are completed on each assigned or attached technician (military and civilian).

Department of the Army Form 3479-9

F-29. DA Form 3479-9 will be used to maintain a record of the status of each individual in the certification program for the associated facility/shop. It specifies the technician's certification authority by the system/subsystem/ equipment for which there is an associated examination. The information on the form includes, but is not limited to, the following:

- All certification authority issued, including interim.
- All certification-related schooling, correspondence study, OJT, out-of-house training, and certification program examinations. The information shall also include examination results (passed, failed) and completion dates of the training and examinations.
- Signature/initials of responsible officials (maintenance chief/maintenance training personnel).
- The beginning and ending dates of acquired experience.
- The date that certification authority was revoked on specific systems/subsystems/equipment.

F-30. DA Form 3479-9 is used to evaluate a technician's progress toward becoming certified or to assess unsatisfactory progress in a training program. The technician will be told what he must do to improve and why. This information may include study assignments or additional OJT.

F-31. The maintenance chief must review the technician's folder contents annually and annotate "Annual Review" in blocks 7 through 10 of the DA Form 3479-9. As the technician becomes certified or completes related training, the record will be annotated within 15 days. Once the maintenance chief reviews and signs the records, all performance examination results will be placed in the order that the examinations were taken with the latest on top. These results will be retained in the record as long as equipment certification authority remains valid. These folders are permanent records and will remain active while the individual is an ATC maintenance technician. The records of any reclassified technician will be returned to the individual upon completion of reclassification actions.

F-32. Instructions for completing DA Form 3479-9 (figures F-9 to F-11, pages F-24 to F-26) are as follows:

- **Block 1, Name:** Enter the technician's name.
- **Block 2, Grade/Rank:** In pencil, enter the technician's grade/rank (for example, GS-11 or SSG).
- **Block 3, System/Subsystem/Equipment:** Enter the specific system/subsystem/equipment on which the technician is qualified or will qualify (for example AN/FRN-41(V), AN/TSQ-71B, FSC-92, or ASR-9).
- **Block 4, Theory:** In column *a*, enter the method by which system requirements were met (refer to footnote 1 or DA Form 3479-9). In column *b*, enter the date (DDMMMYY) the technician successfully completed the theory (concepts) requirements (for example 101199). In column *c*, the responsible official writes his initials
- **Block 5, Performance:** In column *a*, enter the method by which performance requirements were met (refer to footnote 1 on DA Form 3479-9). In column *b*, enter the date (DDMMMYY) that the technician successfully completed performance requirements. In column *c*, the responsible official writes his initials.
- **Block 6, Certification:** In column *a*, enter the date (DDMMMYY) the certification authority requirements were fully met and the theory (concepts) examination was successfully completed

(refer to footnote 2 on DA Form 3479-9). In column *b*, enter the date (DDMMMYY) the certification authority was revoked.

- **Block 7, Duty Station:** Enter the technician's duty station (for example, Robert Gray AAF, Fort Hood or Company B, 164th ATS Group).
- **Block 8, Date of Action:** Enter the date (DDMMMYY) of that particular action
- **Block 9, Type of Action:** Enter the type of action or remarks that pertain to the entry in block 9.
- **Block 10, Maintenance Chief's Signature:** Self-explanatory.
- **Block 11, System/Subsystem/Equipment:** Enter the system/ subsystem/equipment for which the technician took the training or examination.
- **Block 12, Course Number:** Self-explanatory.
- **Block 13, Training of Examination:** In column *a*, enter C or P (refer to footnote 3 on DA Form 3479-9). If the training or examination does not pertain to either, leave blank. In column *b*, enter the edition number of the theory (concepts)/performance examination. In column *c*, record the results of the examination or course by entering either P or F (refer to footnote 4 on DA Form 3479 9). In column *d*, enter the start date (DDMMMYY) of training, examination or course. In column *e*, enter the completion date (DDMMMYY) of training, examination or course.
- **Block 14, Remarks:** Enter remarks pertaining to the technician's training; if desired, continue remarks on an attached sheet.
- **Block 15, Initials:** If the entries in blocks 11 through 14 pertain to examination results, the examiner writes his initials in block 15. If the entries pertain to training, the maintenance chief writes his initials in block 15.

**ATC MAINTENANCE PERSONNEL CERTIFICATION
AND RELATED TRAINING RECORD**

For use of this form, see TC 3-04.81; the proponent agency is TRADOC.

1. NAME (last, first, MI) JONES, JOHN H.	2. GRADE/RANK SFC

SECTION I. QUALIFICATION AND CERTIFICATION RECORD

3. SYSTEM/ SUBSYSTEM/ EQUIPMENT	4. THEORY			5. PERFORMANCE			6. CERTIFICATION	
	a. Qual Meth [1]	b. Date Qual	c. Init	a. Qual Meth [1]	b. Date Qual	c. Init	a. Date Acquired [2]	b. Date Revoked
AN/TPN-31	CEXAM	11 MAR 2008	MD	PEXAM	11 MAR 2008	MD	18 MAY 2008	
AN/TSQ-221	RTRN	18 MAY 2008	CR	RTRN	18 MAY 2008	CR	18 MAY 2008	
AN/TSW-7A	CEXAM	6 JUN 2008	SH	PEXAM	6 JUL 2008	SH	10 JUL 2008	
AN/TSQ-198A	CEXAM	7 JUN 2008	SH	PEXAM	7 JUL 2008	SH	10 JUL 2008	
AN/TRN-30(V)1&2	CEXAM	8 JUN 2008	SH	PEXAM	8 JUL 2008	SH	10 JUL 2008	

DA FORM 3479-9, OCT 2010   PREVIOUS EDITIONS ARE OBSOLETE.   Page 1 - ____

APD PE v1.00ES

Figure F-9. Sample DA Form 3479-9, page 1

SECTION II. CHANGE OF STATION ANNUAL REVIEW AND VALIDATION RECORD			
7. DUTY STATION	8. DATE OF ACTION	9. TYPE OF ACTION	10. MAINT CHIEF'S SIGNATURE
1-245 AOB LEXINGTON, OK	10 FEB 2008	Assigned	
1-245 AOB LEXINGTON, OK	8 FEB 2009	Annual Review	
1-245 AOB LEXINGTON, OK	8 FEB 2010	Annual Review	

DA FORM 3479-9, OCT 2010

Page 2 -
APD PE v1.00ES

Figure F-10. Sample DA Form 3479-9, page 2

SECTION III. RELATED TRAINING RECORD AND EXAMINATION RESULTS

11. SYSTEM/ SUBSYSTEM/ EQUIPMENT	12. COURSE NUMBER	13. TRAINING OR EXAMINATION				14. REMARKS	15. INIT
		a.Type [3]	b.Number	c.Results [4]	d.Date Comp		
AN/TPN-31	102-35D10			P	5 FEB 2008	AIT	SH
AN/TRN-30	102-35D10			P	5 FEB 2008	AIT	SH
AN/TSW-7A	102-35D10			P	5 FEB 2008	AIT	SH
ETVS	102-35D10			P	5 FEB 2008	AIT	SH
DVRS	102-35D10			P	5 FEB 2008	AIT	SH
AN/GRT-21/22	102-35D10			P	5 FEB 2008	AIT	SH
AN/GRR-23/24	102-35D10			P	5 FEB 2008	AIT	SH
T-1428/FRN NDB	102-35D10			P	5 FEB 2008	AIT	SH
R-2176/FRN NDB RECEIVER	102-35D10			P	5 FEB 2008	AIT	SH
AN/TPN-31		C		P	5 FEB 2008	AIT	SH
AN/TPN-31		P		P	11 MAR 2008	CERTIFICATION EXAM	MD
AN/TSQ-221				P	18 MAY 2008	NET/GC/CERT REDSTONE, AL	MD
AN/TSW-7A		C		P	6 JUL 2008	CERTIFICATION EXAM	CR
AN/TSW-7A		P		P	6 JUL 2008	CERTIFICATION EXAM	SH
AN/TSQ-198A		C		P	7 JUL 2008	CERTIFICATION EXAM	SH
AN/TSQ-198A		P		P	7 JUL 2008	CERTIFICATION EXAM	SH
AN/TRN-30(V)1/2		C		P	8 JUL 2008	CERTIFICATION EXAM	SH
AN/TRN-30(V)1/2		P		P	8 JUL 2008	CERTIFICATION EXAM	SH

[1] Enter RTRN for resident training, PEXAM for performance examination, EXP for experience, CEXAM for concepts (theory) examination, PC for prior certification, and NTRN for nonresident training.

[2] If other than regular certification, enter I for interim.

[3] Enter C if action pertains to concepts (theory) or P if action pertains to performance.

[4] Enter P for passed or F for failed.

DA FORM 3479-9, OCT 2010

Page 3 - _____
APD PE v1.00ES

Figure F-11. Sample DA Form 3479-9, page 3

Department of the Army Form 3479-10

F-33. DA Form 3479-10 (figures F-12 and F-13, pages F-28 and F-29) is also used to officially assign certification responsibility/authority to the technician. Instructions for completing DA Form 3479-10 are as follows:

- **Block 1, Type:** Enter an *X* in the appropriate box. Enter the revision number if applicable. Initial assignment block is checked when the form is generated to document the technician's assigned maintenance or certification responsibilities for the first time. The revision block is checked each time the form is generated to document technician's equipment or certification responsibilities change. The revocation block is checked when the form is generated to document the technician's lack of proficiency on the system.

- **Block 2, Date:** Enter the date (DDMMMYY).
- **Block 3, Page Number:** Self-explanatory.
- **Block 4, Name:** Self-explanatory.
- **Block 5, Location:** Self-explanatory.
- **Block 6, Position Title and Rank/Grade:** Self-explanatory.
- **Block 7, Immediate Supervisor:** Self-explanatory.
- **Block 8, Location/Phone Number:** Enter the location and office telephone number of the immediate supervisor.
- **Block 9, System/Facility/Equipment:** In column *a*, enter the type of equipment for which the technician is assigned responsibility (for example, AN/FRN-41(V)1, MARK 1F or MARK 20A). In column *b*, enter the identification of the station or location (for example, PTK CNS or Starns Beacon, Cairns Tower).
- **Block 10, Responsibility (Refer to maintenance and certification codes on the back of DA Form 3479-10):** In column *a*, enter the appropriate maintenance responsibility code. In column *b*, enter the appropriate certification responsibility code.
- **Block 11, Effective Dates:** Enter the effective starting and ending dates (DDMMMYY) of the responsibility. The ending date is when the responsibility is no longer required or has been revoked.
- **Block 12, Comments:** Enter comments pertaining to certification responsibilities; if there are no comments, so state by entering *None*.
- **Block 13, Special Instructions/Restrictions/ Limitations/Remarks:** Enter special instructions for restrictions/ limitations, and enter other remarks. (If certification code LC is entered in block 10, the limitations must be shown in block 13. If code SSC is entered in block 10, the equipment must be listed in block 13.)
- **Block 14, Technician:** Enter the technician's name, title, and grade/rank. The technician will sign in this block.
- **Block 15, Immediate Supervisor:** Enter the immediate supervisor's name. The immediate supervisor will sign in this block.
- **Block 16, Examiner:** Enter the name of the examiner. The examiner will sign in this block.
- **Block 17, Copy To:** Enter an *X* in the box marked FILE if this is the file copy, and indicate who was given a copy of this DA Form 3479-10. If an *X* is entered in the OTHER box, specify the personnel or element receiving a copy.

RESPONSIBILITY ASSIGNMENT

For use of this form, see TC 3-04.81; the proponent agency is TRADOC.

1. TYPE		2. DATE	3. PAGE NO.
☐ Initial Assignment ☐ Revocation ☒ Revision No. 2		25 Nov 1998	1

4. NAME *(last, first, MI)*	5. LOCATION
JONES, JOHN H.	F Co, 1-58th Aviation, Fort Hood TX

6. POSITION TITLE AND RANK/GRADE	7. IMMEDIATE SUPERVISOR	8. LOCATION/PHONE NO.
ATTCS Supervisor, SGT/E-5	SMITH, FRANK A.	Fort Hood, TX: DSN 737-0143

NOTE: As recorded on DA Form 3479-9-R, you have demonstrated proficiency on the equipment listed below. You are hereby assigned maintenance and certification responsibility for this equipment. The kinds and levels of responsibility delegated to you are shown by the code designations, which are explained on the reverse side of this form.

9. SYSTEM/FACILITY/ EQUIPMENT		10. RESPONSIBILITY		11. EFFECTIVE DATES		12.	COMMENTS
a. Type	b. Ident or Location	a. Maint	b. Cert	a. Start	b. End		*(If none, so state)*
AN/TPN-31	Fort Hood	RWA	FC	25 Oct 1998			None
TRN-30	Fort Hood	RWA	FC	25 Nov 1998			None

DA FORM 3479-10, OCT 2010   PREVIOUS EDITIONS ARE OBSOLETE.   Page 1 of 2
APD PE v1.00ES

Figure F-12. Sample DA Form 3479-10, page 1

13. SPECIAL INSTRUCTIONS/RESTRICTIONS/LIMITATIONS/REMARKS

14. I understand the nature and extent of the responsibilities listed on this document.

NAME, TITLE, AND GRADE/RANK *(typed)*	SIGNATURE OF TECHNICIAN
JONES, JOHN H., ATCS Supervisor, E-5/SGT	

15. NAME AND TITLE *(typed)*	SIGNATURE OF IMMEDIATE SUPERVISOR
SMITH, FRANK A., Maintenance NCOIC	

16. NAME AND TITLE *(typed)*	SIGNATURE OF FACILITY MAINTENANCE CHIEF/CERTIFIER
SMITH, FRANK A., Maintenance NCOIC/Certifier	

RESPONSIBILITY CODE DESIGNATIONS

MAINTENANCE

CBO	Callback only; not regular workload.
FIR	Facility inspection responsibility.
R-AST	Regular workload assistance as assigned by supervisor.
R-ASTCS	Regular workload and/or callback as assigned by supervisor.
RWA	Regular workload assignments.
RWCS	Regular workload and callback responsibility.
STAF	Duties as assigned by the facility maintenance chief such as analytical, diagnostic, evaluation, major modification, inspection, relief, training and supervisory duties.

CERTIFICATION

FC	Full certification for complete system.
FIC	Full installation certification.
LC	Limited certification; subject to listed limitations.
SSC	Subsystem certification; limited to listed equipment.

17. COPY TO

[X] Technician   [ ] Maintenance Supervisor   [ ] Maintenance Chief   [ ] File
[ ] Other
    (Specify)

DA FORM 3479-10, OCT 2010   PREVIOUS EDITIONS ARE OBSOLETE.   Page 2 of 2
                                                                           APD PE v1.00ES

Figure F-13. Sample DA Form 3479-10, page 2

CONTESTS AND APPEALS

F-34. Trainees/technicians may agree or disagree with the review and make the comments they feel are necessary. They will place their comments on a separate sheet and attach the sheet to the review. The reviewing authority ensures the forms are filled out properly, makes the appropriate entries/comments, and signs and dates the form. Technicians may contest or appeal the entries on DA Form 3479-9. Complaints will be directed through channels to Commander, ATSCOM, AFAT-ATS-CT, 2805 Division Road, Fort Rucker, Alabama 36362-5265.

This page intentionally left blank.

Glossary

A3O	Operations Directorate
AA	assembly area
AAF	Army airfield
ABCS	Army Battle Command System
AC2	airspace command and control
ACO	airspace control order
ACOM	Army command
ACP	airspace control plan
AD	air defense
ADIZ	air defense identification zone
AFI	Air Force information
AFJPAM	Air Force joint pamphlet
AFIS	Automated Flight Inspection System
AFMAN	Air Force manual
AHP	Army heliport
AIC	airspace information center
AMOS	Automated Meterological Observing System
AMTP	air traffic services maintenance training program
AN/FPN	Army-Navy/Federal part number
AN/TSQ	Army-Navy/tactical signal equipment
AN/VRC	Army-Navy/very high frequency radio communication
AO	area of operations
AOB	airfield operations battalion
APA	aeromedical physician's assistant
APG	aviation procedure guide
APM	approach path monitor
AR	Army regulation
ARAC	Army radar approach control
ARIMS	Army Records Information Management System
ARNG	Army National Guard
ARTCC	air route traffic control center
ARTS	Automated Radar Terminal System
ASCC	Army Service Component Command
ASHRAE	American Society of Heating, Refrigeration, and Air Conditioning Engineers
ASIC	Air and Space Interoperability Council
ASOS	Automated Surface Observation System
ASR	area surveillance radar

AT&AO	air traffic and airspace officer
ATB	aeromedical technical bulletin
ATC	air traffic control
ATCME	air traffic controller medical examination
ATCRBS	Air Traffic Control Radar Beacon System
ATCS	air traffic control specialist
ATCSCC	Air Traffic Control Search Coordination Center
ATCT	air traffic control tower
ATIS	automatic terminal information service
ATNAVICS	Air Traffic Navigation, Integration, and Coordination System
ATS	air traffic services
ATSCOM	Air Traffic Services Command
ATTP	air traffic training program
C2	command and control
C3	command, control, and communication
CA	conflict alert
CAB	combat aviation brigade
CARDA	continental United States airborne reconnaissance for damage assessment
CATS	combined arms training strategy
CD	clearance delivery
CERAP	combined/center radar approach control
CFR	Code of Federal Regulation
CFM	cubic feet per minute
CI	coordinator
CIC	controller-in-charge
CIS	communication and information system
CIV	civilian
CM	configuration management
COA	certificate of authorization
CONUS	continental United States
COP	common operating picture
CPX	command post exercise
CRAF	Civil Reserve Air Fleet
CTL	commander's task list
CTO	control tower operator
DA Pam	Department of the Army pamphlet
DA	Department of the Army
DAC	Department of the Army civilian
DALR	digital audio legal recorder
DAR	Department of the Army representative
dB	decibel

DBRITE	digital bright radar indicator tower equipment
DCS	Deputy Chief of Staff
DD	dial division
DH	decision height
DHS	Department of Homeland Security
DME	distance measuring equipment
DND	Department of National Defense
DNIF	duties not to include flying
DOD	Department of Defense
DOT	Department of Transportation
DOTD	Directorate of Training and Doctrine
DP	departure procedure
DRU	direct reporting unit
DSIP	domestic security integration program
DSN	defense switch network
DSS	data systems specialist
DTM	digital terrain map
DVD	digital video device
DVR	digital voice recorder
DVRS	digital voice recorder system
EAA	estimated approach altitude
EATPL	emergency air traffic priority list
ECHUM	electronic chart updating manual
ECP	engineer change package
EIP	engineering installation package
EMC	electro magnetic current
EML	emergency manning level
EOD	explosive ordinance disposal
EOS	end of statement
ESCAT	emergency security control of air traffic
ETS	end term of service
ETVS	enhanced tower voice switch
EUSA	Eighth United States Army
FAA	Federal Aviation Administration
FAA DEN	Federal Aviation Administration Domestic Event Network
FAA-E	Federal Aviation Administration equipment
FAA JO	Federal Aviation Administrative Joint Order
FAAO	Federal Aviation Administration Order
FAF	final approach fix
FAR	Fedral air regulation
FARP	forward arming and refueling point

FBPAR	fixed-base precision approach radar
FC	final control
FD	flight data
FDB	Fahrenheit dry bulb
FDC	feeder control
FDIO	flight data input/output
FF	flight following
FI	flight inspection
FLIP	flight information publication
FM	field manual, frequency modulation
FOIA	Freedom of Information Act
FRN	Federal Communication Commission Registration Number
FS	full stop
FTM	facility training manual
FTP	facility training program
FTX	field training exercise
FWB	Fahrenheit wet bulb
G-3	Assistant Chief of Staff, Operations and Plans
GA	ground angle
GC	ground control
GCA	ground-controlled approach
GPA	glide path angle
GPI	ground point of intercept
GPS	global positioning system
GRT	ground radio transmitter
GS	General Schedule
GTM	general terrain map
HAA	height above airport
HAL	height above landing
HAT	height above touchdown
HF	high frequency
HIRLS	high inensity runway lighting system
HQ	headquarters
Hz	hertz
IAW	in accordance with
ICAO	International Civil Aviation Organization
ICOM	integrated communications security
IFF	identification friend or foe
IFR	instrument flight rules
IIMC	inadvertent instrument meteorological conditions
ILS	Instrument Landing System

IMCOM	Installation Management Command
INV	inverse
JOG	joint operational graphic
kHz	kilohertz
kw	kilowatt
LA	low approach
LAN	local area network
LC	local control
LCN	local control North
LCS	local control South
LEA	law enforcement agency
LITE	local integrated tower equipment
LOA	letter of agreement
LOGSA	logistics support activity
LOP	letter of procedure
LV	live
LZ	landing zone
MAGVAR	magnetic variation
MALS	medium intensity approach lighting system
MEARTS	Micro-En Route Automated Radar Tracking System
MEDEVAC	medical evacuation
METAR	meteorlogical aviation report
MHz	megahertz
MIL-STD	military standard
MIRLS	Medium Intensity Runway Lighting System
MLS	microwave landing system
MMDF	master maintenance data file
MOA	memorandum of agreement
MOS	military occupational specialty
MSA	minimum safe altitude
MSAW	minimum safe altitude warning
MSL	mean sea level
MTP	mission training plan
MVA	minimum vectoring altitude
MVAC	minimum vectoring altitude chart
NAS	National Airspace System
NAT	national agreement
NATO	North Atlantic Treaty Organization
NAVAID	navigational aid
NCO	noncommissioned officer
NDB	non-directional beacon

NFDD	national flight data digest
NFPO	National Flight Procedures Office
NGA	National Geospatial-Intelligence Agency
NOE	nap-of-the-earth
NORDO	no radio
NOTAM	notice to airmen
NTFS	New Tactical Forecast System
NVD	night vision device
NVS	night vision system
OCE	Office of the Chief Engineer
OCONUS	outside continental United States
ODALS	Omnidirectional Approach Light System
OJT	on-the-job training
OPM	Office of Personnel Management
OSF	Open Software Foundation
PAO	Public Affairs Office
PAPI	precision approach path indicator
PAR	precision approach radar
PDC	pre-departure clearance
PIREP	pilot report
PLT LDR	platoon leader
PMCS	preventive maintenance checks and services
PQ	position qualified
PSG	platoon sergeant
PZ	pickup zone
QTB	quarterly training briefing
RA	radar assistant
RAIL	runway alignment indicator light
RBDER	radar bright display equipment replacement
RCO	remote communication outlet
RCF	remote communication facility
RCP	retention control point
RDP	radar data processing
RF	radio frequency
RH	relative humidity
RL	readiness level
RN	radar North
ROC	required obstacle clearance
ROZ	restricted operating zone
RPI	runway point of intercept
RPL	runway parallel line

RS	radar South
R/T	receiver/transmitter
RTA-2	radio transmitter antenna-2
RTR	remote transmitter receiver
RTS	return to service
RVR	runway visual range
S/S	supervised or simulated
SALS	Short Approach Lighting System
SATCOM	satellite communication
SAVES	safe aviation via exceptional service
SD	special duty
SID	standard instrument departure
SIGMET	significant meteorological information
SINCGARS	single-channel ground and airborne radio system
SJA	Staff Judge Advocate
SL	shift leader
SNMPc	Secure Network Management Program-computers
SOP	standing operating procedure
SPECI	special observation
SPINS	special instructions
SSALS	Simplified Short Approach Lighting System
SS Pam	supply support pamphlet
STAFFEX	staff exercise
STANAG	standard agreement
STARS	Standard Terminal Automation Replacement System
STVS	small tower voice switch
STX	situational training exercise
SUA	Special Use Airspace
SVFR	special visual flight rules
TAC	tactical
TACAN	tactical air navigation
TACT	tactical team
TAIS	tactical airspace integration system
TAOG	theater airfield operations group
TAPS	Tactical Approach Publications System
TC	training circular
TCH	threshold crossing height
TD	touch down
TEER	training events execution review
TERPS	terminal instrument procedures
TG	touch-and-go

TM	technical manual
TMDE	test, measurement, and diagnostic equipment
TTCS	Tactical Terminal Control System
TTE	training time extension
TVO	tower visibility observation
TVOR	terminal very high frequency omnidirectional-range
TWR	tower
U.S.	United States
UA	unmanned aircraft
UAS	unmanned aircraft system
UCS	unmanned control system
UFC	unified facilities code
UHF	ultra high frequency
UPS	uninterrupted power supplies
USAACE	United States Army Aviation Center of Excellence
USAAMA	United States Army Aeromedical Activity
USAASA	United States Army Aeronautical Services Agency
USAASD-E	United States Army Aeronautical Services Detachment-Europe
USAF	United States Air Force
USAISC	United States Army Information Systems Command
USAR	United States Army Reserve
USN	United States Navy
USR	unit staus reporting
UTC	coordinated universal time
VASI	visual approach slope indicator
VCC	visibility checkpoint chart
VFR	visual flight rule
VHF	very high frequency
VOR	very high frequency omnidirectional radio range
VORTAC	very high frequency omnidirectional radio range tactical air navigation aid
YTB	yearly training brief

References

These publications are sources for additional information on the topics in this TC. Most JPs are found online at http://www.dtic.mil/doctrine/. Most Army publications are found online at http://www.apd.army.mil.

SOURCES USED

JOINT PUBLICATIONS

ICAO Annex 11, *International Standards and Recommended Practices, Air Traffic Services,* July 2001.

ICAO 7910, *Location Identifiers,* March 2007.

JP 1-02, *DOD Dictionary of Military and Associated Terms,* 12 April 2001.

JP 3-52, *Joint Airspace Control,* 20 May 2010.

STANAG 2999. *Edition 8, Use of Helicopters in Land Operations – Doctrine – ATP-49(E) Volume 1,* 31 October 2008.

STANAG 3596. *Edition 6, Air Reconnaissance Requesting and target Reporting Guide,* 26 November 2007.

STANAG 3680. *Edition 5, NATO Glossary of Terms and Definitions (English and French) – APP-6,* 23 December 1998.

STANAG 3700. *Edition 7, Joint Air and Space Operations Doctrine – AJP-3.3(A),* 5 November 2009.

STANAG 3736. *Edition 11, Allied Joint Doctrine for Close Air Support and Air Interdiction – AJP-3.3.2(A),* 11 September 2009.

STANAG 3805, *Edition 8. Doctrine for Joint Airspace Control – AJP-3.3.5(A),* 5 April 2006.

STANAG 4184, *Edition 3, Microwave Landing System (MLS),* 27 November 1998.

STANAG 4586. *Edition 2, Standard Interfaces of UAV Control System (UCS) for NATO UAV Interoperability,* 8 November 2007.

STANAG 7204. *Edition 1, NATO Minimum Requirements for Personnel Proving Air Traffic Services (ATS) in NATO-Led Operations,* 17 March 2010.

Title 5 Code of Federal Regulations Section 339.202, *Administrative Personnel.*

Title 14 Code of Federal Regulations Part 65, *Certification: Airman other than Flight Crewmembers.*

Title 14 Code of Federal Regulations Part 73, *Special Use Airspace.*

Title 14 Code of Federal Regulations Part 91, *General Operating and Flight Rules.*

Title 14 Code of Federal Regulations Part 99, *Security Control of Air Traffic.*

Title 14 Code of Federal Regulations Part 105, *Parachute Operations.*

Title 14 Code of Federal Regulations Part 171, *Cost of Flight and Ground Inspections.*

Title 32 Code of Federal Regulations Part 245, *Plan for the Emergency Security Control of Air Traffic (ESCAT).*

UFC 3-535-01, *Visual Air Navigation Facilities,* 17 November 2005.

UFC 3-260-01, *Airfield and Heliport Planning and Design,* 17 November 2008.

UFC 3-260-05A, *Marking of Army Heliport Operational and Maintenance Facilities,* 16 January 2004.

AIR FORCE PUBLICATIONS

AFMAN 15-111, *Surface Weather Observations,* 19 December 2003.

ARMY PUBLICATIONS

AR 25-50, *Preparing and Managing Correspondence*, 3 June 2002.

AR 25-52, *Authorized Abbreviations, Brevity Codes, and Acronyms*, 4 January 2005.

AR 40-8, *Temporary Flying Restrictions Due to Exogenous Factors*, 16 May 2007.

AR 40-501, *Standards of Medical Fitness*, 14 December 2007.

AR 70-1, *Army Acquisition Policy*, 31 December 2003.

AR 95-1, *Flight Regulations*, 12 November 2008.

AR 95-2, *Airspace, Airfields/Heliports, Flight Activities, Air Traffic Control, and Navigational Aid*, 10 April 2007.

AR 95-30, *Participation in a Military or Civil Aircraft Accident Safety Investigation*, 8 July 2004.

AR 115-10, *Weather Support for the U.S. Army{AFI 15-157(IP)}*, 6 January 2010.

AR 115-11, *Geospatial Information and Services*, 10 December 2001.

AR 190-13, *The Army Physical Security Program*, 30 September 1993.

AR 190-51, *Security of Unclassified Army Property (Sensitive and Nonsenitive)*, 30 September 1993.

AR 220-1, *Army Unit Status Reporting and Force Registration-Consolidated Policies*, 15 April 2010.

AR 385-10, *The Army Safety Program*, 23 August 2007.

AR 420-1, *Army Facilities Management*, 12 February 2008.

AR 570-4, *Manpower Management*, 8 February 2006.

AR 700-138, *Army Logistics Readiness and Sustainability*, 26 February 2004.

AR 710-2, *Supply Policy Below the National Level*, 28 March 2008.

AR 725-50, *Requisition, Receipt, and Issue System*, 15 November 1995.

AR 735-5, *Policies and Procedures for Property Accountability*, 28 February 2005.

AR 750-1, *Army Material Maintenance Policy*, 20 September 2007.

AR 750-43, *Army Test, Measurement, and Diagnostic Equipment*, 3 November 2006.

AR 25-400-2, *The Army Records Information Management System (ARIMS)*, 2 October 2007.

CTA 50-909, *Field and Garrison Furnishings and Equipment*, 1 August 1993.
   (https://webtaads.belvoir.army.mil/USAFMSA)

DA Pam 25-30, *Consolidated Index of Army Publications and Blank Forms*, 14 July 2009.

DA Pam 25-403, *Guide to Recordkeeping in the Army*, 11 August 2008.

DA Pam 385-10, *Army Safety Program*, 23 May 2008.

DA Pam 385-30, *Mishap Risk Management*, 10 October 2007.

DA Pam 385-90, *Army Aviation Accident Prevention Program*, 28 August 2007.

DA Pam 611-21, *Military Occupational Classification and Structure*, 22 January 2007.

DA Pam 710-2-1, *Using Unit Supply System (Manual Procedures)*, 31 December 1997.

DA Pam 710-2-2, *Supply Support Activity Supply System: Manual Procedures*, 30 September 1998.

DA Pam 750-8, *The Army Maintenance Management System (TAMMS) Users Manual*, 22 August 2005.

DA Pam 750-3, *Soldiers' Guide for Field Maintenance Operations*, 28 September 2006.

FM 3-04.120, *Air Traffic Services Operations*, 16 February 2007.

FM 3-21.38, *Pathfinder Operations*, 25 April 2006.

FM 3-25.26, *Map Reading and Land Navigation*, 18 January 2005.

FM 3-52, *Army Airspace Command and Control in a Combat Zone*, 1 August 2002.

FM 3-52.1, *Multi-Service Tactics, Techniques, and Procedures for Airspace Control {AFTTP 3-2.78}*, 22 May 2009.

FM 3-52.2, *TAGS Multi-Service Tactics, Techniques, and Procedures for the Theater Air Ground System {NTTP 3-56.2; AFTTP(I) 3-2.17}*, 10 April 2007.

FM 3-52.3, *Multi-Service Procedures for Joint Air Traffic Control {MCRP 3-25A; NTTP 3-56.3; AFTTP(1) 3-2.23}*, 23 July 2009.

FM 4-25.11, *First Aid {NTRP 4-02.1.1; AFMAN 44-163(1); MCRP 3-02G}*, 23 December 2002.

FM 4-30.3, *Maintenance Operations and Procedures*, 28 July 2004.

FM 7-0, *Training for Full Spectrum Operations*, 12 December 2008.

FM 10-27-4, *Organizational Supply and Services for Unit Leaders*, 14 April 2000.

FMI 6-02.70, *Army Electromagnetic Spectrum Management Operations*, 5 September 2006.

MIL-STD-1472F, *Human Engineering, Design Criteria for Military Systems, Equipment, and Facilities,* 23 August 1999 [https://assist.daps.dla.mil/online/start/ (password required)].

MIL-STD-3007F, *Standard Practice for Unified Facilities Criteria and Unified Facilities Guide Specifications*, 13 December 2007.

SB 11-573, *Painting and Preservation of Supplies Available for Field Use for Electronics Command Equipment*, 8 February 1969.

STP 1-93C1-SM-TG, *Soldier's Manual and Trainer's Guide, MOS 93C, Air Traffic Control, Skill Level 1*, 1 June 2002.

TB 11-6625-3263-25, *Test Equipment Modernization (TEMOD) Program Guide and Replacement Lists*, 2 December 2004.

TB 43-0118, *Field Instructions for Painting and Preserving Communications-Electronics Equipment*, 15 June 1986.

TB 43-0129, *Safety Requirements for Use of Antenna and Mast Equipment*, 15 June 1986.

TB 43-0133, *Hazard Controls for CECOM Radio Frequency and Optical Radiation Producing Equipment*, 15 November 2000.

TB 43-180, *Calibration and Repair Requirements for the Maintenance of Army Materiel*, 1 June 2010.

TB 385-4, *Safety Requirements for Maintenance of Electrical and Electronic Equipment*, 1 July 2008.

TB 750-25, *Maintenance of Supplies and Equipment: Army Test, Measurement and Diagnostic Equipment (TMDE) Calibration and Repair Support (C&RS) Program*, 7 October 2008.

TB Med 523, *Control of Hazards to Health From Microwave and Radio Frequency Radiation and Ultrasound*, 15 July 1980.

TB Sig 222, *Solder and Soldering*, 5 March 1985.

TM 5-811-3, *Electrical Design: Lightning and Static Electricity Protection*, 29 March 1985.

TM 9-6140-200-14, *Operator's, Unit, Direct Support and General Support Maintenance Manual for Lead-Acid Storage Batteries; 4HN, 24 Volt (Dry) (NSN 6140-00-059-3528) M11188/2-24V; 4HN, 24 Volt (Wet) (6140-01-396-68) M11188/2-24V; 2HN, 12 Volt (Dry) (6140-00-057-2553) MS35000-2; 2HN, 12 VOLT (Wet) (6140-01-390-1969) MS35000-2; 6TN, 12 Volt (Dry) (6140-01-441-1697) 6TLFP; 6TMF, 12 Volt (Dry) (6140-01-446-9498) 6TMF; 6TMF, 12 Volt (Wet) (6140-01-446-9506) 6TMF; 6TGEL, 12 Volt (Gel) (6140-01-444-2545) 6TGEL; NBB248, 12 Volt (Gel) (6140-12-190-9024) NBB248; NBB248GTW, 12 Volt (Gel) (6140-01-439-0616) NGB248,* 11 September 1998.

TM 11-5825-266-14-1, *Operator's, Organizational, Direct and General Support Maintenance Manual: Radio Transmitting Sets, AN/FRN-41(V)1 (NSN 5825-01-070-5843) AN/FRN-41(V)2 (5825-01-070-5842), AN/FRN-41(V)3 (5825-01-088-9391), AN/FRN-41(V)4 (5825-01-088-9392) and AN/FRN-41(V)T1 (5825-01-083-7365)*, 28 January 1980.

TM 11-5840-377-13-2, *Operator's, Unit, and Direct Support Maintenance Manual, Volume 2 of 4 for Radar Surveillance, Central AN/FPN-66 (NSN 5840-01-320-3687) (EIC: KJ8)*, 1 March 1996.

TM 11-5840-382-23, *Field Mantenance Manual for Fixed Base Precision Approach Radar System (FBPAR) AN/FPN-67 (NSN 5840-01-450-8127) (EIC: LZ4)*, 1 December 2007.

TC 11-6, *Grounding Techniques*, 3 March 1989.

TM 43-0139, *Painting Instructions for Army Materiel*, 30 June 2008.

FEDERAL AVAITION ADMINISTRATION PUBLICATIONS

FAA Publications can be located at http://www.faa.gov/library/.

FAA Advisory Circular 70/7460.1, Obstruction Marking and Lighting.

FAA JO 1900.47, *Air Traffic Organization Operational Contingency Plan*, 22 October 2009.

FAA JO 6130.3, *Maintenance of Flight Data Input/Output (FDIO) Equipment*, 7 May 2009.

FAA JO 6191.3, *Standard Terminal Automation Replacement System (STARS)*, 16 November 2006.

FAA JO 6310.19, *Maintenance of Airport Surveillance Radar -9 (ASR-9)*, 1 February 1999.

FAA JO 6310.30, *Maintenance Handbook for Airport Surveillance Radar, ASR-11 Facilities*, 6 June 2007.

FAA JO 6310.9, *Maintenance of Airport Surveillance Radar (ASR-7, ASR-7E5, ASR-7F, and ASR-8)*, 3 December 1990.

FAA JO 6360.1B, *Maintenance of Air Traffic Control Beacon Interrogator (ATCBI) Equipment (Except ATCBI-5)*, 9 March 1979.

FAA JO 6360.14B, *Maintenance of Air Traffic Control Beacon Interrogator (ATCBI-5) Equipment and Mode-S Collocated with Solid-State Radar Beacon Decoder (SSRBD)*, 1 August 1985.

FAA JO 6410.18, *Maintenance of the Digital Bright Radar Indicator Tower Equipment (DBRITE)*, 4 October 1991.

FAA JO 6480.6, *Maintenance of Air-to-Ground (A-G) Communications Facilities*, 20 June 1990.

FAA JO 6580.5, *Maintenance of Remote Communication Facility (RCF) Equipment*, 18 June 2008.

FAA JO 6740.2, *Maintenance of Nondirectional Beacons (NDB)*, 6 March 1989.

FAA JO 6750.49, *Maintenance of Instrument Landing System (ILS) Facilities*, 28 July 1999.

FAA JO 6670.13, *Maintenance of Digital Voice Recorder (DVR) Equipment*, 3 December 2008.

FAA JO 6770.2, *Maintenance of 75mhz Fan Marker (FM) Facilities*, 5 June 1989.

FAA JO 6820.7, *Maintenance of Navigational Aids, Facilities and Equipment- VOR,DVOR, VOR/DME, VORTAC*, 21 January 2009.

FAA JO 7110.65T, *Air Traffic Control*, 11 February 2010.

FAA JO 7210.3. *Facility Operations and Administration*. 11 February 2010.

FAA JO 7220.1B, *Certification and Rating Procedures for Department of Defense (DOD) Personnel*, 20 October 2008.

FAA JO 7340.2, *Contractions*, 27 August 2009.

FAA JO 7350.8, *Location Identifiers*, 8 April 2010.

FAA JO 7400.2, *Procedures for Handling Airspace Matters*, 10 April 2008.

FAA JO 7610.4, *Special Operations*, 12 March 2009.

FAAO 6000.6B, *Interagency Ground Inspection Guidance*, 5 August 2005.

FAAO 6000.15, *General Maintenance Handbook for NAS Facilities*, 1 February 2010.

FAAO 6190.16, *Maintenance of the Micro En Route Automated Radar Tracking System (MEARTS)*, 29 February 2008.

FAAO 6700.20A, *Non-Federal Navigational Aids and Air Traffic Control Facilities*, 11 December 1992.

FAAO 7900.5, *Surface Weather Observing*, 11 May 2001.

FAAO 8020.11, *Aircraft Accident and Incident Notification, Investigation, and Reporting*, 2 February 2010.

FAAO 8020.16, *Air Traffic Organization Aircraft Accident and Incident Notification, Investigation, and Reporting,* 13 September 2005.

FAAO 8200.1, *United States Standard Flight Inspection Manual (USSFIM),* 1 October 2005.

FAAO 8240.41, *Flight Inspection/Air Traffic On-Site Coordination Requirements,* 1 October 2005.

FAAO 8260.15, *United States Army Terminal Instrument Procedures Service,* 2 February 2007.

FAAO 8260.19, *Flight Procedures and Airspace,* 16 September 2007.

FAAO 8260.3, *United States Standards for Terminal Instrument Procedures,* 12 November 1999.

FAA-STD-019E, *FAA Standard, Lightning Protection, Grounding, Bonding, and Shielding Requirements for Facilities and Electronic Equipment,* 22 December 2005.

DOCUMENTS NEEDED

The following documents must be available to the intended users of this publication. DA Forms are available on the APD web site (http://www.apd.army.mil).

DA Form 2028, *Recommended Changes to Publications and Blank Forms.*

DA Form 2696, *Operational Hazard Report.*

DA Form 3479, *Training and Proficiency Record-Air Traffic Controller (LRA).*

DA Form 3479-1, *Trainee/Controller Evaluation (LRA).*

DA Form 3479-6, *ATC Facility and Personnel Status Report (LRA).*

DA Form 3479-9, *ATC Maintenance Personnel Certification and Related Training Record (LRA).*

DA Form 3479-10, *Responsibility Assignment (LRA).*

DA Form 3479-11, *Commander's Task List (ATS) Tower Operator.*

DA Form 3479-12, *Commander's Task List (ATS) GCA Operator.*

DA Form 3479-13, *Commander's Task List (ATS) AIC Operator.*

DA Form 3479-14, *Commadner's Task List (ATS) ATS Maintainer.*

DA Form 3501, *GCA Operations Log (LRA).*

DA Form 3501-1, *Precision Approach Radar (GCA) Data (LRA).*

DA Form 3502, *Daily Report of Air Traffic Control Facility (LRA).*

DA Form 3503, *Air Traffic Control Position Log (LRA).*

DA Form 4186, *Medical Recommendation for Flying Duty.*

Unless otherwise indicated, all NSNs are ordered through normal Army Supply channels/systems. AR 750 series and a number of supply handbooks detail how the order process works for the Army.

FAA Form 6030-1, *Facility Maintenance Log 1.* (Available at http://www.faa.gov/forms/)

FAA Form 7210-9, *En Route Minimum IFR Altitude/Minimum Vectoring Altitude Obstruction Document.* (NSN: 0052-00-911-3000)

FAA Form 7220-1, *Air Traffic Control Specialists Certificate.* (Controlled item, not avialable for distribution. Obtained through FAA Certificating authority.)

FAA Form 7230-7.2, *Flight Progress Strip: Terminal Continuous Without Center Perforation.* (NSN: 7530-01-449-4250)

FAA Form 7230-8, *Flight Progress Strip: Terminal-Cut.* (NSN: 7530-01-449-4239)

FAA Form 7230-21, *Flight Progress Strip: FSS.* (NSN: 7530-01-449-4244)

FAA Form 7460-2, *Notice of Actual Construction or Alteration.*(Available at http://www.faa.gov forms/)

FAA Form 8000-5, *Certificate of Designation.* (Controlled item, not avialable for distribution. Obtained through FAA Certificating authority.)

FAA Form 8260-7, *Special Instrument Approach Procedures*. Available at
http://www.faa.gov/about/office_org/headquarters_offices/avs/offices/afs/afs400/afs420terps_forms/.

Index

By Order of the Secretary of the Army:

GEORGE W. CASEY, JR.
General, United States Army
Chief of Staff

Official:

JOYCE E. MORROW
Administrative Assistant to the
Secretary of the Army
1018105

DISTRIBUTION:

Active Army, Army National Guard, and U.S. Army Reserve: To be distributed in accordance with the initial distribution number (IDN) 110717, requirements for TC 3-04.81.